T0282016

PI

Adventures on Land and Sea

"Bumpus exudes the French countryside in this latest book. If you're planning a trip to this region of France, the details are enticing, and one wants to replicate Carole's journey. *Adventures on Land and Sea* reads as if we're perched on Carole's shoulder, learning about the Provençal villages, the history, and cooking. Sip a glass of wine and lazily read the recipes dotting the chapters, and if you close your eyes, maybe you'll even smell croissants baking."

—Leslie Johansen Nack, author of *The Blue Butterfly*

"Don't read this book on an empty stomach or drool will be left on every page. Appetites are whet by the many mouth-watering delicacies dished out on the book's three culinary adventures in Southern France. Throughout all three trips, there is always plenty of great-tasting wine. So, put on a bib and devour the author's sixth book about food, wine, fun companions, and gorgeous scenery."

—Evelyn LaTorre, author of *Love in Any Language*

"It is Carole's clear and generous desire to share her travels so we can experience her rich discoveries in all their sensory detail: So we, too, can talk the morning away over *a petit déjeuner* of chocolate croissants and *café*, or laze on the beaches along the French Riviera, a mix of clothed and fully nude sunbathing, or delight in days and nights of camaraderie in a little farmhouse in Clavier, or glide away in our boat through the ancient port of Nice."

—Kate Farrell, storyteller and author of *Story Power: Secrets to Creating, Crafting, and Telling Memorable Stories*

"Carole Bumpus's own unique writing style is bursting with delight, energy, and humorous observations. That style quickly made me feel like one of her travel companions, hungry for whatever adventure or enticing feast was ahead on the road."

—Elise Miller, author of *The Berkeley Girl in Paris in 1968*

"Bumpus offers a delightful tour of small French towns' traditions, landscapes and culinary delights. It will make your mouth water and your soul pine for visiting Provence. And if you cannot make the trip, the recipes included will bring the richness of this French region to your home."

—Isidra Mencos,
author of *Promenade of Desire, a Barcelona Memoir*

"Bumpus explores Provence from three different perspectives: as a couple, as a sister, and as a friend. With her eye for detail and color, Carole once again immerses the reader in the particulars of French culture and food. I would travel anywhere with her."

—Martha Conway, author of *The Physician's Daughter*

"Bumpus has written yet another book that beautifully sings the praises of France. She so accurately captures the best of Provence through all the senses. Readers will be right there with her as she smells, sees, touches, hears, feels, and tastes the south of France. From the sound of cicadas to the smell of lavender, rosemary, garlic and the taste of rose wine and Provençal seafood, Bumpus delivers the full experience of her travels. Like all great travel literature, this will have readers planning their next vacation and rushing to book their flights to Marseille and Nice."

—Marianne C. Bohr, author of *The Twenty: One Woman's Trek Across Corsica on the GR20 Trail*

"This culinary travel memoir is a fabulous romp through the food-loving, light-filled, old world feel of Provence and the Cote d'Azur!"

—Martha Engber, author of *Bliss Road* and
The Falcon, the Wolf and the Hummingbird

"Embodying the Francophile dream, Carole's explorations of Provence are a pilgrimage of sorts, a return to the land and sea she worships, for the friends she meets along the way, the blunders and banter with her gang, and her manna from heaven—French cuisine. Reading *Adventures on Land and Sea* you can't help but agree with her and yearn to be invited next time!"

—Janine Marsh, Good Life France Productions and author of
My Good Life in France, My Four Seasons in France,
and *Toujours La France*

"Carole Bumpus's latest installment in her Savoring the Olde Ways series is simply wonderful! I savored each chapter as I journeyed along with Carole and crew. More than just a travelogue, this is a love letter to Provence—a true gem!"

—Michelle Cox, author of *The Fallen Woman's Daughter*

"The delicious romp of Carole Bumpus's The *Savoring the Olde Ways* series continues in *Adventures on Land and Sea*. The gorgeous recipes, insightful dips into locals' lives, and living color descriptions of mountains and menus, castles and coastlines are Bumpus at her best. Sailors delight! For a cruise on the Cote, we are treated to husband Winston's journal featuring his voice as an added attraction."

—Barbara Stark-Nemon,
author of *Even in Darkness* and *Hard Cider*

"Enchanting, delicious, and enlivening. Beautifully written but also intimate and relaxed—like the best kind of friend just home from Provence bursting to tell you all her discoveries and adventures. Memoir, travelogue, or cookbook? All three! Full of relish, curiosity, and joy. A tour of Provence like no other. I loved it!"

—Neroli Lacey, author of The Perfumer's Secret

"Mme. Bumpus is once again Savoring the Olde Ways in an ongoing love-filled adventure with life in Europe, fueled by a passion for good food, drink, and new friends. Far more than a narrative collection of recipes, it is a roadmap for happy living."

—Terrance Gelenter, The Paris Insider

ADVENTURES *on*
LAND *and* SEA

SAVORING THE OLDE WAYS SERIES

ADVENTURES on LAND and SEA:

SEARCHING *for* CULINARY PLEASURES *in* PROVENCE *and* ALONG *the* COTE D'AZUR

BOOK FOUR

by

CAROLE BUMPUS

SHE WRITES PRESS

Copyright © 2024 by Carole Bumpus

All rights reserved. No part of this publication may be reproduced, distributed, or transmitted in any form or by any means, including photocopying, recording, digital scanning, or other electronic or mechanical methods, without the prior written permission of the publisher, except in the case of brief quotations embodied in critical reviews and certain other noncommercial uses permitted by copyright law. For permission requests, please address She Writes Press.

Published 2024
Printed in the United States of America
Print ISBN: 978-1-64742-772-6
E-ISBN: 978-1-64742-777-3
Library of Congress Control Number: 2020917548

For information, address:
She Writes Press
1569 Solano Ave #546
Berkeley, CA 94707

Book design by Stacey Aaronson

She Writes Press is a division of SparkPoint Studio, LLC.

All company and/or product names may be trade names, logos, trademarks, and/or registered trademarks and are the property of their respective owners.

Names and identifying characteristics have been changed to protect the privacy of certain individuals.

Years ago, before the love of my life was known to me, I would often profess that "the only trips I take are guilt trips." Since my marriage to Winston Bumpus, the doors to my world have been thrown open as travel is one of the many endeavors we enjoy sharing. From treks back and forth across the Colorado Rockies in the VW camper, to summer vacations in Cape Cod, forays to Europe, and sailing along the Côte d'Azur, we discovered our "almost always best selves" in each other's company—all while traveling.

As it turns out, this was especially true in 1997 when my dear husband agreed we should follow in the steps of Peter Mayle and spend two weeks in the South of France searching for culinary pleasures in Provence. It was with great delight we shared our journey with two other couples, including my lovely sister, Melody.

In the year 2000, my husband encouraged me to return to France with Melody to join a group of women on a culinary tour of Provence. Then, in 2006, he succumbed to his love of sailing by arranging for us to sail the Côte d'Azur with two other marvelous couples. Each trip was a dream come true!

I dedicate this book to him—Winston Bumpus—for being the spark that ignited my love of travel and fostered my deep and abiding interest in other cultures, peoples, and the celebration of life through food. It was these specific adventures included in this book that awakened my desire to capture the stories we were told and to continue my career as a culinary/travel writer. Again, his belief in me and his reassurance of my efforts have been the catalyst. Plus, he has become a Book Sherpa Supreme. I am most grateful to him.

INITIAL TRIP *to* PROVENCE, 1997

"We had been here often before as tourists, desperate for our annual ration of two or three weeks of true heat and sharp light. Always when we left, with peeling noses and regret, we promised ourselves that one day we would live here. We had talked about it during the long gray winters and the damp green summers, looked with an addict's longing at photographs of village markets and vineyards, dreamed of being woken up by the sun slanting through the bedroom window."

— PETER MAYLE, *A YEAR IN PROVENCE*

"When the Good Lord begins to doubt the world, he remembers that he created Provence."

—FREDERIC MISTRAL

CHAPTER ONE

On a Clear Day,
You Can See the Mediterranean Sea

*T*he eucalyptus and redwood trees rose so high above the square, the California morning sun was blocked from view. Only a slight filtering of light slipped through those ancient boughs, and I found myself immersed in semi-darkness. What I expected to find in the village of Mill Valley was a mill, or perhaps a river or two, but there I was standing in a flat space just before entering town—was I even in the town?—while staring up at the face of a canyon wall. Was the address correct? Yes, I double-checked. I could decipher that tidbit of information from the string of mailboxes lining the square. But it was obvious no one lived *in* the square. It appeared they lived at the top of a long, rough-hewn staircase that led up to the crest of the canyon wall.

I shifted in my heels, realizing I was not prepared to scale up the side of a mountain; or any mountain or canyon wall, for that matter. Nor was I prepared to climb up two hundred steps at an almost vertical incline to the address I had been given. I had driven over an hour and a half from our home on the other side of the San Francisco Bay to meet a woman I had never met in Mill Valley to hand over a check. I was only vaguely familiar with her, as we had spoken only once on the phone. Yet here I was preparing to climb this rickety stairway to hand over the amount of $3,000. In '97, that was a bit of cash to hand to an absolute stranger. But this was all in exchange for a ten-day stay in her farmhouse in Provence. Yes, it was sight unseen. And, in the minuscule village of Claviers! What was I thinking? What were we thinking? My husband, Winston, and I had no plans to farm! We just wanted to learn what was so provocative about the magical place called Provence! Yes, we wanted to know about the land that Peter Mayle had so charmingly described.

How was it that his writings had enticed us to drop everything and travel to the South of France? Was it the idea of dipping our toes in the Mediterranean or, as they say, the Côte d'Azur? Was the allure and beauty of lavender fields beckoning us to trundle through purple blossoms to inhale a most intoxicating aroma? Were the local Provençal wineries and olive orchards waving us over? Or was it the idea of meeting the locals in the regions that were steeped in history of a long forgotten, yet slower way of living?

Yes, yes, I confess! After we read Mayle's hilarious book, *A Year in Provence*, our juices were definitely flowing. The saga about his move with his wife from England to Provence was more than hysterical. But it was also through the discovery of Marcel Pagnol's books, *My Father's Glory and My Mother's Castle* and his rendition of his own childhood in Provence, that captured our hearts. Oh, those unforgettable, yet delightful characters carried wonder and magic through every page. (Didn't Alice Waters name her infamous Berkeley restaurant, Chez Panisse, after one of his characters?) I blinked my eyes once, then twice, and with beguiling thoughts of Mayle's and Pagnol's delightful stories awaiting us, I began to thump up that lengthy staircase.

"No," I answered Maggie Cornell, "we have never been to the South of France. In fact, we've only visited France once before, and that was a trip to Paris in '92."

"Well," she said as she sized me up. I was taking on her rental house in Claviers, so she did have a right. "You'll not have to fight big city traffic in this little village; in fact, there is very little traffic at all," she stated. Which, in retrospect, was an understatement now that I think of it.

"Your best bet is to fly into Nice, rent a car, and make your way northwest to my village, which is up in the mountains. Lots of mountain driving there. Are you up to that?"

I must have grinned broadly as she took a step backward. "My husband, Winston, and I have just moved to California from Colorado. We know all about mountain driving."

"Switchbacks?" she asked again, with a bit of concern in her eyes.

"Oh, we know them well; no problem!" I said, picking up the pen lying on the contract.

Maggie ignored me, as she was continuing the description of the house. "I just want you to know what all you are getting here. So, there are three large bedrooms and three bathrooms spread out on three floors, but the main living area is on the second level, which in France is considered first floor. Yes, I know, it's confusing. But you will adjust right away. Oh, and there is a balcony off the living room/dining area, which has a lovely large table for outdoor dinners. And on clear days, you can see to the Mediterranean Sea!"

". . . on clear days, you can see to the Mediterranean Sea," I repeated, in awe. Just think of that! Again, I picked up the pen and signed the contract before handing over the check. I was sold and said so. She then continued to detail what we would need to do once we arrived: how to get into the house; who to contact in an emergency; where and what days to buy groceries; and, last but not least, what markets were open on what specific days.

"You see," she explained, "'Don't forget to find out where the nearest grocery store is located and know the opening and closing time of day and day of the week for the local farmer's markets, which is essential." But I was so excited, I didn't tune into all the specifics. I figured most of the directions and particulars were written on the back of the contract, and I blithely floated out the front door and down the stairs, as if on an escalator. We were going to Provence! We were going to Provence! We can see the Mediterranean on a clear day! Yes, our dream of traveling to Provence was finally going to be fulfilled.

CHAPTER TWO

Arriving in Nice,
June 1997

"The journey is part of the experience—an expression of the seriousness of one's intent. One doesn't take the A train to Mecca."

—ANTHONY BOURDAIN

There is something terribly exotic, almost ethereal even, about flying into a city along the French Mediterranean coast. The crystalline blue waters of the Côte d'Azur were lazily lapping along the shores of Nice as flecks of gold reflected the afternoon sun. I also recall the dream-like experience disappearing once I stepped off the air-conditioned plane. The sweltering June heat slammed against me, taking my breath away. The air felt thick, like wet gauze, and I was certain I would ooze onto the tarmac. I listed under the weight of jetlag—too many hours enroute from San Francisco to Paris to Nice. But at last, we had arrived! My husband, Winston, and I were embarking on the trip of a lifetime. Provence!

As I looked around me, the sights of a tropical paradise

mixed with the salty tang from the sea, along with the heady aroma of heavy garlic from nearby restaurants, all wafted through the air and . . . suddenly an unexpected energy and exhilaration rose up and I realized, yes, we were at the threshold of our new adventure. With a quick snap to my step, I picked up the pace and followed my husband up the ramp and into the *aéroport.* We had places to go and people to see, so we were off to collect our luggage and pick up our rental car.

Although we knew only a word or two of French, our adventure was about to begin. The rental car company at the airport provided us with a long black station wagon, as we were accommodating two couples with plenty of luggage. This looked to fit the bill. With several wild hand gestures indicating the door, the petrol slot, the steering wheel, and the gas pedals, the car rental agent handed my husband the keys along with a French instruction manual and a map. The only word I caught from their conversation was, *'Meh-se-des'* or maybe, *Mercado?* Like I said, we knew little French, but this looked like the perfect-sized vehicle for a shared two-week vacation with my sister, Melody, and her husband, Dan. A Cheshire cat smile enveloped my face. Boldly we flung our bags into the back of the car, laughed at the thought of driving around Provence in a car used only by funeral directors or ambassadors, and we popped into the car.

"Why, we could place an ambassador flag on each bumper," I quipped. "We just need to decide which country we might want to represent." My husband, feeling a tad more sophisticated in world travel than I, smiled politely in my direction but did not yield to my attempts at humor. We had maps in a foreign language to sort out and I was the official map sorter.

We clipped along the Promenade des Anglais, which led us into the heart of Nice with its stark white luxurious hotels and villas facing the coast. Even posher hotels, like the famous Hotel Negresco known as The Palace, stood tall with its bright, pink-domed roof, as an elegant invitation and fashion statement to all. My head snapped backward to take another peek. I remembered from my guidebook that this hotel had been known as the Legend of the French Riviera for over one hundred years.

"Oh, won't it be fun to just to have a look inside," I bantered. My husband ignored me, as he was focused on driving a foreign car, in a foreign city, with only foreign directions at hand and a wife who was not fulfilling her job as map sorter.

But, just then, and with no comment whatsoever to me, he made a quick turn to the left, drove around a large park, and pulled into an underground parking garage like he had done this every day. I was duly impressed. He hated parking garages! But, voilà! Across the street from the park, known as Jardin Albert 1er, sat our night's destination, the Park Hotel. Clever name, I thought. Venturing into the hotel's elegant lobby, I heard my name called out across the room. My big sister, Melody, who is older, but much shorter than me at 5', padded quickly across the lobby to swoop me up in her strong arms. Swedes do this type of thing.

Years and years before, when our children were toddlers, we had made a promise to each other that when the time was right, we would escape the drudgery of diapers, sticky fingers, snowsuits, Slinkys, Play-Doh, and peanut butter sandwiches—and flee to France. It had taken over twenty years, but we had finally done it! We spun around together in that splendid foyer making a purely midwestern spectacle of ourselves. That was until our husbands, Dan and Winston, wheeled us out of the middle of the room and corralled us into a side salon where they ordered *vin blanc* (white wine) for each of us and sat us down.

Dan, a tall drink of water of a man at 6'2" who reminded me of an attractive Abe Lincoln, was a shy sort and not used to displays of attention. Neither was my husband, come to think of it, who, at 5'7" and from the shores of New Bedford, Mass., was also not one for the overly dramatic! For their sakes, we needed to reign in our excitement and settle down. With giggles of glee contained, we picked up our glasses and made our first toast to Provence. *Tchin-tchin!*

It had been several years since we had last seen them, and there was much catching up to do . . . about home and family. Jokes and funny stories were shared, and we all leaned into the laughter with ease. This would be our first trip together and we were looking forward to this time.

Since Melody and Dan had flown in the morning before from Iowa and were already quite refreshed and anxious to show us around, they encouraged us to check in. So, after an hour of catching up, my husband and I were escorted upstairs where a lovely large room awaited us. Our room oozed the aura of Provence with a mustard-yellow flowered comforter and draperies, and an unusually large bathroom. Our room, which had a black wrought-iron balcony, faced the same Jardin Albert 1er park we had parked under, and off in the near distance lay those same azure blue waters. We quickly unpacked and refreshed ourselves before rejoining Melody and Dan. They were excitedly waiting to show us around.

As we walked arm in arm, Melody began to tell us about their first day in Nice. She was jubilant! As we crossed the street into the park and meandered under the cooling shade of the palm trees, she began, "This morning, we took a bus up the steep escarpment high above the old city of Nice." Her hand swept the air to the north of us in a direction we could not see. Deep green palm fronds blocked our vision.

"We toured the Musée Matisse, including his original home where we caught stunning views of the sunlit Mediterranean. The main part of the museum was underground and even though I'm not a fan of Matisse, I became one after seeing the extent of his artistic work in this beautiful setting."

I leaned into her as we strolled through the lovely park, catching sight of the bubbling fountains, glorious gardens, a colorful carousel, and historic statues as we passed.

"We wandered through a park—different than this one—filled with children playing and enjoying *glacés* with their parents. We found it interesting," she continued, "that the *allées* in the park were named for American jazz musicians. On the other side of the park, we encountered a cemetery with elaborately carved gravestones and a Roman Catholic structure, Monastere de Cimiez, built on the ruins of a Temple to Diana. So far, we've both been enchanted with Nice and have found her to be quite the genteel old lady." She looked at me; a twinkle lit her eye. Rarely had I seen her so expressive. I had always known her to be the steadfast quiet one. But Nice had charmed her. *Bon!*

"Wow," I said. "Your time here sounds marvelous!" I knew Winston and I would not have extra time in Nice, but perhaps, when we returned from Provence? By this point, Winston and Dan had moved quickly through the park and had popped out on the other side just across from the beach.

Awe, the glorious beach! Skittering across the many lanes of traffic on the Promenade des Anglais, we made our way down onto the rocky beach. Yes, sand must have been there somewhere, but mostly the beach was covered in smoothed rocks. Not exactly what one would expect when the idea was to kick off your shoes, sink your toes in the warm sand, and make your way to test the waters, so to speak. But, yes, I had to try. Stumbling, staggering, whimpering, I attempted the mad crab scramble toward the water. Yes, the water was warm and delicious, and I wanted to swim, but . . . my sister's call brought me back to a bank of beach chairs where we sat and soaked up the wonder of being together at that very spot on the Côte d'Azur.

Of course, hunger kicked into high gear as we made our way into Vieux Nice. In the Cours Seleya, an open-air market from the Middle Ages, fresh produce and flowers were sold during the day but bistros and sidewalk cafés rule the night. This was where we succumbed to the seductive and garlic-infused flavors of Niçoise traditions. Here, hundreds of years of blended Italian and French recipes were on full display. Plenty of fresh seafood abounded, such as our favorite *moules et frites* (mussels and French fries), plus local olives, anchovies, garlic, olive oils, and capers. The favorite local dishes were *Niçoise* Salad (tuna, boiled potatoes, French green beans, anchovy salad), *Ratatouille* (fresh eggplant and tomatoes baked with spices and splashes of olive oil), *Pissaladière* (thick pizza topped with caramelized onions, anchovies, black olives), a hearty *Daube* (wine-soaked roast beef with vegetables), and of course, *Socca* (a crispy chickpea pancake).

First of all, I must tell you we were charmed by the Socca Woman who stood in the marketplace casually preparing the pizza-shaped cake on an enlarged heated metal pan. A wild discussion between Winston and Dan ensued as they discussed if it was an enlarged hubcap or a flattened steel drum she was cooking on. We ordered a couple of *soccas*, which became an immediate hit as hot hors d'oeuvres, along with glasses of rosé. We were ready to begin our first Niçoise meal with our first glasses of wine from Provence.

Because my husband and I had sampled mussels bathed in

butter-wine sauce during our honeymoon, we were suckers for indulging in this specialty again—and again. Not sure what the other two had, as I was completely immersed in my literal bucket of *moules* with a haystack of French fries. Plus, I was feeling no pain after several glasses of wine and jet lag kicking in.

The next morning, following our *petit déjeuner*, or breakfast of golden croissants and *café*, we made our way back to Cours Seleya for the Marché aux Fleurs, or Flower Market that Melody was anxious to share. Depending on the season, she explained, the local hills are filled with glorious floral colors and are brought in bunches down to the city for others to share. "This market was the first in the world to sell cut flowers and it has been over a hundred years of tradition in the making!" she recounted. We made the most of our time wandering around the flower market, photographing the bounty of seasonal blooms.

And then we checked out the produce market, which had mountains of fresh melons, a bounty of ripe tomatoes, massive arrays of marinated olives, an abundance of cheeses, pastries, oh my! We had no choice; we each purchased little packets of cheese, links of cured sausages, an assortment of olives, two baguettes, and one bottle of local olive oil to take with us to our new home in the mountains.

Having completed our morning market tour, and because we had been inundated with the succulent aromas of sizzling fish and meats, plus fresh spices and herbs, we stopped for a lunch, or *déjeuner*, and I tried *pan bagnat* (a classic Niçoise sandwich loaded with chopped olives, fresh tomatoes, radishes, oil-packed tuna, and tons of basil). No, it is not carefully layered; instead, it is mashed together and spread on an incredible bun, like tuna salad. Scrumptious!

We were biding our time, as our next guests were due to

fly into Nice that afternoon. Yes, our good friends, Bob and Shirley, were on their way. We looked forward to the six of us enjoying days and nights of great camaraderie and food in the little farmhouse in Clavier, as well as traversing Provence together.

CHAPTER THREE

Do You Know the Way to Clav-i-ers (Clav-e-ay)?

The four of us checked out of the Park Hotel, packed up our enormous Mercado, and rushed out to greet Bob and Shirley at the airport. At last, our dear friends were here from Denver. We had been fast friends for a couple of years before moving from Colorado to the San Francisco area, so we looked forward to spending time with them again. With the camaraderie and all the jokesters in the mix, we knew this would be a great time.

We met Bob and Shirley outside the car rental agency, as they had rented their own car, a Citroen coupe, which was smart as it would have been extremely tight if they had piled in with us. Bob was a short man, about Winston's height, slight of build and with a twinkle in his eye, strode with the confidence of a bantam rooster. His wife, Shirley, did her best to keep up with him, and was also short like me, with long blonde hair, blue eyes, and the sweetest face I had ever seen. I greeted them with a hug, then introduced them to my sister, Melody, and her husband, Dan, as we were about to become the *Provençal Six*!

We helped them put their luggage in their car, then Winston went back to get our car and pulled up beside us. "We obviously wouldn't fit in with you," Bob quipped. "Besides, we might prefer to take off on our own."

With Winston in the lead, we headed straight out of town. Before the days of GPS, Michelin Road maps were the only game in town. They were so expansive in size, the map needed to be stretched across the entire front seat in order to read it. I carefully unfolded said map, and with my left hand slipping under Winston's nose on my left side and my right hand sticking out the window, I was able to serve as the designated map sorter or navigator, despite knowing little French.

My second little peccadillo for the day involved misunderstanding the French language in translating the word, *péage*. As it turns out, a *péage* is a toll booth, but not knowing this in advance, I experienced several frantic moments until a French-English dictionary was retrieved from the clutches of my sister's purse to figure out the meaning. "Ah, we can handle that," I breathed.

Then we needed to know how many francs were necessary to throw into the coin hoppers. Comedy capers were on full display with Americans doing what Americans do best: ignoring the need to learn a foreign language before leaving home. But, from the triumphal moment of translating the word *péage*, we laughingly referred to this booth as a "*péage*-you-go," or "pay as you go."

At this time in France, francs were still being used and Bob had not had the time to convert his dollars into francs at the airport. So, when he followed us into the *péage*, he was brought up short. Panic again set in. The guards would not let him continue, and dollars or change tossed into the hopper was not acceptable. Winston stopped our car in the middle of the road, ran back to the toll booth, and threw coins into the hopper until the bell rang and the gate opened. Then, off we went, racing west repeating this scenario at all the péages along the coast, past Antibes and Cannes, before we headed north and deeper into the mountains.

"The guidebook states," I said reading the words aloud to anyone who would listen, "Claviers is a community in the Var department in the Provence-Alpes-Côte d'Azur region in southeastern France, approximately sixty kilometers west of Cannes. Noted as a 'perched village' it is located on the tiny D55 road winding through the pine forests just south of Bargémon . . ."

"Wherever that is," I heard mumbled from the back.

I continued reading. "Nestled in the beautiful, forested mountains, Claviers has an outstanding view of the surrounding hills all the way down to the Mediterranean."

"Wasn't that part of the sales pitch for our little house in Claviers?" Winston asked. "That from our balcony we would be able to see all the way to the Mediterranean?"

"Exactly right," Melody chimed in. "This already sounds divine!"

I continued reading.

"The main part of Claviers is a 'typical' medieval village with narrow streets winding their way between the tall, old houses, with several passing through low archways beneath the houses. Yet the village somehow maintains a feeling of light and open-ness."

"Ah," they all echoed, nodding as we each looked forward to what we were about to discover.

"And here is another special little tidbit," I said, as I contin-ued reading aloud, totally ignoring the beauty of the mountains and hills we were passing.

"The heart of Provence is in the hills that bind the sea to

the Alps. These are the sloping vineyards, cultivated lands, and the colorful scenery that charmed Cezanne, Van Gogh, Chagall or Giono . . . In Provence, or the Midi, the local people have a soft singing accent which evokes their whole relaxed lifestyle. They have no greater pleasure after a hard day's work than to enjoy a delicious and hardy meal shared with friends . . ."

"Right up our alley," Dan chimed in. "I'm ready!" I think both Dan and Melody were ready to leap from a moving car at that point due to the many hairpin turns and the length of the trip. Thank gawd, we finally reached our destination!

Arriving at the petite village of Claviers, both cars pulled into the town square, which was not a square at all, but a tapered triangle. It was then we realized there were no parking lots available inside the village, so we backed around and headed to the parking spaces on the outskirts of town. I quickly reread the directions to our rental and this time we made our way by foot to the farmhouse—which was not a farmhouse at all but one section of a stone building most likely built between the twelfth and thirteenth century. The confined streets that linked the houses together were cobblestone and our walk down to the house was along steep declines and stairs. No glamorous streets winding through low archways. Only stairs. No motorized vehicles had ever driven through here, and possibly only donkeys had made the trek along these slim passageways. Yet, we persevered.

The house was quite a lovely sunlit surprise with three floors and three separate large bedrooms, so each couple had their own floor and bathroom. Just like the owner had said. Marvelous! And a large bowl of fresh peaches with a vase filled with fresh lavender sat on the dining room table with a welcome note. "How very nice," I said, as I attempted to decipher the note. "I believe it is from the housekeeper, as she left her phone number." All nodded, but no one attempted their hand at translation.

The kitchen, which was equipped with mid-twentieth-century appliances (thank gawd), had a stove, oven, microwave, and fridge . . . plus plates for six, pots, and pans—why, almost all the accommodations of our own kitchen back home. Ah, but not so fast! What was this gas mark thing printed on the gas stove? What's a mark, other than a blemish one wants to be rid of? And if this is for centigrade, what does that mean in real degrees? We searched for instructions and found them conveniently tucked into a kitchen drawer, still in the plastic packaging, and all written in French. Of course, it would be. Oh, we knew we were faced with another learning curve of a different magnitude. At least the kitchen was well supplied with cooking utensils and a few spices. (But what does *cerfeuil* mean?) My kingdom for a compact but complete English–French dictionary!

We pulled out our prized edibles from the farmer's market—cheeses, bread, salamis, olives, oh, yes, we had picked up several bottles of wine—they were all ceremoniously placed into the small but reasonable refrigerator. We were set for . . . snacks!

The dining room was an extension of the kitchen with chairs for six conveniently set about a table draped in a traditional Provençal tablecloth of deep yellows and blues, with several armchairs and a small sofa scattered about the space. The dining room led out to a large balcony that had another trestle table for outside feasting.

"On a clear day," my husband said, echoing my only conversation with the owner of the house, "one can see the Mediterranean Sea from here." All but Dan took turns standing on tiptoes and peering down through the range of mountains below us. Someone with better vision or younger eyes than ours must have made this proclamation, I figured, but we squinted through the house binoculars . . . just in case the clouds on the coast disappeared. Melody picked up a conch shell that had been lying on a nearby shelf and sauntered over to the railing and stood on her tiptoes. She put the shell up to her eye, then announced, "I believe I can see the sea clearly." I must confess I was almost suckered into peeking through her shell as I hadn't seen the azure waters yet myself. But Bob sauntered over to the edge of the balcony, looked straight down, and said, "We're hanging off the side of the ramparts!"

"What?" we all said, scrambling back to peer over the side of the balcony. Directly below us, and near where we had entered our front door, was a narrow ledge, which, if Bob was correct, meant that we were, indeed, hanging over the ancient ramparts of this medieval village of Claviers.

"So, what is a rampart again?" Shirley asked, scooting closer to the railing to peer over.

"Why, that, my dear, is the outer wall of a fortress or of a walled city," he said with great aplomb.

"Well, I'll be," Dan said, as he took another look below. "And way down below the wall is . . . that's quite a drop, isn't it!" Again, we all raced back to the edge to see that, yes, he was also correct. Down below were steep hills and olive trees planted in no particular pattern. Their silvery leaves lifted with the warm air that was circulating around, giving us a much-needed break from the summer heat. Somewhere down in the thicket I caught the sound of the cicadas calling up to us.

"Do you hear that, Melody? I think the sound we are hearing is from the cigales or cicadas. One of the most famous symbols of all of Provence!"

"Why yes! They remind me of our locusts in Nebraska and Iowa, right Dan?"

Dan, being the quiet somber sort, broke into a laugh. I was sure he had a tale to tell about life out on the farm in Nebraska, but instead he said, "I believe it was in Peter Mayle's book where he talked about the French myth of the cicada. I'll have to find that and share it with you later."

From the banter around the group as they warmed to each other, it was clear we were all here with similar interests and loves in mind. And we all had read Peter Mayle's book, *A Year in Provence*. Yes, we'd have a great time together.

We continued the tour of the house before the guys raced down to the cars to bring back our bags. The bedrooms were fairly spacious with wide windows that flung open to bring the whole valley into view. Ah, but no window screens, so beware of bats in the night, we were forewarned. The bathrooms were plentiful, which was a nice surprise. Of course, every room presented a challenge, and the bidet was one of mine. A back room housed, yes, a washer and dryer. No, actually, a washer with a clothesline.

The walls throughout were freshly painted creamy white with ancient unfinished oak beams stretching across the ceilings. One could only marvel at how long those beams had held their place. Colorful artistic touches were splashed here and there throughout with artwork, potted plants and ceramic jars filled with dried lavender. And fresh lavender was tucked into little pots on the living area side tables.

The center island, which extended from the kitchen into the dining area, became the place for all food preparation and was also the congregating place for discussion of the daily menu. We divided up the nights of cooking among us three couples, taking into consideration the nights we would sup at restaurants—if we could find any—as Claviers had appeared rather miniscule. And we efficiently made lists of the necessary ingredients for breakfasts, lunches, snacks, and wine we were likely to consume.

We knew a trip to the local grocery store would become a major focus of our days at the farmhouse. Plus, we had come to imbibe in wines, sample olive oil in olive orchards, visit museums, the Grand Canyon of France, and flip-flop our way to the local beaches. But the highest priority was to either make plans ahead for a trip to a local grocery store or make reservations. That became a daily challenge, and one that caught us up more times than I'd like to say.

After careful inspection of the house that first afternoon, we women decided to join our men and trooped back to the cars to collect our luggage. We were told we could not drive closer to our abode, even though the narrow road we had spied from the balcony was near the back door of our dwelling. But the fact that we had already surmised the overgrown pathway was perched on top of the medieval walls of the village was a clue we quickly added to our bit of local knowledge. So, we all lugged and shoved our bags over cobblestones, banged them down steep stone staircases, and clacked them merrily down to the entrance of our little rental in the mountains of Provence.

And because we had not arrived in time to purchase food from the only local grocery store—had forgotten to heed that warning—we happily trooped back through the town to eat dinner at a lovely little restaurant, Le Clavis, which was near where our cars were parked and near the *boules* (also known as *pétanque* or bocce) court. Little did we know at that time, this was the only restaurant in town, and would be closing for good the following week. Alas, we were delighted to be caught up in this magical place as we had ten days to explore!

CHAPTER FOUR

What Makes the Cicada Sing?

*A*fter settling in that first night, some of us got up more slowly than others the following day. The call of the mourning dove along with the singing of the cicadas quickly became a welcome sound for me beginning that Provençal morning. But Bob, being an early bird, made a hasty escape, as he was determined to be the first to ramble down to Bargemon for croissants and baguettes at their local boulangerie. And, somewhere, bless him, he was able to pick up ground coffee.

We were mighty delighted with his early morning exploits, and once the coffee in the French press was pressed, we laid out a platter with cheese, peach slices, and salami to go with our croissants and this became our go-to easy morning breakfast, or un petit déjeuner.

As we were sitting around the table out on the balcony, Dan brought up the subject once again of the cicadas. It seemed he read into the night, and since it was a few years before the birth of Google, I don't know where he came up with his tidbits of information. But he began by asking, "So, what was your experience with cicadas?"

The five of us looked at him with curiosity, as each slipped back into his own childhood memories. At this point, the sound of the cicadas was picking up steam, as was the heat of the day.

"I don't recall hearing cicadas, where I grew up in Southern California," Shirley replied. "This is all new to me," she said as she bit into a flaky croissant. "How about you, Bob?" They both had grown up near Bakersfield, so I expected the same answer. But, no, Bob had memories of climbing trees to capture them live.

"As for me," Winston continued, "I don't have much of a memory of the cicadas, as we called them locusts. And I don't think they are the same insect, but they supposedly have a seventeen-year cycle in New England. It seems like when I was six or seven, I recall dashing after my brothers, who were chasing after the sound in the woods behind our house in Massachusetts. I don't recall much about it, other than when my brothers caught one, they used it to scare me. Of course, Mom would take after them. What about you, Melody?"

"I remember hearing their call as a kid each summer growing up in Nebraska. Right, Carole? And we also called them locusts, and they would spend their time hanging on the bark of the . . . well, now that I think of it, they might have been hanging on our locust trees."

"Yes," I interrupted, "I remember when they died, our little brothers would collect their empty little carcasses and keep them in a bucket. Not that we could do anything with them, but I guess that's what you do in Nebraska when you can't go hunting for seashells."

"How about you, Dan, since you brought up this topic?" Bob asked.

"Well," Dan said, rocking back in his chair, coffee cup in hand, "I lived out on a farm in central Nebraska, with plenty of open fields for crops, but we also had a wind break with poplar and locust trees. I think we also had a spreading Weeping Willow tree in our front yard that my mother loved. I do remember hearing them, but I think my father always felt they were just a 'damned nuisance' and didn't encourage us to investigate. So, it's interesting that here in Provence, it is a genuine sign of their traditions. Maybe we can find out more about them, but I did run across a bit on it in a guidebook:

According to Provençal folklore, the cicada was sent by God to rouse working locals from their afternoon siestas in order to stop them from being too indolent. As it turns out, the plan backfired. Instead of being disturbed by the cicada, the peasants found the sound of their buzzing relaxing, which in turn, lulled them back to sleep.

"Oh, Dan, that's lovely," Shirley said. "Yes, we'll have to keep our ears open to finding out more folklore." We all nodded our heads in appreciation.

"Well, we must get going," he said as he slapped the guidebook closed from which he had just read.

I blinked as if coming awake. "Speaking of being lulled," I said, "I'm sure we would love to wile away more time, but this is our first full day in Claviers. We have places to go; people to see!"

We all popped up from the table and scrambled into the kitchen to clean up before we headed out on our first adventure. But first, we knew we had to find the grocery store—the only grocery store in town as it turns out—as we had taken the owners cautionary words to heart. *"Don't forget to find out where the nearest grocery store is located and know the opening and closing time of day and day of the week for the local farmer's markets..."*

We ladies ambled up the cobbled steps and down to the town square/triangle where we had spotted the little grocery the night before. We waltzed in for essentials like we knew what we were doing, and gathered up items such as milk, eggs, orange juice, more ground coffee in a can, plus other canned goods, such as tuna fish, Spam, packages of dried pasta, and a jar of tomato sauce for spaghetti, just in case nothing else came to light. So, after our larder was somewhat filled, we felt a bit relieved . . . and the rest of the day we set aside as one of discovery.

As I mentioned before, the only flat street we found was in the town square, but it wasn't a square, but a narrow isosceles triangle crowned with large plane trees. Plane trees are much like our sycamores in the US. Originally, we were told, they were planted in the mid-nineteenth century along roadsides throughout France on the orders of Napoleon to provide shade for his troops. (No worries about troops now, though.) We were thrilled we knew their importance when we recognized the trees later sprinkled throughout Provence. In the summertime, they formed the famous lush green canopy-like *allées.*

St. Sylvestre, a medieval church rebuilt in the nineteenth century, stood at one end of the triangle, and was known (in the guidebook) for its elaborate wrought-iron campanile or belfry that obviously towered over the town. But we never saw it due to the buildings or houses having been built so close together on the perch of this narrow hill. Like many medieval villages, one building was built using the wall from the one before, and so forth. Like tin soldiers, all lined up leaning on each other for support. All were a combination of stone and mortar construction with stone plinths and balustrades, undergirded with those trusty wooden beams we spied in our own abode. Some façades were more rustic or original than others. Some had cloaked their stones beneath a slathering of golden plaster. All of the homes in these tall buildings were separated by distinctive doorways or tall green or golden shutters. They were mixed in between with businesses such as the post office, the grocery store, and one little bistro. Cats lazed about in open windows with music wafting down from unseen tinny transistor radios and along the street geraniums grew rampant in the largest pots I had ever seen. Dogs of all shapes, sizes and pedigrees roamed about freely and acted as a welcoming committee of sorts.

After leaving the village behind, we clamored up rugged paths, past age-old rock walls with bright yellow Scotch broom cascading down the sides, and wildflowers staging a colorful rebellion along the undergrowth. We continued up through forests of pines with olive trees woven into the mix. And then, we found ourselves standing at the northern-most edge of Claviers. The ridge overlooked the valley to the north and down to the village of Bargemon. We already had a fondness for this little place, as this is where Bob, now known as "Bun Boy," ventured down for the day's daily ration of fresh croissants and baguettes. To the south, we could see Claviers, along with St. Sylvestre's bell tower. Ah, yes, it *was* quite delicate and lovely in latticework wrought iron from this vantage point!

Also perched on this ridge and ensconced in a wrought-iron fence was a large (possibly eight feet by six feet) sandstone monument to the *Résistance* in WWI. The elegantly carved nude young woman stood next to a boulder from the same stone. Not sure of the meaning behind all of this, as the signage was in . . . French. Sigh! As we would find out in our travels throughout Provence, monuments and signage of wars past— from Roman to WWII—were often a common part of the landscape, because history abounded. But I couldn't help but

37

wonder what the meaning was for this particular monument. Alas, I was unable to find anyone who could translate the few words chiseled in the stone, and this would be my experience throughout the entire trip—missing the gist of the story because my French was lacking.

We walked back into the village of Claviers, passing by the boules court, where a game seemed to be going on. Both old and young men who were playing appeared to be the same as the ones we had seen the day before. Grizzled in appearance, the old gents wore baggy pants held up with loose suspenders over an old flannel shirt, which seemed like a hot choice that summer afternoon. The younger ones were more modernly dressed, but they were equally invested in their game. I realized that these folks were the ones Peter Mayle had written about, as well as Provençal writer, Marçel Pagnol, who would know best. I lamented that I would not be able to chat with them due to my language barrier, but, oh, how I would love to share a beer with them, or a glass of wine. Perhaps Pastis would be the drink of choice!

That evening, one of us was smart enough to have made reservations to dine at the lovely Le Relais de Garron, which, as we were to discover, was a delightful restaurant in Seillans/ Fayence only a few kilometers to the east. Housed in an *auberge*, or hotel, this was our first experience at a *relais*, but we would come to seek them out from then on. They set a standard of excellence just in their name.

The food was Provençal comfort food with plenty of vegetable tartes and roasted meats to fill us. This was the first of many meals to come of having course after course, ending with the cheese course, and then desserts. We should have walked home, but, of course, we crammed all six of our well-fed bodies into the Mercado and took the easy way back.

Once back in Claviers, we sauntered from the car park, arm-in-arm, through the village streets, as the stars and moon above were kind enough to light our way. It had been a sweet first day.

CHAPTER FIVE

Fearless in Fréjus

"We had a crisp, oily salad and slices of pink country sausages, an aioli of snails and cod and hard-boiled eggs with garlic mayonnaise, creamy cheese from Fontvielle, and a homemade tart. It was the kind of meal that the French take for granted and tourists remember for years."_

—PETER MAYLE, *A YEAR IN PROVENCE*

On one of our first forays from Claviers, we trekked (in two cars because Bob did not enjoy being wedged into the back hold by himself) to the coastal city of Fréjus—once an ancient Roman port city on the Côte d'Azur. We all were eager to see some of the many Roman ruins which, we had read, litter most of Provence. And even learn some history that predated the Romans. With guidebooks in tow, we made our way to the city center of Fréjus, where we discovered a conveyance on which would be the first of our many favorite excursions—Les Petits Trains. Small, white, almost child-sized trains were used for tours to traverse up and down the city streets, bumping over cobblestones, rocks, and ruts before continuing out into the countryside. It appeared to be the easiest way to pick up local tidbits, history, and folklore enroute while getting the lay of the land—as long as your headphones were plugged into an English translation of said tour. In this case, we were relieved and pleased to be able to nod, smile, and sigh in understanding of this twangy yet voluble, mechanical English voice who provided us with description of place, monuments, and points of interest, all accompanied with up-beat music.

We rambled along in the little train cars through the narrow streets, up and down hills, and then out into the fields to the north, east, and south of the city where we caught sight of the many listed Roman ruins. We also bounced along to the coastal shores of St. Raphaël, as well as the port of Fréjus.

The origins of Fréjus probably lie with the Celto-Ligurian people who settled around the natural harbor of Aegytna. The remains of a defensive wall are still visible on Mont Auriasque and Cap Capelin. The Phocaeans (Greeks from Western Turkey) of Marseille later established an outpost on the site.

"And that was in English!" I said, confused. "So, what do you think that meant?" I asked Winston but was shushed. As it turns out, the history of Fréjus began long before the Romans, and the creation of the port and harbor were something ready for the taking by the Romans when they showed up two thousand years later. I was so impressed! I looked around for signs of the *Phocaeans*, as the Romans had clearly left their imprint all over the place—in amphitheaters, aqueducts, theatres, along with their city walls, city gates, lighthouses, and no less than five public baths. So much to see and find, as many of these were crumbling buildings left standing by themselves in the middle of open fields. But then, they had lasted another two thousand years.

So, when we saw a place, like a Roman arena or a monument

we wanted to check out, we popped off Le Petit Train to make our way to these ancient stones to physically check them out for ourselves—up close and personal. To touch the past, so to speak, while walking along the paths created over three thousand years before seemed like a dream.

Once we reached the amphitheater, we plunked down on the steps where I began to read aloud from the Fréjus guidebook we had picked up before we took the train:

> One of the most notable of the Roman remains is the amphitheater of Fréjus which was possibly built in the first century in the city of Forum Julii, which today is known as Fréjus. The Forum's dimensions were 113 meters long (339 feet) and 85 meters wide (255 feet); it could accommodate 10,000 to 12,000 spectators.

Our heads pivoted about, checking the steps and the columns as we tried to imagine these seats filled with so many people clad in togas and sandals.

Under the steps of the entrances were the "carceres" which gave way to the French name "incarceration" and served as cells for the gladiators. It appears the arena held shows that consisted of gladiator fights (munera) or hunts for beasts (venationes), even fights between gladiators and animals or between animals only (bestiari), which gave way to the French name "bestiary," as well as naval battles (naumachiae).

"Naval battles? Here?" my husband asked as everything on the sea held a great interest for him. It was hard to imagine, but we knew that this type of event had taken place in the Roman Coliseum so, perhaps, battles were held here also, as the sea was just a short distance away.

Within these ruins celebrated by Victor Hugo during his visit to Fréjus in 1839 he wrote about the amphitheater: "I was in the very square where lions, gladiators and tigers writhed 2000 years ago. Tall grass now grows there, peacefully grazed around me by a herd of skinny horses . . ."

Yes, our heads were bobbing and nodding as each of us imagined the pageantry and the gore having occurred where we were sitting. The tall grasses, though, continued to grow, albeit not with a herd of horses.

Gathering ourselves together, we walked back through the fields to the road, and continued south to check out the port, Fréjus. Le Petit Train had long gone without us. As it turned out, our trip with them was over. The marina was filled with bobbing sailboats and fishing boats with modern condos and townhouses surrounding the port. As we all looked across the water, the cloud-filled sky reflected a marine layer of diffused light. Winston, a sailor at heart, looked out at the sea longingly. Little did he realize we would sail into that very marina a few years later.

As we trudged back into town, we discovered remnants of a Roman lighthouse much farther inland than we expected. But then we were just discovering this strange anomaly throughout our travels (in Rye, England; Pompeii, Italy; and even in Ephesus, Turkey).

"Six thousand years ago, the seas were much higher at the time, so ports are now up to five miles inland from the sea. Times change," Winston stated.

We wandered past Cathédrale Saint-Léonce de Fréjus, a noted and famous cathedral, just as they were about to close their doors for lunch. We were told to return later in the afternoon to check out the complex of medieval religious buildings dating back to the fifth through the thirteenth centuries, as Fréjus had been an important religious center of Provence. "The baptistery within the cathedral," we were told, "was a fine example of early Christian or Merovingian architecture. It was built in the fifth century and is considered the oldest Christian structure in Provence and one of the oldest in France. In fact, they were repurposed Roman temples. You'll have to check it out." We promised to return.

Yes, it was after 1 p.m. and we, too, needed lunch. It turned out, this was a good decision on our part, since all other businesses and museums close at 1 p.m. Plus, we needed a bathroom. We spied one sitting prominently and proudly at the edge of a park. Quite modern in construction, there it stood; a sleek plastic booth which could accommodate our needs. Once again, it became apparent that our French was lacking. The translations we were making up didn't seem to match the instructions on this contraption. Yes, it did take francs. The illustrations indicated that once one entered, you would be locked in there during the entire process. As we stood there contemplating our options, we heard all kinds of washing and thrashing about going on inside and didn't know if this washing process included the individual ensconced. We started to back away. But, no, the person did not appear. What had happened? Eventually, Winston committed to being the guinea pig as nature had called long ago. He was able to deposit his francs, the door swooshed open, he entered, and once he safely exited, the washing and thrashing could be heard once again. Totally sanitized for the next willing . . . guest? Oh, to misunderstand the order of such things could be disastrous!

Now, to find a restaurant or bistro! As it turned out, the restaurants were all open for our benefit at that hour. But this was our first encounter with the pace and rhythm of French restaurants at lunch time, and we came to conclude they were not in a hurry. No other businesses reopen for three hours, so why rush? With the six in our cohort taking time to share a bottle or two of Provençal rosé, we made the best of a long wait for our food. No, they were not being rude; just following the natural order of things! The valuable lesson we learned was to relax, enjoy ourselves, and most especially shift gears to live life at the pace around us. We were on European time!

So, what can one expect for a simple lunch in France? Well, as it turns out, since it lasts up to three hours, each course being served takes about an hour. So, again, relax. The French love to eat, chat, and do not believe in digesting on the run. No, no, no! And the food was worth the wait.

First of all, appetizers were ordered. Slowly sipping our rosé, we devoured a couple of small terrines of golden baked goat cheese *gratin* infused with fresh herbs. Bowls of marinated olives and chunks of tuna were plunked down on the table along with baskets of fresh sliced baguettes for the spreading. Those too disappeared in quick order.

All the while, dear Dan, who had ordered coffee the moment we entered the bistro, waited for his much-desired cup of coffee. Used to drinking multiple cups per day, he was getting a bit testy with the idea that he had to wait—yes, a couple of hours. Yes, they heard his order, but no, they couldn't possibly serve him until after the entire meal was over. It just wasn't their way! Possibly, he'd need to carry a thermos for moments like this.

The daily menu had savory ratatouille, made with zucchini, fresh plum tomatoes, plenty of garlic, thyme, oh my! The pasta dishes, which I had once considered to be Italian, were more than prevalent, as this area of Provence had once been part of Italy. Spaghetti alla Carbonara and Spaghetti with *palourde,* or clams, were chosen by some! Yes, we were in our glory! The eggplant dish I chose was a gift from the gods, with fresh tomatoes, onions, and peppers dancing through the olive oil and baked with a golden crust of grated cheeses.

The ingredients for all the dishes, whether fish, fowl, vegetable, or meat, were obviously purchased fresh a few hours before from the nearby farmer's market or off the nearby boats. Everything was prepared daily with regard to availability and seasonality. So, this concept of seasonality meant that we saw plenty of the same ingredients appear in a variety of scrumptious ways throughout our trip because it was their season. But this was a luscious beginning. Somehow, we found room for dessert. A decadent little fresh strawberry and chocolate delicacy. Oh, and coffee. Yes, finally the much-needed coffee. Dan was finally able to relax and enjoy his dessert.

Well into the afternoon, we made our way from the table and staggered up the street to find—yes, a butcher shop, as such stores are not available in Claviers. Winston and I were scheduled that evening to cook dinner. So, in short order, despite being stuffed to the gills from lunch, we found ourselves pressed up to a chilled meat counter in a *boucherie*. We were there to pick out fresh chicken or *poulets* (thighs and breasts) for dinner. Our eyes were a bit bleary from the wine on a hot afternoon. But, as we tried to decipher how to ask for what we needed, we found ourselves attempting to read the fine print in a miniscule English–French dictionary. Finally, I gave up and resorted to the age-old method of pointing. I pointed at the chicken, and then slapped my individual body parts in order to get the message across. They loved my English translation! Bend down and slap your thighs! Stand up tall and slap your chest! They grinned at my antics but followed my detailed order to a tee. "*Mais oui*," I stated once they wrapped the breasts and thighs in white butcher paper and tied the package with a string. My face was beet red, but Winston carried a couple of packages of thighs and breasts under his arm as we made our escape into the open air of the town square. The rest of our troops awaited.

Huddling together, we gave them the blow by blow of how to handle such shopping dilemmas for future reference. They took copious notes, then we broke the huddle and raucous laughter could be heard as we headed back to the car park to pick up our cars. It was time to head home to Claviers and . . . yes, start dinner.

I'm not sure how one handles cooking dinner on nights you have spent a percentage of the afternoon sipping wine! But I would have given my kingdom for a nap! Instead, we wrestled our *poulets* into the oven to roast—after determining what number to set for the heat—splashed them with olive oil, sliced up fresh vegetables, and topped it all with tomato sauce. Visions of lunchtime aromas danced in my head as I was leaning on the Italian side of my culinary talents. With the entirety of roasted chicken and sauce tossed over pasta, and a fresh salad on the side, we were set. And I was spent! It had been a good day, but good night! *Bonne nüit!*

CHAPTER SIX

Gorg du Verdun, Here We Come

The following day, we decided to head north and deeper into the mountains, Les Alpes du Haut, to discover the French Grand Canyon, known as Gorg du Verdun. Because it was going to be an all-day trip, we packed accordingly and also kept our raincoats at hand. The weather had been extremely comfortable the previous few days, although sometimes a bit warm. But the clouds looked threatening as they made their way south across the mountains heading toward the Mediterranean. And, no, we hadn't spotted the Mediterranean Sea yet from our balcony!

Bob and Shirley disappeared up the road before us, as was their way. They wanted to check out the terrain beforehand, seeking out the best cafés, or overlooks we might want to see. What a nice treat for us, as we could leisurely make our way along without a care in the world. And if we had had cell phones back then, I can't tell you how much time we would have saved when trying to track them down. Ah, but ignorance is bliss!

The route around the entire Gorg *was* about 72 miles, so

we determined that we should pick up the loop closest to the eastern corner and journey along the northern ridge to the village of Moustiers-Sainte-Marie, which was our ultimate goal. As we drove through the mountains, the clouds seemed to boil, foment, and then sporadically give way.

"The guidebook says," I stated matter-of-factly, "parts of this tour are particularly mountainous, so drivers must be aware of hairpin bends and narrow roads with sheer drops." We all gasped.

But Winston drove fearlessly as we zigged and zagged our way through the numerous spates of rain, along many hairpin turns—yes, we encountered many of these tricky turns like the owner of our farmhouse had professed—all the while the rest of us attempted to peer deep into the Gorg we were skirting.

"Ah, there's Bob!" Winston said as he pulled the car off the road at a roadside café—La Bonne Table—D.J. Point Sublime. We popped out of the car to greet the couple but sped past them in order to take a bathroom break. Then, before leaving, we ducked into the restaurant for what was going to be a quick café to go. I was sure that this was what the doctor ordered for Dan. But Melody, feeling a little peckish after only a light breakfast before we left, opted for a plate of something fresh and healthy to eat. She'd confess to you even to this day that she somewhat self-righteously ordered a healthy item from the menu . . . a platter of fruit. To her delight, she received a heaping platter of *pomme frites*, or French fries. Her mispronunciation resulted in a delicious indulgence of eating a *grande* amount of French fries for breakfast. Of course, she was most delighted and burst into joyful exclamations and laughter. "O, happy *pomme frites* fiasco!" she called it. Well, we couldn't help ourselves as we three joined in her merriment. And French fries! A table of four stout German men sitting near us looked at us quizzically, especially with all of us in fits of laughter. But, of course, it would have been lost in translation! Or, mistranslation, as it were! As we were waiting patiently for her to finish her indulgence, we realized the nearby windows were facing the gorge. The clouds had shifted enough that we were finally able to see across to the opposite side. "Where's Bob?" Melody asked.

No one had mentioned anything about Bob and Shirley while we were gorging on French fries, but now, we were beginning to feel mighty embarrassed. When we first piled out of the car and saw them, we all needed that bathroom break, then there was the French fry fiasco . . . No, there was no bloody excuse for our collective behavior.

We walked across the street to see what we had missed before as the roads had been a bit hairy with the cloud cover and all. It was still difficult to make out how close the road was to the actual Gorg. We peered over the edge of the road to see the deep ravine before us, and we thought we could make out the Verdun River at the bottom. Wisps of clouds swirled up and over us, but there near the bottom—some two thousand feet below—was a thin thread of a river we assumed was the Verdun.

Other than that quick pitstop, I can't say that we "saw" the Gorg at all on the trip up to Moustiers-Sainte-Marie, which probably was a blessing. I suppose it's like driving north through the fog on Hwy 1 along the California coast. You are grateful you are not the ones dangling off the edge over the ocean, like those on the trip south. Ah, but we would have a return trip.

"So, what are we going to be doing here," Winston asked as he pulled into a car park. He had done a mighty good job of driving not to know where he was going or what our purpose was.

Even before exiting the car, I pulled my trusty guidebook out and read:

> Moustiers Ste. Marie is an unbelievably charming village set up high on craggy heights overlooking a deep ravine. It has been listed as a *Plus Beaux Villages de France* or designated as one of the most beautiful villages in France. The church, the old village walls, the chapels, the aqueduct, the fountains represent an alliance of water and stone. The pastel colors of the tiles and the limestone create a living architectural whole. The core of its economy is focused on tourism and the ceramics or earthenware tradition known as *faïence*.

"*Faïence?*" I asked Melody. "Do you know what *faïence* is?" She was already out of the car with Dan, and they were moving upward along the steeply sloped streets. I loved that about my sister. Being an independent sort, she had such a wonderful way—but she also needed to keep up with her long-legged husband. Winston and I, short-legged, trundled along behind. Way behind.

As it turned out, Melody and Dan were headed to a brasserie for lunch. Yes, it was that time again, and we found a lovely little inn that had a—well, look there! There was Bob and Shirley casually sipping a glass of rosé while awaiting their meal. We made a bit of a commotion but were able to wheedle a table near them and catch up on all we had missed. And bless that Bob, he didn't miss much.

While we lunched on *croque-monsieur*—hot little ham and cheese sandwiches—along with cups of French onion soup, Bob and Shirley filled us in on all that they had already seen and done in Moustiers. No, they didn't leave a single stone unturned. But we were determined to check just in case.

After lunch, we headed up higher along the steep cobbled streets where artisan shops and houses alike were beautifully festooned with flowers—everywhere. Along rock walls, hanging out of window boxes, along hedges, hanging from porches, potted in ancient stone bowls—bright crimson and magenta geraniums, climbing pink and red roses, white daisies, yellow . . . oh, whatever they were! It was glorious!

Way above us and along a narrow winding path was a twelfth-century chapel that stood prominently overlooking the entire valley. Known as the Notre-Dame-de-Beauvoir, it truly looked lovely, but it was way, way up there.

We turned down a side street, which was much like Claviers in that no motorized vehicles could venture, when we spotted an overlook with a little park—no, I was wrong. It was another boules court. Without fail, wherever these little parks were situated—and we've seen them in several villages we had passed through so far—we noticed both old and young men alike competing against each other, their arms swinging as the metal balls or boules spun down the course. Whooping and hollering was heard, and somehow the cheers and sound of the *pétanque* (when one ball hits another) adds a special little joy to a community—along with the clink of their glasses!

We then discovered the museum that was dedicated to— yes, *faïence*. More than three hundred pieces of stunning ceramic or earthenware were on display. We were told these highly glazed pieces had been manufactured right there in Moustiers in four or five factories from 1679 to the 1800s. The guide, thankfully in English, filled in the next: "The art flourished because of a little Italian monk who had been visiting the Monastery of the Communauté de Lérins. He came with the secret of white enamel (tinned ceramics) in 1668. Not long after, Louis XIV ordered all the gold and silver tableware to be melted down to restore the royal treasure in order to go to war and replaced them with the faïence of Moustiers. It was at that moment Moustiers' earthenware acquired high renown all over European courts."

We walked along with the guide as she talked, moving from one room to another, *oohing* and *aaahing* at the beauty that had been created into such magical pieces.

"Originally, the pure white glazed pieces, whether soup tureens, plates, platters, or bowls were hand-painted with figurative scenes, often copied from engravings of hunting scenes, or with mythological subjects. In the seventeenth century, a Spanish influence added much more color and the images became more of flora and fauna designs."

Our guide finished her tour by saying, "Lovers of culinary arts will also be pleased to see these pieces in more than twenty local restaurants. Even our nationally renowned Chef Alain Ducasse, who has La Bastide de Moustiers near here, teaches cooking classes and serves all of his gourmet dinners on our fine dishes," she said proudly.

I looked over at Melody and we both swooned at the idea of taking such culinary classes. Little did we know we would return a few years later and stay at that very Bastide on our first gourmet cooking tour.

Of course, we were then led next door where, if we were so inclined, we could purchase one of the many pieces of their finest plates. Winston insisted we buy the one with the dancing birds design which were whimsical and mythological in nature. Little did he know that that purchase would be the first of many, many of my purchases of *faïence*. Collections have to start somewhere. Right?

Giddy from the charm of lovely Moustiers and following

the tour of the *faïence* museum, we decided it was time to search for Bob and Shirley as we needed to head back along the Gorg and home. Silly us! They were nowhere to be found! We figured they were long home by then, anyway, and probably busy whipping up some very special dinner for our night's repast. "That would be so lovely," Melody said.

Once we headed out of Moustiers, the skies cleared and now that we were really skirting the edge of the gorge, we were able to see all that we had missed on the trip up. Stopping here and there, we took our time to return as we looked forward to a nice hot dinner. And, yes, we knew that they would magically find some marvelous market along the route, as that was what they were so good at. And, indeed, we dined out on the balcony with a dinner fit for kings and queens—candlelight, wine, and pasta of another sort with a mélange of fresh vegetables.

After dinner, which was always accompanied by local radio music out of Nice or Cannes, we danced and sang to the "Itsy Bitsy, Teeney Weenie, Pas Petite, Petite Bikini" obviously in French, then leaned over the balcony to see if we could catch a glimpse of the Côte d'Azur. Mais oui! *Demain* (tomorrow), we were heading to the Côte d'Azur and the beach.

CHAPTER SEVEN

Along the Bay of St. Tropez

*U*nlike the deep blue for which this French coastline was named, the Côte d'Azur was a soft tinge of blue so pale in color and reflecting such diffused light that I found myself questioning the very adjective *blue*. The smooth and recently preened white sandy beach appeared to be a simple extension of the water—a ripple, a sheen, and a glimmer—as it stretched its broad body into the Bay of St. Tropez.

We—the six of us—stood on the ten-foot-high sea wall of St. Maxine, and as our eyes adjusted to the golden shimmer of light, we panned the coastline, past the marina, the beachside cafés and around the horseshoe of the Bay. In the distance, through a mist of warm coastal fog, we struggled to catch a glimpse of the village of St. Tropez. Oh, so different from the chilly bay we had left in San Francisco.

On that June morning, the air felt thick and heavy like a wet beach towel that clung intimately to every part of one's body. An occasional puff of onshore wind swept past without cooling us but carried a surprising hint of jasmine. As the breeze shifted, an intermingling of aromas rose from sausages, pizza, *pommes frites*, and Coppertone. Techno-music sent its raucous beat into the air as a backdrop to the laughter and French banter from the sunbathers below us.

We were anxious to join them but were not quite prepared. We all plunked down on the sea wall to observe the ensuing activity below. None of us was a seasoned traveler, and I was coming to realize, we were, as a group perhaps a trifle naïve about foreign places and customs. In fact, over the past few days, it would be an overstatement to say we grasped the basics of the French language, much less the cultural norms. The truth was we were desperately attempting to translate any and all signs for a little (*un peu)* understanding of anything around us. With sweaty fingers pawing through an array of totally useless French dictionaries, three of us searched for meaning to the world around us, while three kept watch for clues of understanding. I felt especially responsible as I was the one who had answered the sweet little ad in the *San Francisco* magazine and had swept the others up in the idea of a dream vacation together in the hills of Provence—and along the beach.

Once we understood that *plage* was not a bad, nor a contagious thing, but the word for beach, we sighed with relief and continued to scrutinize the next signs and rules.

"How does one order a chaise?" I wondered out loud, and, "What terms do we use to order wine or a sandwich, for gawd's sake?" But foremost in my mind was: What is the appropriate beach wear at this apparently semi-nude beach before us? Clearly, I was out of my element. I had only heard of a few such beaches on the fringes of the San Francisco Bay, but I had never considered frequenting them. Too chilly!

Below me, I could see the sprawling beach was cordoned off into businesses, separated one from the other by a spectrum of colorful umbrellas and beach chaises: red stars, blue plaids,

pink polka dots and green stripes. Each business was distinguished not only by a specific hue but also by an exotic name:
Canard et Dauphins Plage, La Cannelle Plage, or Paris Plage,
none of which we could translate. Connecting one chaise to
another were small tables where, among the sunglasses and
tanning lotions, *pan bagnat* (tuna on a roll) or succulent *saucisse*
(sausage) sandwiches were being placed. And to our amazement,
patrons were also being served cool, shimmering wine in crystal
glasses—not the regulation paper cups we were used to juggling.
Yes, this one magnificent observation sent promises of soothing
relief from the scintillating heat of the June morning sun. My
eyes continued down the beach to the women casually lounging
in their bikini—bottoms.

Now you may not know this, as I certainly didn't, but the
beaches along the French Riviera are a mix of clothed, semi-
nude, and fully nude sunbathing. Why, only a few sandy
beachheads away in St. Tropez, stardom came to one Brigitte
Bardot in this way. So, as we sat there dazed by the sun, I got
to wondering about whether a girl like me, a bit past my prime,
and on vacation for the first time on the Côte d'Azur . . . Well,
could I? Would I?

I cast a sideways glance at my sister, Melody. I knew she
had never experienced such things on public beaches—she *is*
older, you see—and crystal-clear moments of the two of us
skinny-dipping in our youth along the Platte River in Nebraska
flashed through my mind. But this was different! I was no
longer young. This was no private beach, and we were definitely not in Nebraska. And, to further my dilemma, the sophistication I had achieved as an adult in colorful California
seemed to have slipped below my knee knobs.

I noticed the beach-side women seemed quite relaxed
wearing only bikini bottoms and certainly the smile on men's

faces around them indicated total acceptance. But, for me? No! Definitely not! Not with anyone I actually *knew* around me! It all seemed quite embarrassing. I blanched at the very thought. Again, I glanced at my sister wondering what she was thinking. I couldn't tell. In fact, our entire entourage remained mute, revealing nothing. Could we? Would we?

The enticing aromas of the nearby food display finally moved us into action. It was lunchtime and we never missed a meal. So, while my sister and her husband nonchalantly wandered away from the beach "in search of sustenance elsewhere," we two remaining couples marched down to the closest *plage*. We opted for the green striped umbrella and chaise, bumbled through our orders for food and wine, and took our turns changing in the bathhouses along the beach. All of us came out in, let's say, modest attire. We were hungry, and thirsty—not nudists!

It didn't take us long to feel like we could do this thing—sit on a beach along the Bay of St. Tropez. The sun was warm, and the blue-green waters were cool and refreshing. The sandwiches were delectable, although I must confess, I gave my husband a haranguing he didn't deserve. You see, he knew next to no French, so why I thought he could go up to the booth and order food for us was rather stupid on my part. He marched back to me and presented me with baguette sandwiches.

"What kind of sandwich did you buy?" I asked him nonchalantly.

"It's a *beurre* and *jambon* sandwich," he said proudly. He was so pleased with himself, but the shrew in me came out like a banshee, "Beurre and jambon?" I loudly whispered. (Fortunately, Bob and Shirley were in the water and didn't hear my outburst.) "That's what you ordered? You know that's just plain ham and plain butter, don't you? No mustard; not even

Grey Poupon, no cheese; not even Velveeta; just plain butter on a thin slice of ham wrapped in a baguette!"

Oh, my! I saw how he wilted at this and realized I had made an issue ugly when it didn't need to be; but believe me, I profusely apologized. Then once I took a bite of my sandwich, I was surprised to find it to be quite delicious! Yes, I confess. Food choices are way too important for me, and I needed to get a grip! At this point, we were served wine in real glasses while sitting on the beach, and this was a real and unexpected treat.

Before we knew it, Melody and Dan returned from their midday meal and saunter. They had been gone only for a couple of hours, but we asked them where they had gone as we knew Melody could not spend time in the sun.

"After lunch, we mainly wandered the shady paths near the beach, but did venture down to where a rivulet ran into the Mediterranean. I found an interesting pottery piece there, which will have pride of place in my waterfront rock box," she exclaimed. "I have stones from the shores of Nice, Half Moon Bay, the Bay of Fundy, the Mississippi River, our brother's pond . . ." She held up her now prized piece of pottery for our assessment. And Dan held up a book he had come across from a local bookstore. (He never missed a bookstore!)

"Melody, that's lovely!" Shirley said.

"Yes," I said, "all we have to show for our time is a sun-burn . . . and memories!"

"Not me!" Winston said as his fair skin had been fully pro-tected by a quart of SPF 75 sunscreen and a large umbrella. (It did have a pink hue, though, but we didn't mention it.)

We packed up our gear and headed up to our cars. I must say, I'm never happy to leave a beach or a swimming pool and this was no different. But then, I was also determined to return.

In retrospect, that first day at the beach became a practice session—as if I was mentally working up to an Olympic event. Nothing was ever verbalized, but my mind was a constant buzz. We returned to this, our favorite beach, a number of days and none of us attempted the cultural extravagances of semi-nude sunbathing. I believe I was relieved. But, what if . . . ? I shoved those thoughts aside.

Chapter Eight

Sauntering with Melody

On one particularly exquisite afternoon, after eating a sumptuous brunch on the outside deck, Melody and I decided to take a walk together through the nearby hills. Yes, it was just the two of us, as the guys opted to relax and read at the house, and Bob and Shirley? Well, they were carrying their swimming gear when they crept out the door, and the words St. Tropez were whispered in a way that if spoken outloud, their plans might dissipate. We all shrugged and went on with our plans.

Melody and I took some straw hats, and I recall the dust lifting off the roads as we padded along coating the crystal clean air around us and turning the nearby plants and our feet the color of dirt. The local dogs, which were all characters everyone, began barking as we passed. I guessed they wanted to let us know that, yes, they did have homes and were, at times, frequenting them.

You see, it had become a comedy caper each and every day as we walked through the village center heading for our cars, that the town dogs, would bound out to greet us. They, it seemed, were allowed to go anywhere and everywhere. No leash laws here. When they would come careening through the streets, racing their buddies, or carousing under the tables at the little café, if one was not careful, your legs could get knocked out from beneath you. Ah, but then they would back off, as if to say, "Just kidding!" One hound, in particular, would saunter past us, as if we weren't even there, but clearly his eyes were keeping us in sight. Just in case. Oh, I digress!

So, that day when Melody and I walked down the road leading out to the west of town, we trudged up and over a ridge and past houses set outside the city walls. We had not been aware of where many of these dogs lived, but, they were quick to let us know they saw us coming. And those who were well-fenced, echoed all of the greetings from their rambler buddies. Of course, some came bounding down toward us barking, but then quickly lost interest!

Now, I don't know about you, but I'm not altogether comfortable with unknown dogs lurching about without a tether. But, Melody seemed quite fine. (She did live on a farm in Iowa, so this was right up her alley—or field, so to speak.) But since I was not quite certain how to speak French to people, how could I possibly speak to French dogs? The village of Claviers was not a tourist town, so it was unusual for folks and dogs to deal with the likes of us. But, there we were and somehow, the locals, whether on two feet or four feet, seemed to tolerate us. And in a kindly way!

Lining the road were enormous bushes of yellow broom with their sweet pea-like golden blossoms, a sprinkling of purple irises, random blood-red poppies, and blue-flowered rosemary hedges which competed with an overwhelm of aromas. The area outside of town was surrounded with a smattering of olive, hackberry, or plane trees and off in the distant fields, we could see wide expanses of lovely purple lavender. It was purely idyllic!

"Melody, do you remember when I lived in Illinois with my husband and two small children, and you drove all the way from Iowa to visit us?" She turned to look at me. "I remember sitting on a set of stairs in our apartment hallway, where our preschool-age daughters were able to run and play. The winter winds, which were always whipping up deep drifts around our complex, had once again denied us the ability to go outside. So, this was our only reprieve."

"Yes, Carole, I do remember! We were attempting to hold a conversation but the noise from the kids was so deafening that we couldn't finish a sentence."

"Yes, and that's the reason I bring this up. It was right then and there that you and I made a pact that when our children were grown and gone, we would fly away together! Anywhere, just to be able to spend enough time together to finish each other's sentences. Don't recall if France was our goal, but, I feel as if this was the day we prepared for."

Melody turned and swooped me up in a hug, our hats colliding in the mix. And as we began to talk, she grabbed my hand, and we ambled slowly along, catching up on the years of intimate conversations we had missed. As I recall, the afternoon was not dreadfully hot, but remained like a warm embrace. The aromatic air gently held us as we walked . . . it was such an amber time. When I think back on that memory, I recall it was one of comfort and a congenial joy for this treasured sister time.

Once we returned, Dan looked up from his book and looked at the two of us. I'm not certain what he saw, but he said to Melody, "I think you lived here in another age." *What a sweet observation of his dear wife,* I thought. And I believe he was right. It felt like we had made an almost spiritual connection to this place—this little out-of-the-way village of Claviers.

Years later, I recall reading a description of Claviers, as "A secret surrounded by olive trees; a perched village which manages to preserve the languor of Provence." Yes, that was the experience we came away with. A slowing down of life; and a relaxing into a world lived many years ago.

Melody and I made dinner together that evening—our bond was always strong, but now even stronger. Memories of us as little girls standing on chairs to help with dinner came flooding back, but especially the nightly dish washing duty. Being the two oldest in a family of five children, we were the designated dishwashers. Plus, we were the only girls!

For our hors d'oeuvres that night, we began with little pots of rich black olive and artichoke tapenade. Glasses of rosé were poured, and as wedges of ripened Brie cheese were laid out, Bob and Shirley made their entrance. Totally sunburnt, but excited about their day at the beach in St. Tropez. "We have to go back," they both exclaimed. I voted to join them.

After the two cleaned up a bit, we sat down for a course of mushroom-filled tortellini splashed with vegetable-infused pasta sauce. We might have been in France, but we were in southern France, and were paying attention to the Provençal cuisine which embraced both the Italian as well as the French. Plus, these items were readily available at the local market. Ah, but we did need to stock up again!

CHAPTER NINE

To Bargemon and Moulin de Callas

"And, as for the oil, it is a masterpiece. You'll see." Before dinner that night, we tested it, dripping it onto slices of bread that had been rubbed with the flesh of tomatoes. It was like eating sunshine."

—PETER MAYLE, *A YEAR IN PROVENCE*

"The smell of good bread baking, like the sound of lightly flowing water, is indescribable in its evocation of innocence and delight."

—M.F.K. FISHER

*T*he following morning around eight, we decided to venture out to Bargemon together to collect croissants and baguettes—and to see where on earth our dear friend, Bob, had been disappearing each day. (We had begun calling him "Bob, the Bun Boy"). Not that we didn't trust him to pick up our pastries as he always returned with delicious ones at that. But we were curious and wanted to check out the bakery and village of Bargemon for ourselves. Why, it was only a scant five kilometers. away! So, six of us wedged into the Mercado and attempted to get comfortable. Picture a front seat and middle seat, ah, but no back seat. Just a cargo area!

Bargemon, another picturesque medieval village, lay to the north of Claviers at the bottom of a verdant valley filled with olive groves. Once we parked, I dug out my sun hat and slapped it on my head, as the heat and humidity levels were already climbing. Bob had already taken off, as he was proudly leading the way to the boulangerie. Finally, we were able to meet the mysterious *boulanger*, or baker, Bob had been telling us all about. We felt significantly justified that we had, indeed, checked him out.

Actually, the baker we met was quite busy, but pleasant. You see, there are two boulangeries, but only one was open at a time. Every other day, one baker opened up his boulangerie, and the other one the next day. It seemed to be a kind thing; a friendly thing to do in a small village of only about 1,500 folks. And we were fortunate that in this village the bakers provided bread, cakes, and croissants. In larger towns, these specialties are found in separate stores: a patisserie and a boulangerie, which requires more trekking about.

We trooped down the hill of one of the village's *allées,* or streets, with our own wax paper envelopes of croissants, clutched in hand, while stalwart Dan carried a three-foot baguette thrown over his shoulder. Immediately, we discovered a lovely square, the Place Chauvier, which had nice outside tables near a fountain. While we three ladies held court at the tables, the gentlemen placed orders for *cinq* (five) *café au lait* and *un* (one) *Americano,* which the French consider a large weak coffee.

I took off my hat, leaned back and looked up as the dappled morning sun filtered down through the leaves of the majestic plane trees around us. Bistros, fresh fruit vendors and food markets skirted the periphery of the square and the music of splashing water from the nearby fountain was pleasant to the ear. A flash of color caught my eye as a couple of local children began peeking around corners, trees, and the fountain to keep tabs on us *étrangers*, or strangers, in their midst. It became a game of hide and seek as these precocious children crept closer and closer giggling all the while.

As we lazed away at our table, sipping coffee, and sprinkling croissant crumbs down the front of ourselves, we set about discussing our next plan of action. We hoped to visit a nearby olive mill and winery, so local maps suddenly appeared out of back pockets and purses. Once our plans were set, we began to meander back up hill through the *allées* of the old village back to the car.

As we proceeded up through the village, we checked out the beautiful old houses surrounding the fifteenth-century church. At one point I stopped walking to read from the guidebook. I didn't want to stumble on the cobblestones, even though the rest continued without me.

> Bargemon is fortunate enough to have kept a good part of its medieval enclosure . . . The ramparts and doors date from the twelfth and sixteenth centuries . . . From the top of the old ramparts of the village, you will have a magnificent view of the nature which surrounds it, and you will discover the village of Claviers which stands proudly opposite Bargemon.

"Well, that's the direction we came from," my husband said, "but *not* where we are headed. We're on our way to Callas. Are we ready?"

First, let me remind you again that all six of us were truly wedged into our Mercado station wagon. And even though it was just a few kilometers from both Bargemon to the village of

Callas, my husband promised us wedgees we wouldn't be long on the road. That was a promise missed.

Winston began driving south as he followed the extremely narrow roadway down through one switchback after another through the mountains. It was slow going, but we all tried to make the best of it. Even though it was difficult to catch sight out of all the windows, the village of Callas was surrounded by wild, rocky lands and the gorgeous forest of Pennafort. When we spotted massive pinkish-red, iron-ore-colored cliffs and rocks, I pulled out my guide and attempted to read, although I felt myself getting a wee bit car sick.

"This pretty route near Callas leads you to discover the Gorges de Pennafort. The trail starts at the Gorges car park and goes down to the riverside," I read as our car sped right past it.

"The Pennafort valley stream is framed by high-cut red rocks and a pine forest. It forms beautiful basins that invite you to swim." My audience was, indeed, hot and needed a dip, but we continued. We were on a mission!

"If you want to hike the Cascade de Pennafort, it is better to wait for the summer period." *Check.* "Part of the path is done with your feet in the water. On the way back, a path starting from the car park leads you to the chapel of Notre Dame de Pennafort. In neo-Greek style, this nineteenth-century building is built on a spur at the confluence of two valleys."

"Do you want to take a hike and cool your feet?" Bob asked. I'm sure he was anxious to get out of the crowded car as we were all sweltering.

After what seemed like forever, we finally entered Callas from the north, where we discovered yet another charming, perched village. Mountain goats would do well living in these parts! We careened through the main part of town bypassing steep narrow streets, known as *calades,* and past their ancient village fountains. We were in search of a sign for the "Olivier," or olive oil maker, which was our desired destination.

The car weaved down the roads until the land flattened out and we were able to see broad fields with olive trees spread out before us. We arrived at the mill and piled out of the car. Each one, but the driver took a moment to unhinge their knee knobs from their chins and sort out if they could walk again. Yes, we were capable!

The Moulin de Callas, or the Callas Mill, was small and according to the sign on the doorway had been run by the Bérenguier family since 1928. Originally dating from 1746, the Mill looked to have been made over into the owner's home with a lovely shop attached. We walked in en masse and a young woman in her mid-twenties, her brunette hair pulled up into a regional cap and wearing a bright yellow Provençal print tunic, welcomed us at the counter.

"*Bienvenue!*" she said. We all nodded our heads and muttered "bonjour." Once she recognized we were non-French speaking tourists—*What gave us away?*—she didn't hesitate, but said, "Welcome!" From then on, she peppered her talk with a modicum of English, as she offered us olive oils for sale, along with a complimentary oil tasting following a short tour of the workings of their old facility.

"We will explain about olive oil production and show you through the old workrooms where the rich, luscious golden-green olive oil used to be born. Would you care to join us?"

We nodded enthusiastically and were introduced to another young woman—our guide, Janine—who was a red head and wore the same traditional cap and yellow and blue tunic. She led us through a showroom where I spotted in passing marvelous little gift bottles of olive oil, soap, and ceramics embossed with olives. All called out suggestively to me. Oh, what a great ploy! They knew I'd be back.

We encircled a display of an ancient millstone where the tour began. "As you can see, we no longer make oil at this two-hundred-fifty-year-old mill. Our present mill is a modern facility located nearby but let me begin our story." She threw her arms wide open and exclaimed, "There is nothing more ubiquitous to Provence than its wonderful history of olives and olive oils." Exuberance punctuated every carefully uttered word of English.

We swooned and nodded our heads in agreement. I, of course, was delighted because one of my mottos is: "I brake for olive oils and wines." Honest, I do!

"In Provence, the *Olivades* or olive oil season, takes place between late November and late January. This is when the olives are harvested, and the oil is pressed. There is a local saying that '*A la saint Catherine, l'huile est dans l'olive*' or 'On the Feast of Saint Catherine, the olives are ready to press.' And so it is that if you are in Provence any time from St. Catherine's day which is November 25th through the end of January, you will be able to see, and sometimes even join in, harvesting the olives and pressing the oil.

The traditional way to harvest olives was by hitting the tree branches with long wooden sticks. The olives would fall onto nets that were spread on the ground under the trees. There are also some growers who still pick their olives by hand! No matter how they are harvested, it's crucial to press them as soon as possible. In fact, to qualify for the AOC label, they must be pressed within three days."

"AOC?" my husband asked.

"*Oui*, this label identifies each agricultural product whose stages of production and processing are carried out in a defined geographical area, or the specific terroir, using recognized and traditional know-how. *Comprends?*" We all nodded our heads as if we did understand and she continued on.

"The production of olive oil begins once the leaves are removed, and the olives are washed." She showed us old photos of past pressings. We crowded together to peer at the faded black and white prints.

"The olives are then dumped into a large stone, or granite bowl like this one before you," she said, sweeping her hand over the enormous old press. "And the olives are crushed under two concave stones attached to a central beam fixed to an iron pivot to create the pomace." Pieces of that old equipment were now a figment of our imagination, but we were busy imagining.

"The pomace is spread onto straw mats and again pressed. The liquid is typically drained into a stone settling tank where the oil rises to the top and separates from any remaining water and particles. In the past, the olive oil would then be skimmed off the top and stored in terracotta pots for later use in cooking, medicines, religious ceremonies, and more." She drew in a deep breath and looked at each of us.

"So, are you open to tasting some different olive oils?" We were and we all scurried behind her to inch into the tiny tasting room.

"Should have brought your large baguette for dipping, Dan," Bob said, grinning, until Janine interrupted him.

"Now, let me explain the process of olive oil tasting, as it is not quite like wine tasting." I started to nod my head as I consider myself well-versed in wine tasting, but realized I knew nothing here.

"It is not just a dainty sip or swipe of oil on a piece of bread," Janine said. "Oh, no! In fact, you hold a tiny cup in your hand, swirl the oil around like it is a fine wine, then inhale the aroma," she said, handing out minuscule paper cups of oil.

"When you're ready, you bring a good amount of oil into your mouth, breathe in; actually, suck it in. Delicious, isn't it?"

I let the light floral liquid slip between my lips and slide to the back of my throat, and then swallowed. I nodded at the others like we've got this. But Janine intervened.

"Ah, but you're not finished yet . . . Wait for the first, second, and even the third after-taste. And there's a whole vocabulary that goes along with this ritual. Grassy. Herbaceous. Peppery. Hints of artichoke, apple, or almond. And so on."

We struggled to find our own descriptors, but we were anxious to take another sip. It was at this point Janine lifted a little cup to her glossy red lips and began to suck in—with the loudest *slishing* sound I think I had ever heard in mixed company. We all looked aghast!

"As you can confirm," she said, "it can be quite a noisy affair, as there is this loud sucking sound when you inhale the oil, all in order for it to hit the back of the throat."

I could see there was nothing terribly delicate about this and I was expecting hog calling next, but I found this a unique way to get the tongue and the inside of the mouth coated with oil, in order to identify the flavor.

I took another swig, coughed, and sputtered, but made a suitable sound, *slish*, to confirm to one and all that I could conquer this challenge.

"Ah, I believe this has a hint of grass, maybe some apple, but with a bite of pepper," I stated bravely.

"Quite complex, isn't it," Janine said.

We nodded in agreement and continued tasting until we realized we were, indeed, getting hungry. We felt we had thoroughly expanded our knowledge of the fine art of olive oil pressing and it was time to march through the gift shop and on to a restaurant. I admit I sidetracked the momentum when I stopped in the gift shop and purchased a bottle of olive oil, a ceramic bowl with olive motifs, along with olive-wood salad utensils. Shirley added to the coffers of olive oil. And Melody purchased a ceramic pitcher & trivet with irises in blues and yellows. Always one to envelop the colorful Provençal spirit, she had chosen the proud colors of place. Bless them, our dear husbands nodded their pleasure.

We asked for directions to a good restaurant, and were given several options, but as we stepped out of Moulin de Callas a light rain began. Without hesitation, we immediately ducked into the restaurant next door, where we indulged in excellent savory crêpes and omelets. Some of us enjoyed the conviviality of the local dogs, which were present at all local cafés. And some, not so much!

CHAPTER TEN

Off to the Winery in La Motte

One morning, after a leisurely breakfast followed by catching up on chores, we all decided the day had come to go wine tasting. But, in two separate cars. I doubt that Bob will ever forgive us for insisting he be the designated hatch sitter, but he was the slimmest and most agile.

We had noticed some vineyards on the route going and coming to the beach the other day, so we decided to retrace our course down the highway and headed toward Le Muy. We tried to enjoy the scenery, as it was quite beautiful, but our stomachs were suddenly growling. We were so hungry. Bob had told us about a little restaurant they had spotted on the way back from St. Tropez, so our plan was to rendezvous there.

Once down on the plains, we were surrounded by a myriad of vineyards, with the deep green leaves hiding lush, emboldened fruit.

"Ah, there's a great-looking winery," Dan said, as we drove quickly by.

"Perfect! We'll return after lunch!" Winston responded. We all nodded in agreement, as our stomach clocks were set.

The six of us sat outside in an open-air garden surrounded by olive trees. I had a most superb entrée: lightly batter-fried goat cheese stuffed zucchini blossoms. What an extraordinary taste experience and one I hoped to attempt to replicate once I got home.

"The ability the French have to lightly fry anything is a miracle in my book," I effused, as I popped each one of those delicate petals stuffed with goodness into my mouth. Were there lavender buds mixed in? Whatever it was, it was a magical combination I simply couldn't explain.

I joined the rest in ordering bowls of fresh pasta with a light olive oil sauce, scads of olives, fresh tomatoes, and chervil. This was, of course, followed by a glass of rosé.

After lunch, we drove back up the road, once again passing field after field of grapevines, which appeared like a patchwork quilt spread in every direction, ending at the bottom of the mountains.

We had hoped to take photos of those fields and the winery, but before we pulled into the parking lot of Chateau d'Esclans, the clouds opened, and rain began to pour down. I caught a quick glimpse of a grand chateau through the plane trees, as we followed signs leading up the winding road. Painted golden brown with light blue shutters, this immense Georgian-style house exuded notes of prominence, history, and aristocratic ideals. As I scurried out of the car and into the building, my expectation was of visiting grandeur. I was surprised to find that the large room we entered seemed . . . a bit damp and chilly and was also somewhat bleak. A lackluster bar sat in the middle of the room, but there was no real décor, no fanfare or reception desk, no colorful paintings . . . Why there was nothing on or against the walls other than a poster or two, plus boxes and boxes of bottled wine.

Well, I thought to myself, *they must operate wineries differently here in France. Thankfully, I hid my ignorance with silence.*

A man sauntered in from a backroom and introduced himself as Jean-Claude. Wearing a green ball cap, plaid shirt, and casual blue slacks, he announced that he was the estate manager for the d'Esclans Winery. He welcomed us, and with my urging, explained a bit about the winery's history, but mostly handed me an English language brochure.

"This chateau," it read, "was once the former residence of the Earls of Provence. It also was the property of Jacques Auxile Verrion, Minister for War under Louis XV, and he was the man who then became the Earl of d'Esclans during the reign of Charles X."

When I finished reading from the brochure, I asked if the Earl was the reason for the name of the winery, Esclans. He nodded. Check! I understood the history!

Ah, but he clearly was setting up for wine tasting.

We bellied up to the bar, so to speak, where Jean-Claude pulled out six large wine glasses from under the bar. We inched in even closer. Yes, he knew a bit of English, but much less than at the olive mill from the other day. We, of course, were useless. Nodding and head bobbing had become our usual contributions to language. We all, of course, had visited wineries before in California so, we knew the drill. Or, thought we did.

As I said, the estate manager was eager to have us sample his wines as he was quite proud of their products. He pulled out a gold certificate of award from beneath the bar and showed us the winery's successes. I'm not certain if I heard an inward groan when we mentioned being from California, but after that mere faux pas, we kept our mouths shut. But, in his broken English—we should know more French than "faux pas"—we were able to nod, swish, swirl and sip several of his floral tasting wines as we regaled him with our stories of where we were staying in Provence.

"Most all of the grapes in this vineyard are used in rosés," he said, "and during the hot summer days and nights, you will find this to be a light and lovely gift to your palate." He lifted his glass then held it up to the light, sipping wine right along with us as I'm sure he didn't want us drinking alone.

"The terroir," he continued, "is made of healthy old vines, some of which are more than eighty years of age. Grenache makes up the majority of our grapes, or 60 percent, with Mourvèdre reaching 20 percent, completing with Cinsault and Syrah. And, as you could tell on your drive up here, we have forty-four hectares of vines which are grown on clay-limestone soils that lie in a marvelous position that captures all the warmth of the sun."

Château d'Esclans, as a winery, continued to assert its long history.

We continued chatting as we tasted several varietals. Recalling some of the descriptors from our olive oil tour, we began pulling up adjectives like grassy, herbaceous with hints of artichoke, apple, or almond.

Yes, we liked them as they were quite light and tasty, as he had stated earlier. And we were feeling a bit rosy, ourselves.

"Why, this wine is so good you can come down from Claviers and bring your own bottles or milk jugs and fill them with our wine," he boasted.

"*Oooh*," we said, our heads bobbing in understanding.

But it was when we asked if we could see their bottling process, that his face squinched up. He took a step back from the bar, I guess in order to scrutinize us. Were we serious? He seemed querulous!

"Why would you want to do a thing like that?"

We said we had visited other wineries in the States and were quite interested in their methods, including the bottling process.

He shifted back and forth on his feet, shoved his cap back on his head, and then asked, "Are you sure you want to take the time to see the process?"

"Oh, my yes," we echoed. "We have plenty of time!"

Reluctantly, he led the way to a back room, which was purely utilitarian in nature. There were grey concrete walls and floors, large stainless-steel sinks, and a conveyor belt with boxes filled with wine bottles. But seated in the middle of the room was a group of older women—maybe six in total—wearing white smocks, hair tied up into babushkas, all chatting amiably while perched on tiny stools. They were merrily hand-filling each and every wine bottle by directing plastic tubes into the bottles which led back to the wine barrels across the room. Yes, I was a bit taken aback, as the production line was much more primitive than any I had witnessed before. But then what did I know? It seemed quite effective, and since we were told we could bring in our own wine bottles and/or milk jugs, we were already considering dropping by to do just that.

We all smiled, nodded, and complimented the women on their fine work and immediately went out to the showroom and bought several already hand-filled bottles of wine. If the wine was good enough to produce, who were we to dampen their efforts in getting their products out into the world and down our gullets?

After an afternoon of gallivanting about, we headed back up the hill to Claviers where we hoped to collapse in our lovely home away from home. Can't remember whose night it was to cook, but, surely, we still had the baguettes . . . some cheese . . . fresh olive oil . . . oh, and wine! What else did we need? A nap?

Ah, but, as it turned out, we were not finished for the day. We had been intimating that we wanted to venture out to Avignon and Arles for a day or two, as our guidebooks were filled with the wonders of historical relevance—from pre-Roman through the time of the popes in France. In Avignon to be exact!

So, once we arrived back in Claviers, my husband suggested that "we" call a hotel in Avignon for a reservation for three rooms. We were planning to leave in a day or two and, hopefully, we had not waited until the last minute to consider those little details. Everyone nodded in agreement.

"We must make a reservation!" my husband said.

"Yes, that is something WE should do," we all responded.

And then they all looked straight at me, as I knew a wee bit more (*un peu*) French than the rest. As I stared at the house phone, I knew my normal nodding and bobbing wasn't going to cut it this time. Not over the phone! I sat down and wrote out a script, just in case. We wanted three rooms (*chambres*) with baths (*bain*) and showers (*douche*) for two nights beginning next Monday and Tuesday. Would that cut it?

We all grabbed comfortable seats in the living room, where we each pulled out our own trusty guidebooks. Yes, there were a great many hotels in Avignon, we surmised, but which one should we try? After a bit of back and forth, I struck upon one called Hôtel d'Angleterre, or the British Hotel.

"They ought to speak English there, don't you think?" I asked, with apprehension gilding my words. I looked around the circle as five pairs of eyes stared at me with shared anxiety and anticipation. They then nodded enthusiastically and encouraged me to give it a try. I took another look at the French phrase book to see exactly what I should ask, but, to me, it was not clear.

"Well, nothing ventured; nothing gained," I finally said as

my sweaty hand picked up the phone and placed the call. When the hotel receptionist answered with "Bonjour" the rest was an immediate muddle of French. My head began to nod and bob as I hoped this would help. But no! I then began to stammer, *"Parlez-vous Anglais?"* I breathed in, breathed out, and waited. There was a pause on the other end of the line, and then there was a clipped, *"Non."*

"Non?" I gasped. My shoulders slumped. The others sagged. Yet I caught glimpses of faith they had in me. They encouraged me on.

I took another deep breath and asked, *"Avez-vous trois chambres dans votre hôtel?"*

"Oui!" she said. Yes, as it turned out, they did! What did I expect? It was a hotel. But I believe she asked me did I want them with a *bain* or a *douche?* Well, my face turned red at the word *douche*, but I felt I should power through. At least I knew that *douche* was the term for a shower and *bain* was a bath so, I figured we needed both.

"Avec a douche et bain, s'il vous plait. Oui! Trois chambres! Pour deux nuits?"

"Quel jours? Quel jours souhaitez-vous votre chambres?" she asked me.

"Lundi prochaine," I mumbled. *"Et Mardi, aussi!"* Ah, but it was enough for me to get things moving as she must have figured I meant the upcoming Monday for two nights.

"Oui! Oui!" I said as my husband handed me his credit card, and the rest went magically forward, as all things with credit cards do. (Except the pronunciation of numerals is also different, but my few years of college French finally paid off.)

After the call, I collapsed onto my bed, wringing wet with sweat and angst. Yes, a nap was called for now. I had earned it!

CHAPTER ELEVEN

*A Leisurely Sunday in Provence and
the Gorges de Pennafort Restaurant*

"If time, so fleeting, must like humans die, let it be filled
with good food and good talk, and then embalmed in the
perfumes of conviviality."

—M. F. K. FISHER

*T*he next day was Sunday, and after a relaxed breakfast,
several of us considered taking a long walk. However,
the morning air, which had been delicious enough to eat earlier,
was turning hot as the sun rose over the mountains in the east.

Bob, who had been pacing around the living room, was
feeling desperate to find fuel for his Citroen. He had not refilled since we had picked up our rentals, and his car, being
much smaller, needed gas. On Sunday, no less! Since a drive
anywhere was fine with me, Melody and I decided to tag
along. Our two-day trip to Avignon and Arles had been
planned for the following day so we would definitely be taking
both vehicles.

"Want to go along?" I asked my husband and Dan.

"Nah," Winston said as he sank behind his book, the

Marcel Pagnol memoir, *My Mother's Castle, and My Father's Glory* gripped in his hands. I had just finished it and considered this book to be the true measure of all the people of Provence. Of course, that was not true, but Pagnol's beautifully described story of his boyhood was written as a love letter to not only his parents, but to the people, the hills, and valleys of his youth outside of Marseilles. It was charming and haunting at the same time.

Dan, too, was relaxing outdoors on the deck with a book in hand, and the radio tuned to his now favorite classical station out of Nice, so all was good.

So, Bob was stuck with all of us 'babes' in his search for a gas station. Always highlights to capture in life!

"Say, Bob," I asked him, blithely, "where should we start?" He didn't answer at first but just hummed a jaunty little tune as he hopped into the front seat and offered Melody the passenger seat. This was the first time a front seat had been offered to anyone other than Shirley, so she grabbed it up. Shirley and I wedged ever so carefully into the back as it was our turn to be the wedgees.

"I'm thinking of driving opposite of where we've been. Hopefully, en route, we'll locate an open *Gazole* station." I knew he had been worried about finding the correct fuel for several days. Poor thing!

My sister looked back at me. No words were uttered but our two sets of eyebrows rose mightily. *Did he have enough gas to cruise around the mountains?* I knew Bob was one who loved to attempt something both radical and/or risky, but could he get us there and back? Stoic Shirley, bless her, said nothing.

We drove east, then headed north to skirt through the Provençal village of Seillans. Classified in our guidebook as one of the many "most beautiful villages of France," we sadly found that nothing was open. It was Sunday, after all. Bob whirled through the main streets of the town and then back out onto the main road.

"Aren't the wildflowers simply gorgeous, all in bloom, and lining the roadside?" Melody said to Bob. "Bright red poppies, the light-blue cornflowers, the yellow broom—Oh, and so many more!" she waxed on effusively. At every turn, she became even more excited.

After several of these exclamations, Bob turned and said, wryly, "Melody, don't they have wildflowers in Iowa where you are from?" Stunned, Melody's euphoria drooped, and she silenced her ebullience.

Farther east, we arrived in Fayence, where we drove through an archway into the main part of town. We were fortunate to spot a station that carried *gazole*. Ah, but it was closed for lunch. Since we had nothing else to do, we ambled through the village. Like many of the villages we had come to know, this, too, was a very attractive town and had a nice selection of cafes and restaurants. An enviable contrast to Claviers. Thoughts of a delectable, little smackeral of something danced through my head as I secretly channeled my inner Pooh Bear.

While we were deliberating, Melody wandered over to the side of one of the city walls and waved us over to see the expansive vista. Below, we could see the lush green valleys which spread out for miles over hills and between villages. The air that wafted past was floral with a punch of rosemary. Again, my hunger alarm was going off.

"Ah, but the guidebook points out," Shirley said, "several places of interest nearby. Like a rustic stone lavoir, which is an ancient trough where women had washed their family's clothes over the past couple of centuries. Also, we could find an age-old communal oven from a sixteenth-century boulangerie, and some carvings etched onto the stone lintels above village doorways."

Well, that sounded intriguing enough. We're all for figuring out a woman's life from centuries ago, aren't we? And where there was once a boulangerie, there might be another one, I surmised. Etchings in stone above one's doorway? Now, that would have been a nice touch.

We walked about in search of these treasures, but as the sun rose to its zenith, the heat beat down with a vengeance. The humidity level, too, had risen and we all began to feel light-headed. It was time for a drink of something! We scrambled to find a place to sit down.

Fortunately for us, there were numerous fountains throughout the village, and we were able to grab a bistro table in the middle of the town square near a fountain. A bevy of establishments was at the ready to serve us, and we quickly ordered our drinks and settled back in our seats with our guidebooks as Bob meandered off to check to see if the gas station was open.

"See that archway we drove through earlier?" I asked anyone who would listen. Melody and Shirley swiveled their heads in the direction I was pointing.

"That archway is a fourteenth-century entrance through the original ramparts of their walled city. It is known as the Saracen Gate! Who knew?"

"Saracen?" Melody echoed me. "What were they doing way up here in France? I wonder if this had to do with the Crusades?"

I looked back at my guidebook. I was really too warm to think this through, but it mentioned Saracens from the Middle Ages, whether Arab or Turk, who had come from the Sinai Peninsula. It seemed impossible there would be a need for this gate; almost incomprehensible. Yes, I was too warm!

Thankfully, the waiter returned to serve us bottled water and scoops of raspberry sorbet to each of us. I could have given him a big kiss . . . oh, I do get melodramatic!

Bob had not returned at this point and his dish of sorbet became a foamy drink of sorts. As it turned out, Bob had somehow failed to mention that he needed someone to help him remove the gas cap. It seemed he had been in such a hurry to pick up his rental car at the Nice airport, that he had not received adequate instructions regarding the removal of the cap. Who knew that would be a thing? Unfortunately, the gas station attendant wasn't able to open it either, although he suggested a screwdriver to pry it open. Visions of irreparable damage to the car must have flashed through Bob's mind, as he decided to wait until the next day to grab a tank of gas. When he described these decisions, we stared at him as if he had a screw loose. How was he going to get this problem resolved? I kept quiet.

Bob was a delightful, but sometimes odd guy! One was never certain where his mind was, or what plan he was hatching. But his lovely wife seemed to take him in stride in all the best possible ways. No clue was given as to how Shirley really felt! No worries! And in no time at all, we were back on the road, laughing and joking, as we headed back to Claviers. I was looking forward to a respite of reading and a nap!

Ah, but my nap was short-lived. We had made reservations that evening at a very plush (or do they say posh?) restaurant, The Gorges de Pennafort Restaurant. It was located near the same Gorges du Pennafort we had driven through en route to the olive oil shop the other day.

The Hostellerie Les Gorges de Pennafort, only a few minutes from Callas, faced the majestic red walls of the Pennafort gorges. The gastronomic 4-star hotel-restaurant, once an authentic Provençal country house reflected the late after-noon light, with its coral pink walls and light blue shutters peeking out from behind tall cypress trees. Hydrangeas, roses, peonies, and oleander flooded the gardens, and yellow broom and bushes of lavender perfumed the early evening air.

The doorman, who kindly ushered us into the reception room, led us over to the hostess. I was so in awe of the taste-fully appointed space I almost walked right past her. The room was filled with French country furnishings, (and where more obviously would one find French country furnishings than in . . . yes, here!) Baskets of palm trees and pots of roses exuded an ambiance of gentility. The hostess immediately whisked us into the dining room, which was also a composition of subtle elegance. Fresh-cut roses in crystal bowls reflected the shim-mering candlelight off a myriad of wine glasses. The country armchairs, upholstered in soft peach damask, again matched the tones of our surroundings. As we were seated, a hint of setting sunlight streamed in through the windows enhancing the entire setting and everything became aglow.

There were a couple of menus to choose from the waiter informed us: The Discovery Menu and the Gourmet Menu. This was going to be more difficult than I thought. "The Dis-covery Menu, he meticulously explained in excellent English, "had a smaller sampling of choices beginning with the requisite foie gras, escargots de Callas, lemon granita, and tarragon sorbet as an *amuse bouche,* which is a small taste to delight the mouth. Then, as the main course, Mediterranean rockfish, or braised veal with mushrooms with mashed saffron potatoes. Then a selection of fine French cheeses, or a terrine of grated goat cheese with whipped cream."

My mouth simply watered with the reviewing of the first menu, and then, after the waiter left us, I began speed-reading through the Gourmet Menu. It also began with foie gras, but the fried *langoustines* (shrimp) with local rosemary honey caught my attention. And the roasted rack of lamb with thyme along with a tian of vegetables simply shrieked at me from the menu. Yes, it was a few dollars more per person, but this was a meal to remember. I was especially delighted to note that the produce and products used by the restaurant were from local sources, including our new favorite olive oil from Moulin de Callas.

Our waiter returned with an elegant flourish and served us *Kir Royales,* which was a most delightful mix of champagne and *Créme de Cassis,* a liqueur made from black currents. I tasted my aperitif and sat back to soak up the ambiance. The time was filled with the sipping of fine wines, along with the sampling of delightful *amuse bouches.*

I must admit that the camaraderie of our little group could have gotten out of hand as we began recalling some of the most perplexing moments of the trip. Or, most embarrassing! True confessions of "vacation faux pas," we called it as we rec-ollected moments of bumbling through French directions or misunderstanding cultural norms.

I recounted one of the days we happened down to the beach and then went shopping for groceries at the Super Marché in St. Tropez. I had made a huge faux pas by asking where the brie cheese was located in the store. We are in France, you know! I'm so embarrassed to confess even now but when I asked the salesclerk for brie at a cheese counter, no less, she kindly reached across the counter, grabbed my hand, and began to walk around the counter with my hand clearly ensconced in hers. Once we reached the next aisle, she waved with her other hand, as with a wand, and voila! There before me was an entire aisle of brie cheese which seemed to extend for a full block. She did not point out my ignorance, but it was clear I was a novice as I should have figured this out on my own.

Then there were the tales of finding we had driven up streets too narrow to continue to move forward. If there had been signs of instruction, we would have ignored them, because . . . why? They were in French. With our rental car larger than any self-respecting Frenchman would attempt to drive, we were forced to slam our mirrors up against the side of the car in order to pass between narrow stone walls unscathed. Or we were forced to back up along narrow alleys or make a point-by-point-by-point turn until finally inching back out the way in which we had come. Sheesh! Or the beach day in St. Maxime when we were tempted by the gods with going top-less . . . and Bob chose to move down the beach where totally nude sunbathing was the forte. Oh, we were so out of our league! And before we had even touched on some of the more comical tales, our main course was served.

I moaned with delight at every savory mouthful! Of course, I began with pâté de foie gras, followed by a rack of lamb with thyme, but the chocolate-praline soufflé, which was the seventh course, sent me into a sugar coma! Ah, but it was worth it!

Three hours after we entered the restaurant, we wandered outside wearing a beatific glow across our faces. The trees along the Hostellerie path sparkled with shimmering points of light reflecting upon the pink canyon walls. I took my honey's arm as the balmy summer evening wrapped itself around us and we headed back to our car. The evening's experience was like stepping into a fantasy for royalty, and we were feeling a bit like kings and queens.

CHAPTER TWELVE

All Roads, Even to Orange,
Lead to Rome

he next morning, I must confess, I found it difficult to rise. Too much of a good thing (food and wine) the night before was . . . just that, too much of a good thing! But we had a full day planned and I needed to kick butt to get going! After a quick breakfast and a strong espresso, Winston, Dan, Melody, and I popped into our "Mercado" and made our way out of Claviers, down through Draguignan, and onto the A8, which would take us west through Aix-en-Provence, then north to the ancient city of Orange. It took us about three hours. Bob and Shirley, still hampered by the gas cap debacle, headed out before us. Promising to find a car dealership to open the gas tank, they assured us we would meet up at the amphitheater in downtown Orange at noon.

For the last couple of hours of our drive, we had been following one mountain range. Although it was mid-June, the slopes appeared to be covered in snow. How could that be? Dan pointed at Mount Ventoux on our map as the focal point of the nearby range, but we all were surprised to learn this was geologically part of the Alps. All I knew was that this was the one which towered over all the Provençal plains.

"Mount Ventoux?" asked Winston. "Wasn't that where Petrarch went to write poetry to his beloved Laura?" We had taken classes on the Renaissance and Petrarch's name had popped up on occasion.

"I thought Petrarch was the Father of Humanism in Florence," I said. "This was in the 1300s and the beginning of the Italian Renaissance."

"Right, but he is the same person. I remember reading that he fell in love with Laura but could never get her to take notice. Even after he moved back to his hometown of Florence from Avignon, he still longed for her and wrote his most famous of all poems as a love sonnet," Melody chimed in.

"And, they say, he never even saw her or talked to her," I said. "Talk about unrequited love."

"I suppose that's why he found time to become the Father of Humanism," said Dan. "After rediscovering Cicero's papers, and never getting a date, he must have had a few hours on his hands." We laughed.

Dan rarely spoke, but when he did, we listened. Even though his voice was soft, he had a delightful sense of humor, and we didn't want to miss a lick of it.

Although we were all familiar with parts of the Petrarch story, it was Mount Ventoux we were tracking. And sure enough, the ancient city of Orange, which was built on the banks of the Rhône River, stood in the shadow of Mount Ventoux.

As Winston and Dan navigated through the city, I pulled out my trusty guidebook. "Do you know that Orange is one of a number of former, illustrious Roman cities in France?" I paused for my words to resonate. "Well, this one, in particular, contains two—count them—two UNESCO World Heritage sites."

I should have been quiet while the guys were navigating, but I was excited about being in Orange. They heard nothing, but Melody said, "Really? Oh, I can't wait!" Ah, *she* is my audience!

We all had felt the pull of ancient history before we came to France, but once we visited Fréjus a few days before, we were on the hunt for even more Roman glory. We decided to begin at the northern edge of the city where the monument known as the Roman Triumphal Arch or *Arc de Triomphe* was located.

We whipped into a parking lot nearby, and made our way on foot to the base of the Arch. I continued my job as unsolicited tour director. "The guidebook points out that this Arch was constructed, not as a triumphal arch, but rather as a commemorative, dedicated to the glory of the veterans of the second Gallic legion, who were the founders of the Roman colony of Orange. This construction began at the beginning of the first century. Later, the Arch was bestowed upon Emperor Tiberius, and is considered an exceptional monument of Provençal Roman art." I looked around for some response, but everyone was busy walking back and forth through the Arch.

We *oohed* and *aahed* and trooped around and back through the Arch again, before meandering around the sides. One more time I realized my lack of height made it difficult for me to see the detail of these beautifully etched stones.

"The Arch is known to be the 'Entry to the Aurelian Way'," I said aloud as we marched through the three-vaulted passageway. "It was built during the first century AD and is considered an honorary passage. This marks the limits between the world of the dead and the ancient city."

Winston's head bobbed up. "Now, that's a line of demarcation I had never considered. This was a city gate dividing what again?" he asked.

"I guess, the dead from the living." I shrugged. I suppose that's what it was meant to do, but even as I said it, I couldn't wrap my head around this way of thinking. I continued reading to whomever was interested.

"The monument was built of large limestone blocks and measures approximately sixty feet high, over fifty-six feet wide, and twenty-five feet deep. It was endowed with an abundance of sculpted scenery and décor." Our eyes all went skyward once again taking in the immensity of the gate.

We walked to the northernmost side, which, as it turns out, was Winston's favorite side. It had carvings depicting prows of ships, oars, and ropes which represented the naval victory of Rome over Massalia (or Marseilles). Higher up on the monument, we were told the décor depicted land battles waged against the ancient Celts. On the southern face, the sculptures were not as well-defined as time and wars had damaged them badly.

After walking back and forth through all three arches, we posed for photos—not exactly like gladiators or Roman warriors—but as us, Americans thoroughly impressed with the immensity of the structure, its history, and the fine artistic detail which remained. Yes, hands on hips or in the air as if victory was in our grasp!

Hopping back into the car, Winston maneuvered through the side streets of Orange where we located a parking lot and made our way to the Roman Temple and the classical Theater of Augustus. We looked around hoping to see Bob and Shirley near the temple or theater, but they were not there. The time was exactly noon. We stood in the hot sun for a while then decided to begin our tour without them.

As it turned out, there was, sadly, not much left behind to be seen of the second CE Roman temple. Other than weathered vestiges of an ancient stone arch, only a few Roman columns which surrounded the hollowed-out ruins of the temple remained. Plus, there was very little information to help us understand its true history. Since it was located next door to the Roman amphitheater, we exited from the Temple by stepping over a fallen pillar.

Directly from the main street, we made entrance into the amphitheater past a plain but massive sixty-foot-tall stone wall and ambled to a set of corridors. From there we continued through one of three arches which were equally tall, known as the royal door and the guests' door. Surprisingly, we all ended upon an enormous central stage. Would everyone end up walking onto this stage? We missed our turn.

Uncomfortable with finding ourselves on stage while other tourists flowed in behind us, my sister and I skittered off to the side and down a stairway. From there, we headed up another staircase which led to four levels of stadium seats which spread out into a massive semi-circle above us. We climbed to the center of the seats on the second level and stared down at the immense stage we had just left. Our significant others had disappeared somewhere. Maybe needing a costume change? No problem! I wanted to know more about the amphitheater, so I dragged out my guidebook and once again began to read the description of the amphitheater.

"This is said to be the most well-preserved theater in the ancient Roman world and also a UNESCO monument," I read to Melody. Her attention had drifted.

I continued undaunted, "Designed to accommodate the Gallo-Roman public, it was built at the end of the first century AD under the reign of Emperor Augustus. It was the first of its kind in France." I paused and looked around to take in the majesty of the arena.

"Caesar conceived the idea of a theater for spreading Roman culture and of keeping the population's mind off any ideas of political unrest. The theater's interior, the cavea, could accommodate up to 9,000 spectators, seated according to their social status. Just above the half-moon-shaped orchestra pit, the first rows of seats were reserved for the Equites, or knights. The Merchants and Roman citizens took their seats in the middle rows."

"That's us," Melody said, swiveling about again.

"And the highest (and most vertiginous) rows of seats were left to the prostitutes and slaves," I rambled on.

"Vertiginous?" Melody echoed. "Now, that's not a word I've often heard. Must have something to do with vertigo."

I turned in my seat to look above us. Yes, it was quite a steep climb to the loftiest of bleachers.

We turned back around to look at the stage. "Where on earth could our husbands have gone?" Melody asked. We now had lost track of four members of our party, and this was only a party of six.

"Isn't that lovely!" Melody said, as she pointed to the elaborate back wall of the stage. Columns, friezes, and niches, which had once been adorned with colorful marble mosaics and statues, anchored the center niche that still held a ten-foot-high sculpture representing Augustus Caesar.

"It's difficult to believe that after over two thousand years, Caesar remained lording it over all who passed through the portals," I quipped.

"I'm trying to imagine what it must have been like to sit here in Roman days," Melody sighed. "And to see a play or a comedy . . ."

As if on cue, out on the stage appeared our two husbands goofing off and making like rock stars. Well, let's just say, playing air guitars which was probably not what the Romans had in mind, unless this was a true comedy act. We watched the shenanigans and wondered if we should remove this act before others joined in.

"We've been in Orange for only one and a half hours," Melody announced, "and already we've visited two—count them—two UNESCO World Heritage sites!"

"And seen one air guitar show! Time to go?" I asked.

Melody nodded, and we rejoined our troubadours and searched once again for our friends, Bob, and Shirley. Having no luck, we headed to a nearby restaurant for lunch. It was after 1 p.m.

Chapter Thirteen

A Chateau of a Splendid Sort

After lunch, we wandered through the streets of Orange and into a couple of museums, until the oppressive heat rendered us limp and exhausted. So, we decided to drive south toward Avignon, where our night's hotel reservation awaited.

Winston suggested we take a side road closer to the Rhône River and through one of the most opulent of wine-producing regions in France known as Chateau-Neuf-de-Pape to find yet another winery. And, yes, the name of the region means the Castles of the New Popes. This is where the papal vineyards were established in the 1300s when the papacy moved from Rome to Avignon, just a few short miles further south.

After our recent wine-tasting experience, we thought we might step up our game a bit. No more fair maidens squatting on a plastic bucket to hose wine into the bottles. Both Dan and Winston had researched the regional wineries and had concluded that if we wanted to sample truly excellent wines, Château La Nerthe would be one of the places! And so, we headed up a long driveway that led between vineyards, holm oaks, cypress, and olive trees to a park surrounded by majestic plane trees and century-old pines. Through the trees, we could make out a magnificent golden stone bastide known as Château La Nerthe or The Nerthe Castle. We had arrived!

The car's air conditioning had reenergized us, and we immediately sprang from the car to enter the iron gates of the beautiful winery. The entrance to the tasting room was off the car park where a wooden door, inset into a cylindrical rock and stone tower sat opposite the doorway to a row of buildings constructed of the same rough composition. An efficient young woman met us at the doorway, ushered us out of the heat and into a cool reception room. Before sinking into comfortable seats, she introduced us to a formidable older man, Martín, who, thankfully, had an excellent command of English. His job was to fill our minds with the wonders of viticulture and the history of the place. He kept us moving down a long hallway as he regaled us with the history of the Château, the surrounding vineyards, and a litany of the natural environment in which these wines were produced. Obviously, we had arrived in time for the last tour, and he was in a hurry!

"The 227 acres of vineyards," he began, "are divided into fifty-seven plots each of which has its own identity, the result of the unique combination of soils and grape varieties."

"Ah, are we talking *terroir?*" I asked. He nodded in my direction and continued his talk at a fast clip.

"Indeed, if the whole of the vineyard benefits from a typical Mediterranean climate, fortunately, tempered by the northern winds, the mistral," he said, sweeping the air with his hand for dramatic effect, "the diversity of the soils and subsoils creates a veritable mosaic of micro-terroirs. And to which was added a palette of thirteen grape varieties!"

Winston asked him, "I see the ground around the grape

vines have a mix of soils and rocks. Some of those rocks seem quite large and smooth, like river rocks. What is the purpose of these stones?"

"I'm glad you noticed that as this is one way, we in the Chateau-Neuf-du Pape region, are able to control the formation of sugar in the grapes. The heat of the day, you see, is absorbed into the stones, so the cool of the night does not drop the temperature of the grapes so drastically."

Martín continued his talk. "For five centuries, generations have succeeded each other here at Château La Nerthe in the search for the perfect match between soil, subsoil, and grape varieties."

"Wow! Five centuries?" I asked. "So, are you saying this winery was established three hundred years *after* the Popes began vineyards in this valley in the 1300s?"

"*Mais oui*," he responded. "Established in 1560, the history of Château La Nerthe began at that time and became intertwined with the ancient history of the Châteauneuf-du-Pape region since. It was five centuries ago when the natural springs along with a mosaic of soils and subsoils gave the wines of this estate freshness and elegance."

He then regaled us with the history of the three families—yes, only three over all those years—who brought their wines to international prominence. "Today it is the Richard Family who imagine the wines of tomorrow and continue to write the history of Château La Nerthe, with the ambition of preserving and revealing this unique heritage, both viticultural and architectural."

"When did this winery come to the Richard Family?" Melody asked.

"I'm glad you asked," Martín said, "as it was only after a troubled period, marked in particular by the requisition of the castle by the German occupying army in 1943, that the Richard family acquired the estate in April 1985. They immediately brought the winery up to the original values of excellence and meticulously restored the castle before they dug a modern wine cellar."

"Wine cellar?" I piped up. "Are we going to tour the wine cellar?"

"Yes, after I complete my talk," he said, persevering despite my distractions. "It took years of hard work, along with scientific breakthroughs, but the wines which are most characteristic of this winery are Grenache, Syrah, and Mourvèdre, or GSM, plus Counoise, which are all red grape varieties, giving warmth, richness, and softness to their wines. Our Clairette and Picpoul, not as well known, are white grape varieties intended to bring finesse, freshness, and a particular bouquet."

After having first been indoctrinated by our guide, we were led down some steep but narrow steps, and deep into their wine cave. We passed barrel after barrel covered in layers of dust. The only lighting shone from candlelight in ancient chandeliers which gave us a taste of the ways of the past. *Alors,* no electric lights were in here!

"Obviously, this was not 'the modern wine cellar' he mentioned earlier," Dan pointed out. He ducked his head so as not to hit the low beams in the ceiling, also layered with the dust from the past.

We were then, thankfully, led through a passage where we arrived in a charming and, yes, modern section of the wine cellar. Finally, it was time for our first wine tasting. How was the wine after this build-up, you ask? If you enjoy a liquid that tastes as soft as velvet while undulating over your tongue with deep rich tones of plums, chocolate, or cherries, then this would be it! They were purely sumptuous!

I luxuriated in the tastings and felt gratified that I had a better understanding of the importance and elegance of these wines. Yes, we took a few bottles home to our own castles. They were divine!

After the winetasting, we made our way from the chilly wine caves into the searing hot sun. We continued south to Avignon, giddy from the wine and for having found such a magnificent winery in the famed Chateau-Neuf-de Pape region. But we were also concerned for our friends, Bob, and Shirley. We had not seen hide nor hair of them and we were anxious to reach the hotel to see if they had arrived.

We reached the northern suburbs of Avignon, before making it into the historic center of the city. Rising above the treetops was an enormous stone wall, the ramparts, which we recognized from brochures as part of the ancient city walls of the city. Only the top of the Cathedral could be seen looming in the background along with the *Palais de Papes*, the Palace of the Popes.

Referring to her guidebook, Melody began to read, "Originally, the walls, known as Ramparts (*Remparts*), were approximately twenty-four feet high and were embellished with battlements and slits."

"We called them 'shootouts'," Winston said from the driver's seat.

"Hmmh!" Melody continued. She was now realizing that being a tour guide is not always a job well appreciated. "The walls were constructed during the time of the Pope in 1356. This massive and solidly built stone structure, with crenelated glacis and numerous towers, encircled three miles of the historic city.

"A large moat, twelve feet deep, with waters from the Sorgue and the Durance Rivers stopped access. The seven city gates, equipped with wooden vents spiked with iron, were closed each evening, and were dominated by towers and their drawbridges. More spikes and descending grilles were added, for extra protection." Melody paused.

I suppose we should have looked for a gate entrance closer to our destination, the Hotel d'Angleterre, but we were so taken by the sight of the Palais de Papes, we entered through the closest gate we came to. Wow! The city was a total maze. We had discovered a labyrinth of sorts. Weaving our way through the narrow yet bustling lanes, we rattled across cobbled streets onto wide thoroughfares. It was like time travel driving through canyons of massive Gothic-style buildings, which butted up against more 19th century art nouveau department stores, museums, and restaurants.

"Were these streets laid before the Popes came from Rome in 1309?" Dan asked. Our heads were swiveling from side to side to catch any glimpse of our surroundings, but it was beginning to be a bit of a blur.

"Surely, this was a Roman town a couple of millennia before that, don't you think?" I replied. "Somewhere I read that this city was once a Phoenician trading center—or maybe it was Phocaean trading center—because it was situated on the Rhône River—the inner highway to the center of France."

"I guess that's what we're here to find out," Melody answered matter-of-factly.

Eventually, we arrived at the Hôtel d'Angleterre and found it to be a small but charming boutique hotel. And who did we find in the lobby fully immersed in the reading of a French newspaper? Why Bob, of course! Shirley smiled and jumped up to greet us. Did they appear frazzled? No, not at all! Did they project a bit of anxiety? No! Were they surprised to see us? Non! Non! I guess we had been frantic for no apparent reason. Well, we knew stories would soon be revealed. But before that could happen, I needed to check on our rooms. Because I had made the infamous phone call to set up our reservations, I felt fully responsible.

Winston and I walked over to the reception desk where we were relieved to find two friendly and completely charming receptionists. Although English was not easily spoken by either, we were able to make ourselves understood. Thank goodness! Universal laughter and self-effacing shoulder shrugs got the job done. The others joined us once they sensed the all clear and we collected our room keys.

Emboldened by our new-found ability to communicate, we all, en masse, stepped over to the concierge's desk to make reservations for dinner. We were getting this down. I can't describe the feeling of jubilation that swept over us once room keys were in our hands and our dinner reservations were confirmed for a nearby bistro. *Oui! Huit heure!* Eight p.m. Such a simple little detail, but extraordinary in the big picture of relaxing into a foreign culture.

I found the bedrooms fresh, clean, and more than adequate. I don't know what I expected, but again, I was skeptical of what I had actually requested as a reservation for the six of us. I was grateful each room came with not only a *douche* (or shower), but also a WC (or water closet). Some rooms shared a water closet at the end of the hall! The queen-sized bed called my name for a nap, but first, Winston waved me over to the window that opened onto Boulevard Raspail. We peered outside, expecting to hear the cacophony on the road we had just driven through but were relieved to find the boulevard was a quiet street, lined with some of

Provence's most prolific trees, the plane (sycamore) trees.

"Supposedly planted throughout France by Napoleon," my husband said as we peered out the window, "in order to provide shade for his troops." I didn't mention that he had told me this historic item before, and yes, the trees did stand regally as if having been called to duty by Napoleon himself. A light breeze fluttered through the leaves and sent some skittering down the street while I took a much-needed nap.

At 7:15 p.m., we made our way down to the small bar to have a little *apératif.* We were not surprised to find Bob and Shirley already seated at a small table with glasses of wine in hand. They were always early! We sat down beside them as they began to regale us with their tale of an extraordinarily frustrating day. Ah, but wait! Melody and Dan joined us, and then Bob began to roll out their story.

Bob had attempted to get gas the day before in Fayence but had no luck. The gas cap did not open, and the option to use a crowbar or a chisel to pry open the cap had not been acceptable. Trying to avoid damage to the rental car, the two left Claviers early that morning to make their way to a car dealership before meeting up with us in Orange.

Unfortunately, they arrived at the dealership just as the shop closed for lunch—again. Was this déjà vu all over again? A complete repeat of the day before! So, for them another day of their vacation was wasted. Oh, but they said, they made the most of it.

"We had a most lavish lunch," Shirley said.

"In fact," said Bob, "it was so filling that we aren't particularly hungry for this evening. I believe we will hang back and have a little cheese plate or something."

I am sure my shoulders slumped. I could certainly understand their decision, but this sounded like a tragedy beyond reason. I can eat anytime, anywhere, and especially at a restaurant. And while in Provence, I refused to be denied. I was hoping this news wouldn't squelch the others' appetites as my goal in life had been to sample my way across France. We had made reservations, hadn't we? I was determined to have a little smackeral of something for sure. I'm ashamed to confess it may have been my woeful look that made the difference. In no time at all, all six of us headed down the boulevard together, arm-in-arm.

My husband and I resorted to buckets of mussels with baskets of French fries. Yes, again! I don't recall what the others ordered—probably burgers—but ours was, indeed, a sumptuous feast that also easily accommodated glasses of *vin rosé.*

Chapter Fourteen

Cavorting through the Ramparts of Avignon

The following day, after a petit déjeuner at the hotel of croissants, juice, hard boiled eggs, and café au lait, we began a busy day of exploration. We were there to see the magnificent city of Avignon. With excellent help once again from the concierge, we navigated our way back down through the city to begin at the Palace of the Popes. This fourteenth century papal palace was no less daunting than Rome's Vatican City. The entire historic center of Avignon had, at one time, been the center of the Roman Catholic Church. Imagine that!

"The Palace of the Popes," I read as we were standing in line for tickets to enter, "took approximately thirty years to complete with changes happening under the reign of three popes (Benedict XII, Clement VI, and Innocent VI). It is said to be one of the largest palaces in existence covering 15,000 square meters or about 161,459 square feet. As we noted from driving in, the outside of the Palace resembled a fortress with high walls pierced with narrow openings (shoot outs) massive, pointed arches, and huge machicolations that made the castle practically impenetrable."

"So, what is a machicolation?" Winston asked. "And is it important?"

"I'm guessing it is a mechanized version of bats using echolocation. But that is just me," Dan joked.

Ah, but the description continued. "In medieval castle construction, it is an opening between the supporting corbels of a projecting parapet or vault of a gate. It was used to throw stones or boiling oil down on invaders. Now, aren't you glad I told you?"

Winston laughed, "Do you think it is like a shoot-out?" I smiled. That was our joke from a trip we took to England one year. Another story.

We signed up for an English-speaking tour, where each of us was given headphones and a small dangling tape recorder. Then the six of us made our way up the steep stone ramp and into the majestic front door.

"At one time, the interior walls were covered with artwork and tapestries," the tape began, "but mostly the interior reflected the Pope in charge at the time." We wandered through the barren, stark grey hallways, the walls completely empty of any décor. I found it difficult to picture what grandeur had once been part of this regal castle as we saw no traces.

"Under Pope Benedict XII, the palace was designed with Romanesque architecture, which made the palace sober and austere, and mirrored the austerity of the monastic temperament despite the fact that he is said to have kept forty trunks filled with gold artifacts, jewels, gemstones, and 600,000 florins, which were all stored in the Treasure Hall."

"So much for the piety of poverty," Melody said. The rest of us nodded at each other, with a thumbs-up gesture. Yes, we would have to search for the holding place of those ancient treasures.

"Clement VI was a lover of art and of the courtly life,

whose propensity was for luxury and embellishment. Under his watch, the architecture changed to the Gothic style to reflect his more grandiose way of life and a reflection of the epoch."

For some reason, nothing was mentioned about Innocent VI's choice for architecture or interior design, but then I believe the popes were called back to Rome on his watch.

We wandered into the Hall of the Consistory, which was huge by any measure. "About 119 feet long, sixteen feet wide, and thirty-two feet high, with elaborate (replacement) tapestries of which three of them almost filled the 119 feet of the length. Not only were tapestries used to tell Biblical stories, but they were also a good way to stanch the chill of the rooms." Portraits of the popes hung at the end of the hall, but we were informed that none of the décor had originally been part of the room. Okay, I supposed they needed to cover those cold drab walls with something. Made sense.

"So, what took place in this room during the papacy?" the recording continued. "It was in this room the supreme council and supreme court of all of Christendom met; where great pomp and magnificence was on parade with cardinals filing in through the room when summoned by the Pope. It was in this room the Pope also received kings, and ambassadors, and handled the business of the Church."

We made our way from the Hall of the Consistory into the Chapelle Saint-Jean where the ceilings and walls, although damaged with time, remained painted in the frescoes from that period. We were directed (by the tape recorder) to climb the steep stone steps to the second floor where we entered another massive room that was just above the Consistory.

"The Grand Tinel had six huge, vaulted windows overlooking luxuriant gardens, with five smaller windows above."

We were told that the pope's meals were kept warm in the fireplace at the end of this 155-foot-long room, yet the pope dined at a table along the opposite end of the hall. Odd! Wouldn't his food get cold by the time he received it? All the other guests were seated at tables along the side walls. Not exactly a friendly bunch! "Papal deliberations and secret ballots of the cardinals took place in a tiny oratory off in a small side room. A passageway from an outside balcony led to the upper kitchen.

Ah, the upper kitchen! Right up my alley of interest. I love this kind of thing! We climbed the steps to a great square kitchen that had a ceiling with unusual pyramidal vaulting and contained a massively tall chimney. It was erected so the smoke from the enormous cooking fires could be jettisoned up and out of the way. And also to keep the kitchen cool when the summer heat was overwhelming.

I pulled Winston over to the side and said, "I saw similar kitchens with this pyramidal-designed chimney here in chateaux in France. Do you remember?" He scratched his head to bring the memory into focus.

"No, I think you were with Josiane?" he said.

Wow! He wasn't even there, and he remembered a detail when I was in France with my dear friend, Josiane. He had traveled with us for part of the trip through the northeastern most regions of France, but not the southern regions as we were searching for answers to her mother's story, of which I turned into the novel, *A Cup of Redemption*.

"I also recall a similar but more ornate model in the Topkapi Palace in Istanbul. Could they all have been fabricated around the same time during the fourteenth century?" Obviously, he was not as tuned into the kitchen tours as I had been. I'd give him a pass.

We wandered into an austere room known as the Lower Treasury Hall. It was just below the Great Treasury Hall. It was a large room in the Angel Tower with stone slabs as flooring, but oddly in one corner of the room a large chunk of that slab had been replaced with plexiglass that lay across a hole in the floor.

We raced over to peer into the hole. A lower chamber had been hidden below where the ledger books, bags of money, and massive amounts of gold and gems had been amassed then hidden. Another great quote came to me from Petrarch. He lived in Avignon with his parents during the papacy, but he detested it. And once he moved back to his beloved Florence, he denounced the Avignon of the Popes as the ". . . most evil place on earth since the days of ancient Babylon." Now that quote made more sense to me.

Despite the avariciousness of the popes, the tour was remarkable, to say the least. But by that point, I felt overwhelmed and needed a tea break. I tried to encourage the others to skirt quickly through the rest of the tour, but each new room we passed through told more of the story. How could they leave? How could I leave?

The Pope's bedchamber was immense and the Antechamber, which was another grand receiving room for the Pope, was set aside for granting special audiences. Originally, we were told, it was decorated with frescoes of which only traces were left after a fire had damaged the room. What we saw were walls once again covered in exotic and magnificent tapestries, but, of course, these were not the originals. The originals had been stolen hundreds of years before.

So, what happened to all the glory and majesty in the furnishings, tapestries, and sculptures? I wondered. And why did some of the walls seem so stark and barren? Well, it seemed that after the Popes left, many marauding hordes rambled in, including those during the French Revolution. The place was picked as clean as a turkey's carcass.

The six of us wandered into a foyer on the ground level, found a handy Coke dispensing machine, and sank down on wooden benches exhausted but awed. I took a photo of Melody and Dan, sprawled out on a bench staring up at the elaborate ceilings and inner balconies with mouths open in wonder. To this day I smile every time I see it, as this one photo told the story of our whole tour! Inspiring, daunting, exhausting!

After our tour of the Palace of the Popes, we quickly headed to the parking lot, passing by some of Avignon's finely crafted churches, seventeenth century mansions, and the fourteenth century cardinals' castles, known as *livrée*. We were in a hurry as we wanted to spend the afternoon visiting Pont du Gard.

Once back in our cars, we followed each other in tandem as we cut through the inner city to one of the gates within the Ramparts and headed to the nearest bridge to cross the Rhône River to reach the Pont du Gard.

"Ah, but what is that bridge we are passing?" my sister asked, slyly.

I spun around in my seat as the Saint Bénezet Bridge came into sight and quickly disappeared over my shoulder. "Ah, Sur la Pont d'Avignon" I squealed.

And all together we began singing the children's nursery rhyme, totally maiming the French language but with all the best of intent:

Sur le Pont d'Avignon
L'on y danse, l'on y danse
Sur le Pont d'Avignon
L'on y danse tous en rond.

Somehow, we got so carried away with singing we must have missed one of the turns, but eventually, we made our way across the Rhône River and west to Pont du Gard.

So, what is the Pont du Gard, you ask? Rising high up above the Gard River is a magnificent feat of Roman engineering, an ancient Roman aqueduct bridge. It was built in the first century AD to carry water over thirty miles to the Roman colony of Nîmes.

We pulled into the parking lot at the Pont du Gard, and once again located Bob and Shirley. They were already in line for lunch, and once we joined them, we all opted to have a little *picnique* of ham and cheese baguettes, sodas, and potato chips. The idea of feasting on the grassy grounds along the Gard River was grand!

Melody was the last to reach the drinks cart, where a young man was working. She asked him for a Coca-Lite, which is the French name for that drink. He reached into the cooler, pulled out a glass bottle and, after opening it, said sweetly to her, "You speak very good English!" She smiled, blushed, and thanked him. Being an occasional cynic, I thought she had been working on her English for quite a few years now. But my kindly sister smiled, warmly thanked him, and accepted the bottle of Coke.

Melody and I have often reflected on this brief yet sweet moment in time. It was a simple exchange between people who did not share a common language. We could only surmise those were the very words he was told every single day from American tourists, "You speak very good English!" But for some reason, that exchange spoke volumes to us. We, as a couple of those bumbling American tourists, struggled to speak French in our attempts to communicate with the locals. But it became clear to us that the locals also found it difficult to speak languages they were not familiar with. Made sense. In this small exchange, if just for Melody and me, our eyes and hearts were opened.

The air was still, the early afternoon weather was hot and steamy, but sitting below the plane trees in the shadow of the massive bridge, we enjoyed an occasional puff of wind off the river. As we dabbed sweat off our brows, we considered the looming masterpiece of human creative genius before us. Le Pont!

"So, how tall do you think that bridge is?" Bob asked Dan. Dan turned to Winston and the three of them began to consider the size and nature of the bridge. All three heads bent to their guidebooks.

"According to my book," Bob said, "the three-level aqueduct is about 150 feet high and extends more than thirty miles from the hills farther north all in order to bring water farther south to the Roman city of Nîmes." He waved his arm over to the west, even though we weren't quite sure where Nîmes was located.

"The bridge was built of concrete," Dan read, "which was a Roman recipe created around 30 BC. And the not-so-secret ingredient is volcanic ash, which is combined with lime to form the mortar."

I looked at the soil as I tried to imagine if volcanic ash had been part of its composition. Was this from a local quarry? I knew there had been plenty of volcanic activity all around this whole Rhône Valley, as the vineyards thrived on it. This soil looked more like clay, but then what did I know?

"I can't imagine how they created such large building blocks in the first place," I exclaimed.

"According to my guide," Winston chimed in, "once they created the mortar, they packed it, along with rock chunks into wooden molds, then immersed them in seawater." His head snapped up and he looked around, trying to get his bearings.

"How far away is salt water from here? About thirty miles or so?" I asked.

"I imagine it's just south of Arles, where we will be going tomorrow. Not sure we'll see the sea, but I think Arles is the largest city on the Rhône before it empties into the Mediterranean," Winston replied.

"But how do you think they managed to soak all of those stones?" I asked, because these were problems I wanted answers for, and the guys were getting into it.

"Well," said Shirley, totally ignoring our historical dilemma, "I think we need to take a walk across the bridge. We've come this far."

Without question or comment, we all hefted ourselves up from the grass and trekked up the incline to the top of the bridge. Slowly, we ambled across the stretch of bridge high above the water, stopping long enough to take one photo after another, and then turning to head back down again.

"Should I say, this is a monumental moment?" I asked. No one laughed. And, before we could even say "Jack Rabbit" we noticed that Bob and Shirley had already headed back to their car and had left us pondering our navels. No matter. We would catch up with them in due time. We were planning on celebrating Dan and Melody's anniversary that evening, and it was going to be a special affair!

CHAPTER FIFTEEN

An Elegant Evening at Hiéley

"It was a meal that we shall never forget; more accurately, it was several meals that we shall never forget, because it went beyond the gastronomic frontiers of anything we had ever experienced, both in quantity and length."

—PETER MAYLE, *A YEAR IN PROVENCE*

*T*hat evening we dressed in our finest attire, because we were looking forward to celebrating Dan and Melody's anniversary. We would be dining at what we understood to be a fantastic, starred restaurant, Le Hiély. We were early, so, after parking, we walked about the open plaza of Rue de la Républic. The evening was warm, but a gentle breeze wafted up from the Rhône, through the buildings, and as I whirled around in my long skirt, I felt a bit princess-like.

We strolled along the boulevard where open craft stalls were set up and artists were selling their paintings or were painting *plein aire*. We passed the carousel, which was rocking out with plenty of children riding with glee. We continued past a monumental building known as the Mairie, or town hall, then turned around.

When the clock tower chimed eight bells, we made our way to the entrance of this highly recommended restaurant. We had previously read the history of Monsieur André Hiély, who had opened the doors in 1938 with his wife assisting, and then his son, Pierre, took over the kitchen and carried a two-star status for over thirty-nine years. This restaurant was known as one bringing some of the best in Provençal cuisine to a comfortable family restaurant.

From the outside, there was no auspicious entrance. In fact, we were surprised that this was the official entrance at all as the signage in front was so discreet—to the point of being invisible. The front door opened off the main street, and we found ourselves taking turns walking through a narrow hall-way to climb a long, dark, and narrow staircase. No elevators visible here.

At the top of the stairs, we found the dining room luminous with candlelight reflecting off the highly polished parquet floors. The large room was divided into a series of smaller dining areas as the space was separated by potted palm trees, curved glass, and delicate arches and swirls of cherry wood sculpted screens. The art nouveau style of design seemed to blithely pirouette through space. Of course, nature played a part in the ambiance as the windows, which overlooked plane trees on the boulevard below, mirrored the subtle color palette in the room—tablecloths in pearl grey, sage green chairs, and mustard-colored accent pieces. It was a room that embraced many eras—from the 1890s to the mid-1950s. Sprinkled sparingly throughout the room were serving carts lavishly loaded with cheeses or desserts for the divine. One cart caught my eye as it was designed in silver with elegant swirls and waves with plump cherubs prancing about the base and wheels, all with a grand swivel top that surely held special delights.

Patricia Wells, a French cuisine cookbook author whom I have met and is held in grand repute, said of her visits to Le Hiély: "It is impossible to put a label on Hiély's menu of the moment: neither regional, nor classical, nor modern. But what do labels matter if, when you get up from the table, you feel thoroughly satisfied?" We would come to learn through first-hand experience, she was so correct. Understated, but correct.

We were greeted in a most friendly manner by the host who led us to our reserved table. Before we were seated, a waiter appeared at our sides and asked if we wanted aperitifs to begin.

"But, of course," we said and ordered a round of Kir Royales. After our extraordinary dinner a few nights before at Les Gorges de Pennafort, we had this Kir Royale thing down pat. In fact, that previous experience had given us the courage to venture into this restaurant in the first place.

Their extensive menus were brought to the table, with even more selections than we had encountered a few evenings before. This menu, which was daunting, was set aside for the wine menu, which had wines from local Chateau-Neuf-de-Pape vineyards, but also came with price tags in the thousands of francs for a bottle.

"I think I need a straight-edged ruler," said Winston as he tried to focus on the small print of the menu. He oversaw choosing the wines, partly because of his knowledge of wines, but also because he was the youngest of us all and his eyesight was the best. Bob and Dan did take a crack at the wine menu but realized they knew even less French, so they again turned the menu back to Winston.

"We do serve rather nice house wines," the sommelier suggested, once he arrived at our table. He could see we were in over our heads with making any educated decisions. Yes, we drank a profusion of wine at home, visited a number of local wineries in California, and now had two wineries under our belts from Provence, but . . .

"I recommend you begin with a carafe or two of house wines before deciding on a couple of bottles of our finer wines for the main courses," he said with a stately bob of his head.

"It appears there are about eight courses here," I whispered to my husband.

"Ah, we only live once," he quipped. I relaxed, the rest relaxed, and we all sank back into our seats to peruse the dining menu. This perusal was enhanced by the delectable aromas that wafted through the dining room as waiters zipped back and forth from the kitchen.

When I try to think of all that we ate that evening, my recollection becomes a blur. I recall mere flashes of *amuse bouche* with thimble-sized glasses filled with cleansing sorbet. Then tiny ramekins filled with flans of foie gras topped with creamy wild mushroom sauce or *pâté en croute* of escargot, one of my favorites, dance through my memory. Moving on to the main course, we were privileged to feast on dishes of either local lamb from Sisteron, trout dishes from Isle-sur-la-Sorgue, or sea scallops from the Mediterranean. Why, we were dining in a culinary heaven that encompassed all the best local foods, wines, vegetables . . . oh my! And lovingly prepared in a Provençal manner. Superb!

The waiters served each course with reverence for the majesty of the dish, the splendid composition created by the chef, and the pleasure that delighted each one of us. Each bite was one of pure joy, a blending of familiar spices and foods with more exotic and even more delectable flavors.

As we sank back into our chairs to take a breather and sip one of the many wines that had come our way, the cheese cart was wheeled up to our table. A whole education began regarding the cheeses on board. We were treated to not just brie as we were accustomed, but to the aged, the soft, the hard, the runny, and the pungent, including a goat cheese wrapped in chestnut leaves called Banon, or the ancient Tomme de Provence. And let's not forget to mention the local fresh goat cheese wrapped in grape leaves. We were invited to choose not only one, but a sampling of each. Some of us begged off as we said we were already full, but then again, whenever would we experience this again? *Oui!* We'd have a taste of each!

Okay, now I'm done, I thought! I can't possibly weasel another morsel into my . . . what's that? Another plate of *amuse bouche* appeared on our table, and there lay a resplendent array of the most delicate of pearl pink meringues. Without any resistance whatsoever, six hands reached forward and grabbed up the little meringues and popped them straight into our mouths.

"They taste like clouds, sweet little clouds! Poof! And they are gone," Melody said. "Did I even chew?" I asked. And like the sweet little clouds that they were, poof, they were no more.

"Did you enjoy them?" the waiter asked with a twinkle in his eye. We all beamed as if we had been bequeathed the most decadent of secret gifts.

"Bon!" he said. "Those were just to prepare you for the dessert course!" And like that, another cart, one much larger than the cheese cart, was pushed up to our table where a most amazing array of desserts was on display.

Silver bowls filled with thick whipped cream, fresh strawberries and blackberries rested in bowls, truffled chocolate cake, profiteroles, crème caramel, pain au chocolate, rum-soaked babas, fruit tarts, fraisiers, strawberries bathed in syrup, plus freshly made sorbets and ice creams with lavender honey or more fresh fruits with tiny mint leaves. Oh my! And did they serve us just one dessert? No, not ever! They offered us one of each of the over twenty different delicacies from the cart.

It was at that moment Dan, who had been waiting for . . . yes, a cup of coffee . . . was able to order the coffee, but after his dessert. No matter! We joined him with cappuccinos followed by miniature glasses of port. This had been an evening filled with sumptuous memories. A dinner of pure culinary delight! And wouldn't you know, Dan and Melody quietly picked up the tab for us all! *Bon Anniversaire* everyone!

Special Note: Just by happenstance, when my husband and I returned home following our monumental trip to Provence, our tenth anniversary popped up on the next weekend. In celebration, we attended a book signing with none other than Peter Mayle. What a delight he was! He was touting his newest book, *Toujours Provence.* Following his reading, a member of the audience asked him how he felt about his whole life being put up in lights for the BBC series *A Year in Provence.*

"Well," he said, "I handled it better than my wife. When she first watched the series and saw her life flash before her eyes, she was most chagrined about one thing. In fact, during the viewing she stomped up the steps of our house in disgust. 'What is wrong?' I asked her, after racing up the stairs after her. 'Don't you like what they've done?' She answered, 'Toute du monde! All the world will think I own those tacky kitchen curtains! Toute du monde!'"

And it was in this newest book we discovered a chapter in which Mayle and his wife are taught the fine art of eating French-style at the Hiély Restaurant in Avignon. A restaurant that was dear to our hearts!

CHAPTER SIXTEEN

Arles, Here We Come

The next morning, after consuming our petit déjeuner of chocolate croissants and café, we checked out of our hotel rooms, bid a fond adieu to the lovely staff at Hôtel d'Angleterre, synchronized our watches, checked our maps, and the six of us headed to our cars to make our way to Arles. "Boys, start your engines!"

We zipped along the autoroute that skirted our old friend, the Rhône River, to our right. And on our left, we passed field after field of sunflowers and lavender, which reminded me of Van Gogh's paintings I had seen with bright splashes of yellow interspersed with subtle grey-blue lavender.

Arles, another historical Roman city, was only a little over twenty miles south, so we were set to meet up at the Roman arena that appeared on the map to be centrally located in the old town. Lo and behold, we did it! We all rolled into the designated parking lot at the same time and popped out of our cars together! Hey! We can do this thing! We slapped high fives all around.

Much like the two other cities we visited along the Rhône River—Orange and Avignon—the historical beginnings included the Phocaean or the Greeks, the Celts, then the Romans . . . plus the mixed and sundry civilizations that followed closely on their heels. But we were there to soak up more Roman culture. If we couldn't go to Rome, we could at least go to the Amphithéâtre Romain or Arènes d'Arles, I always said!

We made our way across the street and up the stairs to the entrance of the amphitheatre. It was designed much like the one we had visited in Orange, but for some reason, this one felt more vital. Tacked along all the outer walls were posters announcing upcoming events, one of which mentioned a bullfight.

"A bullfight?" I blurted out. "They still do bullfights?"

No one listened to me blather on as they were making their way to the ticket counter to tour the grounds. I would check out this issue for myself. "Are there bullfights being held in here?" and "When would that be?" I asked.

"No," came the response, there would be no bullfight that day, but if we came back in a couple of weeks, we might be able to see a *corrida* (bullfight) or enjoy a festival.

"Well, can you imagine that, Melody?" I asked. As I turned around to talk to my sister, I was told she had opted to go to the Van Gogh retrospective across the street. That made sense, I supposed, as she was quite an admirer of his. I took my ticket and caught up with the others. We entered the arena, which was elliptically shaped, about four hundred forty-five feet long, and three hundred fifty feet wide. It reminded me of our recent experience in Orange, but this one was for gladiatorial events only. In an English brochure they gave us, we found that for certain Roman spectacles, the stage was raised to the podium level using a floor structure inclined in slots that we took notice of that day. We entered through one of the multitude corridors and were surprised to read that there had once been an ingenious system used to quickly evacuate the spectators. We weren't sure what that meant, or why that would be necessary, but it did challenge the imagination. Floods? Fire? Marauding hordes? And like in many of these arenas, the basement was used for the wild animal cages and machinery used to lift the animals up on the main stage. Of course, none of that was visible after all these millennia. So, imagination helped!

The summer's day was getting warmer as morning turned into early afternoon. Standing out in the open arena felt like a fool's caper, so we meandered back through the corridors and onto the street. Across from the arena we spotted the Van Gogh retrospective where Melody had ventured. Winston and I strolled inside to search for Melody, but instead found the walls of this small museum covered in splashes of bright purple iris that were erotic in their display. Paintings of peasants wandering through open hay fields, or humbly sitting with their meager meal of the day were also exhibited. We were told that it was here, in Arles, where Van Gogh discovered the power of color. For him it had to do with the diffused light of the Provençal countryside. Or could it have had to do with the marine layer wafting ashore from the nearby Mediterranean Sea? We were told he was quite prolific while living in what is now known as the Maison Jaune, or the Yellow House near to where we were standing. We wanted to check that out.

But first my sister! We discovered Melody in the farthest recesses of the museum, and she was in heaven. With great enthusiasm, she showed us some of Van Gogh's famous paintings: the sunflower paintings, as well as his paintings of the iris and so many more. I, quite honestly, thought the pieces of art were a bit primitive for my taste. They were nice, but I just didn't understand the draw! At least, not then. But when the rest of our group wandered back outside to stand in the shade of the building, Winston pulled me aside.

"Which one of these posters do you think Melody would enjoy most?" he asked.

I was pleased by his offer, but realized he, too, had witnessed the delight she had shown in Van Gogh's art. We snuck to one side of the museum store, selected one of the irises, had them wrap it up in a cardboard tube, and joined the others out front. When she finally came out of the museum, Winston handed her the poster. She was more than surprised, but she was so pleased.

"I am deeply touched," she said. "You have honored what I saw in Van Gogh even though it wasn't art either of you appreciate." She gave each of us a hug. "I will have the print framed and placed in a prominent place in our home. And each time I look at it, I will enjoy this memory as well." She's rather formal, when she exudes!

Our next stop was at the Roman Theatre, which was close to the arena. This time we hovered near an English-speaking guide and carried new brochures. It had been dug out of the side of a hill with tiers of theatre seats created in a semi-circle that climbed the hill with grace and wonder.

"Originally," the tour guide stated, "the theatre was developed under the reign of Augustus but finished under Mark Antony. The theatre was surrounded by three rows of granite arches, of which only one remained. The tiers formed thirty-three rows backing against the wall with seating for 7,000. The stage backed up against a large wall, which was ornamented with statuary, alcoves, and friezes enclosing a semi-circle."

"Much like the arena in Orange," Dan and Winston whispered.

"But only two beautiful columns remain standing. The stage, once paved with pink stone, was where the former chorus stood and partially remains. Later this evening, a musical performance will be taking place here."

That made sense as sound equipment and staging were already put into place. We made our way around the tour, handed him some francs, and headed out to lunch.

The sweltering heat of the afternoon wrapped around us like heavy cotton. As we slogged our way across the cobbled streets, we wandered down into a covered plaza where plane trees added to the coolness of the day. We found ourselves at the corner of the Place du Forum, where a Roman column remained embedded into one of the stone walls. At the head of the plaza was a twelve-foot-tall statue of Frédéric Mistral. We knew he held great sway in Provence as a writer, but it was much later that I realized he became a champion for the independence of Provence and, in particular, for restoring what he thought was the "first literary language of civilized Europe"—Provençal.

Facing the plaza was the mustard-yellow brasserie called Le Café de la Nuit, or the Van Gogh Café, with a large reproduction of Van Gogh's *Starry Night* placed prominently in front. We were thrilled to find space on the terrace where we could sink into comfortable chairs in the shade, order a glass of vin rosé, and peruse the menu.

Fortunately, English was used profusely in this tourist town, so it was easy to dive into the menu with gusto. One of the specialties was a celebration of local food, especially from the Camargue.

"So, what is the Camargue and where is it?" my husband asked the waiter who had introduced himself as André.

"Oh, monsieur, our Camargue is a vast expanse of land at

the mouth of the Rhône River," he said as he waved his arm to an unseen location to the south. "It is a paradise for migratory birds, a nesting area for flamingoes, home to bulls and horses, and also is the home of our famous cowboys—the Gardians. The superb beef, which comes from this region is part of our menu."

He pointed to several dishes listed on the menu, such as *Gardiane de Taureau,* or Bull Stew made with red wine, vegetables, bacon, garlic, and *Herbes de Provence.* Or a *Daube Provençale,* made with beef cheeks, red wine, and juniper berries.

"Most dishes in Provençal cuisine," André continued, "are comprised of fresh tomatoes, garlic, and olive oil, and you can find those ingredients in many of our dishes, such as our Camargue-style paella. Also, in the summer, we feature *Soupe au Pistou,* which is a slightly warm soup prepared with beans, pasta, vegetables, tomatoes, herbs, and garlic and then puréed. I'll leave you to make your decisions," he said with a bow.

Finally, we were able to make our selections, although we chose lighter specialties. The feast from the night before had whittled down our appetites. I relaxed back in my chair and watched as the people paraded by, going in and out of the plaza across the street. Music was playing—an instrument I was not familiar with. Was that a mandolin and a mouth instrument called an ocarina?

When the waiter returned with a couple of carafes of vin rosé, Bob asked, "So what is the story about your famous Camargue cowboys? You called them Gardians? Are they like American cowboys?"

I'm wondering if our waiter, André, knew what an American cowboy was, but he seemed to have been asked this question before. "The mounted Gardians are like the

American cowboy, but more like the men who ride the ranges in Mexico, like the Charro, or in Spain. They work with the bulls and the beautiful white horses from this region. It is considered a noble tradition. Seasonal festivals, bullfights, and parades to celebrate the Gardians are part of our vibrant history. And it's always a thrill to see the majestic white Camargue horses parade through the streets. The horses," he said, "are known as the 'horses of the sea,' one of the most ancient breeds of horses in the world."

"Do many tourists ask you these same questions? The questions regarding the Camargue and the horses?" I asked.

"*Mais oui!* But I grew up here and am quite proud of my heritage." He touched a hand to his heart.

Melody leaned forward and in her soft voice asked, "So what is the history of this restaurant? Why is it called the Café de la Nuit?" I knew she would want to know more about Van Gogh as she had carried a glow since we left the Van Gogh Museum.

"I'd be happy to," André said as he bent down to her. "Actually, this brasserie was here long before Van Gogh came to live in our city in 1888. It was said that his eye for color greatly expanded while in Arles and was inspired to paint *Starry Night* while sitting right here on this terrace."

Although Melody rarely expressed emotion with wild abandon, I could tell she was thrilled to know this bit of history. She turned to Dan and repeated, "Right here; right here on this terrace!" Dan beamed at his wife. He so adored her.

Yes, I thought, *I guess I'll have to take another look at Van Gogh's work.*

It was clear there were so many more places to visit in Arles, but after our late lunch, we decided to head back to our cars. We had a long drive back to Claviers and it would be best to go earlier than later in the day. Plus, our energy level was waning!

"We will be back," I said to André as we were leaving the restaurant. And, I thought to myself, "Yes, we'll be back!"

It had been a whirlwind ten days traveling with Melody and Dan, but their final day at Claviers had arrived. As difficult as it was to bid them adieu, we all headed back to our favorite beach town—St. Maxime—to share some final moments. The weather was crystalline clear, with only a few wisps of clouds lurking around the Bay of St. Tropez. It could not have been more picture-perfect—much like our first venture to those beaches, which seemed like forever ago.

This time before changing into our swimming suits at the beach, we thought of venturing out a bit more through the old part of town. And what better way to do it than on our favorite Le Petit Train? *Mai oui!* This time the little white train pulled us from the quayside up into the surrounding hills. We were not so fortunate to get an English translator on this tour. No, but we certainly had something much more memorable. Music! Music transformed this light-hearted little journey into something that bordered on—what?—the morose?

The theme song from David Lynch's *Twin Peaks* blared out from the little train, draping the entire village and its environs in a moody and foreboding cloud. The melody, which could be ethereal and light at times, could also drop into deep and dark tones once the bassline sounded. It was purely haunting!

Our capricious little uphill trip became a frenzied downhill jaunt as the little train careened—out of control, mind you—around one sharp corner after another. St. Maxime and the Bay of St. Tropez flashed past us, in what felt like the end of a deadly, black-and-white movie! Death and destruction seemed quite inevitable to us.

After that experience, we staggered off to find a bistro along the beach where we could allow the serenity of place to seep back into our pores. Aha! We discovered a fabulous little restaurant that boasted: A lunch with your feet in the water, a dinner under the stars, a quality of service in a sublime setting, and refined and elegantly presented Mediterranean cuisine. Yes, this would do as the last meal our little contingent of six would share together.

Grilled fresh fish, steamed mussels, sautéed pink shrimp or burgers and fries (French, of course), or pasta with seafood, which was one of Winston's favorites. Pitchers of vin rosé were served to us, and we dipped our toes into the nearby water right off their beach. Yes, we would have to make another return trip here too!

In midafternoon, having completed our déjeuner, Winston and I drove Melody and Dan back into Nice by way of the coastal highway. Reveling over the gorgeous Côte d'Azur was worth the extra effort on the drive, despite plenty of traffic. My sister and brother-in-law were spending their final night at Hotel Park, the same hotel we all had first stayed in, as they had an early flight the next morning. It was a sorrowful parting as we had truly enjoyed our time together. That's not always a given for families, but this time was perfection!

Winston and I slowly drove back to Claviers, feeling the emptiness in the car without them. At least we knew that Bob and Shirley would be waiting for us at the house. We spent a relaxed evening talking, listening to the local radio station, snacking on brie, olives, baguette slices, and wine. Oh, and playing cards!

CHAPTER SEVENTEEN

Playing Around Île de Porquerolles

*T*he following day, because the four of us could easily ride in one car together, we opted for another coastal trek. But this time with a boat ride or two. Any time we could be on the water we jumped at it.

We made our way to Hyères, which was just east of Marseilles on the coast. Our plan was to catch a ferry from La Tour Fondue Port on Giens Peninsula, which was just south of Hyères, and cross the water to the Island or Îles de Porquerolles. Known as the Nantucket of the Mediterranean, Porquerolles was our destination for a day trip. We made our way to the ferry terminal and waited for our turn to board the boat. Once the ferry was loaded, it only took fifteen minutes to cross to the island. The cool breeze while on the boat helped to beat down the temperatures in the high 90s. The boat was comfortable for a ferry and surprisingly not overly full during tourist season. And the French banter which rose above the roar of the engines brought a holiday spirit to us all.

Porquerolles, the largest and most westerly of the Îles d'Hyères, or islands off Hyères, was about four and a half miles long by two miles wide, with five small ranges of hills. We disembarked on the north coast at the port, which was also the gateway to the lovely village of Porquerolles, and the famous beaches of Notre Dame, La Courtade and Plage d'Argent. Too bad we forgot to bring our suits.

At the harbor, we, along with dozens of other day trippers, disembarked and headed up a palm tree-lined boulevard that led up and through the middle of the village. I couldn't seem to focus well, as happens when I get too warm. And once off the boat, the stifling heat wrapped around me as my brain slipped into a fog.

"Where on earth are we going?" I asked. But it seemed our destination had been preset. I must not have been paying attention. Without responding Bob, Shirley, and Winston continued to plod up the road toward an unseen fort that was supposed to be at the top of a nearby bluff. As we continued following signs to Sainte-Agathe Fort, I slowed to calm and cool down. A light breeze brushed past me, lifting my awareness of the distinct aromas of nearby eucalyptus, oak, pin parasol pines, fig, and olives trees.

The woodsy scents gave me the boost I needed, and the fog disappeared from my head. I caught up with the other happy wanderers, not that they noticed my delay. We reached our destination, which was a bluff that overlooked the crystalline blue waters of the Mediterranean. Far below, sailboats were tethered at the marina, bobbing along on the water. I looked over at Winston and caught a wistful gaze. I knew he ached to clamor onboard those boats, but that was a dream for another day.

Dating back to the sixteenth century, the Sainte-Agathe Fort was built under François I to protect the coastlines from violent attacks. François I was best remembered for having assembled an immense collection of artworks, a magnificent library, and being the patron to artists such as Leonardo da Vinci, who had fled his beloved Florence, Italy into France. Oh, the stories of the French . . .

The fort was constructed in the shape of a large round stone tower. It housed a large-vaulted room surrounded by a battery terrace, or ramparts. The entirety of the fort was enclosed in a trapezoidal enclosure against which other buildings including a cistern were built.

We walked around and through the empty fort before climbing up to catch the best of panoramic views across the island. We tried to imagine fending off marauding hordes with cannons, but the island seemed so bucolic that my imagination cramped. Far below, we spotted the northern beaches, which were well-known for sunbathing and swimming. Again, we sighed. No bathing suits! Another island bobbed on the horizon to the east. Was that Port Cros? And, across the waterway, the mainland of Provence appeared to be beckoning us home. Not just yet!

We ambled back down the road to check out the charming village of Porquerolles. En route, we picked up a brochure about the town and read that this village was founded in the nineteenth century by the Belgian explorer François Joseph Fournier. "The island," the brochure recounted, "was a gift to his wife, Sylvia, in one of the grandest of gestures. In 1971, the year Sylvia died, the French state bought 80 percent of the island and designated it as a national park. Cars and development were soon outlawed in favor of bucolic blessings and mountain bikes."

Well, come to think of it, we hadn't encountered any cars racing up and down the dry dusty roadways. Only bikes were in use and an occasional wheelbarrow loaded down with luggage was being pushed by a local. The village was enchanting with sorbet-colored buildings enhanced with light blue shutters. Brash-looking bushes of magenta bougainvillea climbed up trellises with wild abandon or clustered around the small town square, Place d'Armes.

Gift shops lined the streets, and Shirley and I sidled close to peek in at their wares. Always the little bundles of lavender, lavender honey, tiny ceramic images of the cicadas, olive oils, and, oh, look at those lovely gauzy . . . The guys encouraged us to move along.

As we stepped back onto the road, we could hear it before we saw it, but a boules game was being played at one end of the square. That scene always brought a smile to our faces—not that we would partake. Next door, a prominent church, St. Anne de Porquerolles, anchored the other end. Restaurants that lined the Place de Armes, such as Le Pélagos and the L'Orangeraie, sent out provocative aromas as messengers advertising their local seafood: *Anchoïade* (piquant dip made with grilled anchovies) with fresh vegetables, fresh gazpacho, grilled razor-back clams with mayonnaise, grilled shrimp in parsley sauce, calamari . . . oh my! We were getting hungry.

But our return boat was due in less than an hour, so we ambled down to the port to find a brasserie that hugged the docks and marinas. "Don't want to miss the boat, do we?" Bob asked. Maybe we did. Shirley and I had been enjoying the idea of shopping.

But there, bobbing along with all the boats, we found a true seafood brasserie called Il Pescatore. You can't get any closer to fresh seafood than feasting at a restaurant called The Fisherman. We were taken to a table along the water, bedecked with—surprise!—a bright yellow, blue, and red Provençal tablecloth, which was ensconced with four red canvas-backed deck chairs. We fell into our seats.

All the aromas that had whetted our appetites a few minutes earlier were now wafting from the adjoining kitchen. Waiters raced in and out of the nearby door hoisting large platters of grilled shrimp and lobsters surrounded with steamed mussels and clams. Could grilled razorback clams topped with savory sauces, or calamari steaks ringed with fresh lemons and parsley, tantalize us? And can you say *Linguine alla Vongole* (or Linguini and clams)?

"Yes," proclaimed my husband, and he ordered a small trough of fresh pasta, bathed in a rich white wine/garlic clam sauce, topped with a mountain of steamed clams. He smacked his lips as this was his absolute favorite! So far, he'd said that about all the seafood dishes!

Yes, we feasted! It had been a long time since breakfast, which was at least seven hours before. Even though the hour was teetering at 3 p.m., we made this our déjeuner, or lunch, and, with a few glasses of beer and/or rosé, we settled back in our chairs and relaxed. After a day of hiking up and down hills and through the village, we were spent. It was much more fun watching all those day-trippers pass us on the quay while ogling sailboats and power boats. The tantalizing turquoise blue water was within a few feet of us, and occasional spray splashed up in our direction as the boats joggled for position.

"Say, take a look at that, Carole!" Winston said. He was pointing at a small fishing boat tied up in front of us. "The name across the transom of the boat is *43° North–Porquerolles.*"

"So, what does that mean in relationship to where we live?" I always want to know the latitude of the places we visit. "Is our latitude at home farther north or south than Porquerolles?" I asked.

"Well," he responded, "San Francisco is located at 38° North, so this means Porquerolles is farther north. In fact, I believe this indicates that Chicago, at about 42°, is approximately the same latitude as here."

"Now, I don't know about you, Shirley," I said, "but I can barely wrap my head around such a statement." This was always a big deal for me. Here we were basking in the heat along the Mediterranean Sea, and Winston was pointing out that this place was equivalent to the cold hinterlands of Chicago! I'd lived in the suburbs of Chicago and the only image that popped into my mind was the horrendously cold winters. Both Shirley and Bob nodded their heads in appreciation, but then they both grew up in the San Joaquin Valley of Southern California. It's all relative, I guess.

Tucking this bit of regional knowledge into my hat, we finished our meal and dashed for the ferry. Our timing was . . . well, almost impeccable! This time the boat was crowded as the day was over for those of us who had come for only one day. Surprisingly, it was a quick but delightful trip back to the mainland and we headed back to our car to go home. Ah, but not so fast!

Now, how can one fit even more fascinating events into one day? Well, on our way home, we took a side trip through the illustrious city of Aix-en-Provence. Once we arrived in the beautiful, historic city, we realized we would need several days to appreciate all that was architecturally, artistically, or historically relevant. Once an ancient Roman city founded in 123 BC, it was named after a local spring. As it turned out, every Roman city that has Aix in the name indicates the purpose and importance of the city. It refers to a most important commodity necessary for human habitation—water!

The city that withstood the death and destruction by the

Teutones in 102 BC, the Visigoths and Franks in 477, the Lombards and Saracens in the 700s, eventually settled down under the houses of Barcelona and Aragon during the Middle Ages and became an artistic center and seat of higher learning. Since then, it has been known as a second Paris, a university city, and a center for the arts.

Having parked near one end of the attractive plane tree-lined boulevard known as the Cours Mirabeau, we began to walk along the shaded street. We passed aristocratic seventeenth century palaces, delightful squares filled with shaded flower stalls and open-air markets filled with foods. One couldn't deny the importance of the artwork of one local son, Paul Cézanne. Prints of his most famous works were on display everywhere. We saw posters in gift shops, prints of famous paintings hung in gallery windows, and painted onto key chains, aprons, napkins . . . and were those ceramic cicadas?

We continued walking past one fountain after another, arriving at the grandest of them all, the Fontaine de la Rotonde. Rising thirty-six feet above the street with a base of almost one hundred feet, the fountain was surrounded by bronze sculptures of twelve lions, sirens, swans, and angels on the backs of dolphins. And at the top of the fountain three female sculptures representing justice, agriculture, and the fine arts crowned it all.

As I stood at the base of this impressive sculpture, I could understand the reason Aix-en-Provence was known as the City of a Thousand Fountains. Of course, it made perfect sense: Aix stands for water. We sat on the base to rest, and a cooling spray lifted off the fountain sending relief to all of us over-heated tourists. Some proposed to strip off their shoes in order to dip their feet. We looked at each other considering the prospect, but we knew we could only stay in Aix for a few hours.

Instead, we slowly made our way back up the boulevard checking out the open-air markets. Always enticed by food in any form or region, I reached out my hand to touch the woven wands of lavender, then the garlands of garlic. I sampled rosemary and then lavender-infused goat cheeses, along with some of the forty varieties of olives. Oh, but let's not forget the vast array of fresh fruits and vegetables. Succulent cantaloupes and strawberries, plus voluptuous eggplants, delicate *courgette* blossoms and sumptuous tomatoes called out to us. Plus bottles of local olive oils and wines, oh my! It was difficult to choose, but we gathered enough food for a couple of nights' dinners left on our vacation.

Continuing down the boulevard, we were charmed by the delightful sidewalk cafés, which spilled out onto the shaded streets like children who don't want to miss a party. Music and laughter echoed through the late afternoon, and as we passed tables filled with pastis-sipping folks, we were sorely tempted!

Ah, but I was searching for specialty shops that sold *tissu*, the French word for fabric. I had become smitten by all the bright, colorful Provençal prints we had seen displayed everywhere during our trip—brash reds, brilliant yellows, deep blues, all splashed across calico fabric and displayed in every magical corner we had come across. Tablecloths, curtains, skirts, scarves, napkins, oh my!

A fellow tourist directed Shirley and I up a hill onto a separate side street, where, lo and behold, we found a real fabric shop. But then I was faced with the daunting decision of what fabric to choose. The shop owner was very patient and gave us time to select several meters of material. Now that I think of it, I'm not sure what I had in mind, other than to simply own those joyous colors, but I purchased a couple of meters of mustard-yellow print, along with two meters of lavender-blue print.

We then scrambled back down the street to find our husbands loitering over cups of cappuccino at the Deux Garçons. No, we would not be eating again, but since this was a well-known brasserie located right on the Cours Mirabeau, we were thrilled our husbands had been able to find a table at all. A sign on the wall to the restroom proclaimed that coffee had been served to the likes of people like Paul Cézanne, Emile Zola, and had also been a prominent place for artists and intellectuals since its founding in 1792. Because we had a lengthy drive back to Claviers, Shirley and I joined the men in cappuccinos and enjoyed a few moments of soaking up the sweet ambiance of Aix.

CHAPTER EIGHTEEN

La Plage de Tahiti

"The reason people find it so hard to be happy is that they always see the past better than it was, the present worse than it is, and the future less resolved than it will be."

—MARCEL PAGNOL

I can never get enough time lazing in the sun, so when Bob and Shirley suggested we go to a beach in St. Tropez, we hopped on it. It would be their last day in Provence, and they wanted to introduce us to a beach they had visited before. I believe the word Bob used to describe it was "unique."

The day was another scintillating day on the beaches of the Côte d'Azur. Almost perfect, with cloudless bright blue skies, a light breeze that lifted off the turquoise waters, and long stretches of white sand that extended as far as we could see.

My husband and I had not experienced this beach before, but from first blush, we were pleased. It had our favorite accommodations: comfortable beach chairs with adjoining tables and umbrellas; hot and cold drinks plus bistro-type food delivered beach-side and a marvelous view of the Bay. We embraced the moment. Yes, life was sweet!

Shirley and I made our way into a comfortable cabaña to change into our suits. I adjusted my hat and took off my sunglasses. Now, I truly could see! The dressing room was decorated like a tropical hut, and it dawned on me then why this place was called Plage de Tahiti. The chaises and umbrellas were also decorated, but without tropical prints, just white and green stripes. It did conjure up in my mind full-tropical climes, and we were going to enjoy it! We joined our gents and settled onto the chaises with as much grace as we could muster and ordered our first drinks. Rosé, Madame? *Mais oui*! I was really getting the hang of this French language!

As I leaned back with my drink in hand, my eyes once again scanned the area around me. I knew Bob had chosen this beach for a particular reason. Yes, "unique" was the word he had used. Certainly, the tiki hut assemblage didn't warrant this decision. So, what made this beach unique? No matter. Despite all the many quirks we had experienced with Bob, truthfully, we had enjoyed the ten days we had shared with him. With Shirley too! Uproarious camaraderie might describe it! But like a burr under a beach towel, I still wanted to discover Bob's thinking.

"So, Bob, why did you and Shirley choose this particular beach? It's lovely, but also much farther away from the others," I asked.

Shirley scooted back on her chaise, shifted her sun hat lower over her face and began to read her book. On the other hand, Bob sat forward taking a professorial stance and began to explain the options he enjoyed or hoped to enjoy at this particular beach, although he explained very little. He ended his short diatribe with the mention of more questionable options.

"So, exactly what options would be questionable?" I pressed him. Now my husband began to squirm a bit and suddenly it popped out. Bob was here for the nude beaches! Really? I looked up and down the beach again, truly mystified. I only saw an expanse of white sandy beaches. I turned to look at him, but then felt embarrassed at my thoughts. No, I won't divulge them. But this was a bit of a surprise.

"How about you?" he asked me.

How could he even ask? I thought he knew the inner workings of my thoughts the last time we stood above the beach, contemplating the nubile beauties before us. And he should have known that as a former Nebraskan who has trouble with toplessness, complete nudity would have been beyond the pale.

And for my husband? Would he be tempted to go nude? I doubted it. He hailed from the Puritans of New England. If I knew him at all, this was a complete no-go for him. As for Shirley, she was perfectly content to let her husband wander down the beach to enjoy life on his own in his own free-spirited way.

"So, how did you find out about this place?" I asked him.

"I read in one of the guidebooks that Tahiti Beach's fame dates to the 1950s. This was where the film *And God Created Woman* featuring Brigitte Bardot was made."

I remember being told about the film but had been too young to see it when it came out. But if memory and deep impressions serve me here, there had been some raunchy sex scenes, and this propelled Bardot into instant fame along with her bikini. Well, probably not just the bikini, but how voluptuous she looked in it. Quite risqué for the times.

"Actually, it wasn't just Bardot that I recall," Bob continued, "but the fact that there were nude beaches here—some of the first in Europe."

Well, now, it all made sense! I confess it was a tantalizing thought, but, then again, I could also imagine all the wrinkled old fogies lazing about. Now, that image could almost take my appetite away.

Ah, but not completely! First, we needed to take a dip and then order a little smackeral of lunch! One cannot contemplate nudity on an empty stomach. Even a *jambon and beurre* sandwich sounded good! The fracas I had caused Winston over ordering these ham and butter sandwiches on our first beach foray taught me a good lesson. I would be open to anything. As it turned out, a French burger and fries was a real hit for all of us! I guess you can't take the American out of us, and the extra-thick burgers dripping with cheese and oozing with yes, Grey Poupon, plus a basket of *real* French fries, was perfection.

Now, to relax and read *Jean de Florette and Manon of the Springs: Two Novels* by Marcel Pagnol. But now that we were near where he grew up in Aubagne, completing the stories he had written seemed even more compelling.

Also made into movies, these stories were based on some old Provençal legends that had haunted Pagnol as a child. This one was the tale of vengeance, which had been exacted by a mysterious shepherdess. With Pagnol's keen sense of place, ambiance, and the development of his characters, I felt I had an inside peek into the Provençal people and their connection to their land and culture.

I would read for a short while, take a dip, return to read a few more pages, nap, then wake to take another dip, and so on. At some point in this flurry of activity, I realized that Bob had disappeared from our little assemblage. I looked over at Shirley, and she simply nodded, smiled, and continued to read her book of choice. I had no idea what direction he had disappeared.

The afternoon lazed on like that for at least three hours and finally Bob strolled back up to our chaises and plunked down with a smug look upon his face. No one asked anything of him, but we noticed that his suntan was markedly a darker tone of red than when he left. And there were obvious bright tinges of red where the suntan lotion had not been adequately applied. Oh, well!

The day had been a beautiful one and before the sun had a chance to set, we rambled off the beach back to our car and made our way back to Claviers. With all the food we had purchased the day before in Aix, we used up every bit of it to concoct a local dish of ratatouille. Made with cubed eggplant, minced garlic, chopped fresh tomatoes, onions, and commingled with an herb-infused tomato sauce before baking, the dish turned out superb.

The last evening was another frenzy of cards, while listening to the sounds of the cicadas and once again to the local radio station out of Nice. We had become charmed by this station as the music was so delightful. All was good!

And wouldn't you know it, but our favorite American song sung in French came on, "The Itsy-Bitsy Teenie Weenie Yellow Polka Dot Bikini." In French, it sounded more like *Itsy Bitsy Teenie Weenie un Petit, Petit Bikini . . .* After today's romp at the beach the song seemed fitting.

CHAPTER NINETEEN

Two Alone in Provence

*T*he following day Bob and Shirley left Clavier early, and since this would be our first day in Provence alone as a couple, we decided there were many places we still wanted to explore. We had four more days of our trip to go.

While in Porquerolles a couple of days before, we had heard about the charming coastal village of Cassis. It was touted for its beautiful waterfront, wines, cuisine, and its rugged fjord-like Calanques, which are limestone ridged cliffs that reach out into the Mediterranean. Was another magical boat ride part of our day trip? With the height of the tourist season upon us, the coastal roads were bound to be heavy with traffic, so we also got off at an early start.

The little fishing village of Cassis underwent many transformations throughout its history, beginning back in 500-600 BC when the Ligures (Ligurians) settled in to take advantage of the prosperous hunting and fishing opportunities. They built a fortified village at the top of the Baou Redon, a limestone bluff that resided higher and slightly inland from where the present-day village of Cassis sits.

Later, the Romans settled into the town to use it to estab-
lish maritime trade with Northern Africa and the Middle East.
By the tenth century, any existing Roman settlers had fled further inland to seek refuge from foreign tribes. I guessed there
were too many marauding hordes anxious to replace the fallen
Romans and usurp their power for any groups to stick around.

Cassis was not typically referred to as a beach town as it
excelled in having hidden coves and cliff-side bathing rather
than the expansive swathes of sand we had experienced in St.
Tropez the day before. But sunbathing was not on our agenda
that day.

We inched our way through the traffic into the center of
the lower village heading toward the harbor and luckily we
found parking just a block or two away from the water. Small
sailboats and sturdy fishing boats bobbled together, with sterns
backed up to the docks, or as was known along the Mediterranean, med moored. Tour boats held sway with clamoring
hordes of those who wished to travel out to see the Calanques.
But first things first—food!

Along the docks was a dizzying array of enticing-looking
seafood restaurants. And why not? We were next to the sea,
and we hadn't had breakfast. We did miss Bob's daily boulangerie run. Rats! We were taken to a dockside table where we
were able to watch all the happenings on the water. And, yes,
we were keeping tabs on those bawdy tour boats. Where were
they going? Did we want to go? And what were they shouting?
"Un, deux, ou trois calanques!" They repeated the mantra, so
what did it mean?

The menu at the La Vieille Auberge was extensive, with
some unusual dishes. Did we want marinated raw scallops, or
mussels gratinée for our first course? Could we be enticed by
the sea bass in saffron sauce, or the *le magret* of *canard* (duck)

for our main course? Or how about *bouillabaisse pour deux*? We were only a stone's throw away from the ancient city of Marseilles but hadn't planned a visit this trip. So we opted for the *bouillabaisse* for two.

As many Provençal dishes do, *bouillabaisse*, a lusty savory fish soup, begins with a tomato base and is loaded with fresh off the boats local seafood. Mussels, clams, shrimp, flaky white fish like red snapper or sea bass, plenty of aromatic seasonings, herbs, tons of garlic, saffron threads, fennel, olive oil and yes, tomatoes. Served in deep bowls with plenty of crusty, toasted baguette slices used to dip and slurp up all the seafood goodness one can take in. And don't forget the zesty, roasted red pepper *rouille* sauce you can smear onto the toasted bread or swirl into the broth—it's delectable! Accompanied by a flavorful but light wine like Sauvignon Blanc or our usual, local rosé, we were set. When in Cassis, drink local wines! Say, was it not the Provençal poet, Frédéric Mistral, who once said, "He who has seen Paris and not Cassis, has seen nothing!"

Now, off to check out the tour boats. As we waltzed down the docks to where the lines were forming for tours, again we heard the call, "Un calanque? Deux calanques? Trois calanques?" Each time the barker would hold up first his thumb, then his thumb with his index finger, and thirdly, he held up three fingers but only with the thumb, index, and middle fingers! What did that mean? We kept pointing to just the two of us! We only wanted a ticket for two people. Finally, it dawned on us that the tours were set up to take us to one, two, or three Calanques, or fjords. So, the appropriate amount of money was paid for the correct number of Calanques: we chose trois! We were gluttons!

Piling onto the largest of the boats with mongering hordes practically hanging off the sides, we found our way to the top deck where we could view all that was available for viewing. The boat began with a loud roar and moved through the inner bay before heading out to the Mediterranean. The pearly white cliffs, created by a millennium of disintegrating limestone, rose high up off the water creating miniature fjords above the sparkling turquoise water. To catch a better view, we focused our binoculars up and down the cliffs in sweeping motions. Small sailboats and power boats careened in and out of the inlets like buzzy flies, while picnickers and sunbathers could be seen on every available sandy beach tucked into every nook and cranny available. Even high up on the rocky ridges we caught glimpses of what? What was that? Yes, nude sunbathers were showing off their wares. Quickly we took note, but just as quickly put our binocs away. The thought of dear Bob from the day before popped into our minds. We hoped his twelve-hour flight home was comfortable. He had awakened that morning with a surprisingly bad sunburn, all where the sun normally does not shine. Sitting may have presented a significant problem!

Once we returned to the Cassis harbor, the day was ebbing, so we made our way to our car passing through a beautiful little park en route. Yes, this village had great charm and we would definitely go back—when there were fewer tourists (like us).

We began driving back along the coastal roads, and when we were not ogling glimpses of the sea, we saw signs for wineries. One had the logo of an ancient sailing vessel. Of course, we perked up! Plus, it was difficult to pass gorgeous vineyards without stopping for a taste. Wines? Sailboats? Yes, we had to stop.

As it turned out, the history of the wine industry began in this coastal area by the Phoceans around 500 BC. Once the

Romans invaded several hundred years later, they became the first to export wines from several ports including the nearby port city of Bandol.

Domaine Tempier winery, where we made a short stop, had been in operation since before the reign of King Louis XV during the 1700s. Their *bastide*, or country house, was built on the family's property in 1834 and the family received their first gold medal in 1885. Unfortunately, later in the 1880s, the phylloxera epidemic ruined the French wine trade, and Léonie Tempier began the renewal by having her vineyard completely replanted on root stocks. However, the 1929 crash caused the wine business to plunge and vineyards were partially replaced by peach and apple trees.

One would think that this would be the end of it as the war years followed, but Domaine Tempier came back even stronger. In 1943, Lucien Peyraud, the son-in-law, bottled his first rosé and 1951 was the year when the first red Bandol wine was produced at the domain. The bottle label, or the logo that caught our eye to begin with, was designed and drawn by Lucie Tempier's father, Alphonse Tempier. It shows the departure of the wine bottles in tartan (sail) boats from the local Bandol harbor. They told us the label had not changed much because it embodied the spirit of the domain so well. We were hooked!

And we found their story similar story to the one we had heard in the Chateau-Neuf-de-Pape region—except without the influence of the sailboats used off the Côte d'Azur. The wines were rich, peppery, and full-bodied. "Almost meaty" one description stated in their brochure. Perhaps! I did love red wines, and these were so deep that it was like swimming in a pool of red velvet. Ah, but that's Mourvèdre, for you!

CHAPTER TWENTY

The Pizza Wagon Family

"It is at a time like this, when crisis threatens the stomach, that the French display the most sympathetic side of their nature. Tell them stories of physical injury or financial ruin and they will either laugh or commiserate politely. But tell them you are facing gastronomic hardship, and they will move heaven and earth and even restaurant tables to help you."

—PETER MAYLE, *A YEAR IN PROVENCE*

*I*n short order, it was time to head back home. Despite the respite over good wine, our first night alone in Claviers loomed before us. Quite honestly, we were saddened that all our friends had gone. Although the sun had dropped behind our thirteenth century hamlet of Claviers, a hint of golden sunlight sent a radiant shaft onto the Provençal village square and across the tiny sidewalk bistro where Winston and I sat. The buildings around us held tight to the heat of the June day and St. Sylvestre's church tower at the end of the square shimmered in the remaining glow. The town square, not a square at all but a minuscule triangle, was quiet. The only sounds were the dry rattle of leaves on the *plane* trees; an occasional bark from a passing but sociable dog; people conversing quietly at nearby tables, and accordion music that floated down from the same tinny radio we had heard before from an upper-story window. On occasion, a muted cheer or groan drifted up from the local afternoon boules players from just around the corner.

The burly but cheerful owner of the only bar on the plaza informed us, in rapid French, then broken bits of English, that he and his wife had just that week opened this little bistro. Food was not available—not quite yet—but the drinks, olives, and nuts were in great supply. As we sat back with our drinks, sunlight suddenly illuminated faces near us. Patrons shifted sunglasses down on their noses as their heads bobbed to adjust to this last flash of light. We, too, adjusted our positions, and our heads drowsily drooped toward our cocktail glasses where the intoxicatingly thick smell of licorice liqueur drifted refreshingly into our noses. What the sun and Mourvèdre had warmed on that hot summer's day in southern France, the pastis cooled. Yes, we had succumbed to the wiles of pastis!

It was hard to believe that only an hour before, we had left the cacophony and heat behind along the Côte d'Azur as we wended our way up thirteen hairpin turns to this remote hill-side village. When we pulled into the car park after a full day in Cassis and wine tasting, there were only two things we were looking forward to and those were a cooling drink—maybe pastis?—followed by a traditional Provençal meal.

"Tchin-tchin." The murmurings of an overheard toast floated past us. We raised our glasses in automatic response. It was Friday night after all. Suddenly, voices were raised as more people were welcomed into the tiny square. The sound of metal chairs scraping across ancient stones grew louder as patrons pushed back to make room at their ever-expanding tables. The camaraderie was immediate as both men and women embraced and kissed—each and every one—before they sat down to enjoy a communal drink. Even though we had witnessed this customary physical touch here in Provence, we, like sly voyeurs, could only silently observe.

Across the square, the last customers from the only grocery store in town came out with their purchases. Once again, the chairs scraped across the floor as people leaped from their seats. Once again, cheek connected to cheek, and those with heavily laden hands leaned forward as elbow touched elbow. Young hands reached out to beckon old ones and eyes sparkled as they exchanged pleasantries. Even teenage boys were seen swaggering through the streets greeting everyone in sight. Were we just seeing this display for the first time because we, ourselves, were alone? Had we been missing this each and every day we had been here?

As my husband and I, now in a semi-lethargic stupor from the heat and pastis, continued our observations, the chimes of St. Sylvestre struck eight o'clock. Just then a heavy door slammed shut across the square, and my attention swiveled in that direction. The sharp rasp of a lock sliding into place ricocheted off the nearby buildings as an elderly woman, the owner of the grocery, locked and bolted her store for the evening. She turned, cast a wave across the square, adjusted her scarf, and trudged off down the street.

We stared numbly after the old woman, then back into our glasses. A small bowl of olives slid back and forth between us. I slowly mulled over the French phrases the bar owner had uttered earlier. "My wife and I have just opened our bistro this very week. No, I'm sorry. There is no food available. Not quite yet."

Suddenly, I sat up straight and shook myself awake. I

ADVENTURES by LAND and SEA

realized our remaining hope for sustenance had just locked her doors and headed home. Yes, this was the first night my husband and I would be alone in the house since all our houseguests had gone, but we still had a few more days of vacation. And as I recalled, after last night's repast, we had no food left in those cupboards. The only thing on my kitchen counter was my lowly shopping list. *Oh, gawd!* I thought, staring into my drink.

One of the wonders of staying in Claviers was its remoteness, but now I could envision only dire consequences. "We are doomed," I groaned to my husband. "We will surely starve to death." Mental images of our busy day flashed through my mind. We had bypassed one *Super Marché* after another en route to Cassis and Bandol, and I had completely forgotten that not all places on the face of the earth have readily available food. And there were no other cafés in Claviers.

Just then we heard a low rumbling sound—a gnashing of gears—a grinding of metal—a mighty roar of an engine—then around the corner, past the church, almost into the square and onto our laps lurched a large white van. Pulling up near our table, a young man leaped from the driver's side of the truck. He quickly raced around to the opposite door and opened it for a young woman, his wife we surmised, and as she stepped out of the truck, he reached behind her, lifted out a golden-haired child, and hoisted her high. The year-old giggled and the crowd in the square swiveled their attention toward the joyous sound.

Once the door in the back of the truck was opened, the wife disappeared inside with the baby. The young man deftly flung up a panel window, rolled down a canopy sunscreen, hoisted a counter up to the window, added a step and, *voila,* Le Wagon de Pizza was open for business.

"Hooray," I said to my husband. "My whining has been answered. We've been saved!"

"Indeed, my love," my husband slurred slightly, "it's a miracle!"

Even before the aroma of garlic-infused tomato sauces, simmering local sausages, and caramelized onions could permeate the air, townspeople began to flow out of their homes and down the streets. It was as if the Pied Piper had come to town. Immediately, a line formed near the van as each person in turn leaned up to the counter—some on tiptoes, some on the small step—all to place his or her order. As the young wife bent down to take their requests, she would chat, then stop and reach for the baby. She carefully lifted the child up and extended her over the counter. Big nose met tiny nose—old cheek touched new—as each person in line kissed and caressed the infant. Time seemed to stop. Nothing at that moment took precedence over the gentle acknowledgment of this cherub, the Pizza Wagon baby.

I slowly looked around. "It feels like we've slipped into one of Marcel Pagnol's books—or his movies," I whispered. "Have we become part of one of his scenes?" Just the day before, I had been busy reading his books when all I needed to do to understand the people of Provence was to spend more time in this little town. Claviers.

My husband blinked as if to refocus. "You're right, my dear," he murmured. "It does feel like Pagnol, but, perhaps, the pastis has gotten the better of us. Maybe you should order a pizza and save us from starvation." He paused, then smiled and sat up in his chair. I could tell he was worn out from all the driving, and as they say in the States, he had been rode hard and put away wet. Exhaustion was taking its toll, but he rallied.

"In the meantime, I'll order a bottle of wine." His smile was kind; lopsided, but kind. I knew he was not eager to negotiate a food line, especially if it meant stringing French words together to accomplish the task. So, I nodded, stood up, and was forced to grab the edge of the table.

"*C'est vrai!*" I said steadying myself. "It's true! I've discovered the dangers of pastis," I giggled and gathered up my own meager snippets of broken French and headed over to join the queue.

After a few minutes of scanning the menu for items I might recognize, I glanced over at my husband who was also perusing a menu—a wine menu—with the striking bar owner's wife standing patiently by his side. Within moments, I saw her sprint out the back door of the bistro, down the street, and into a house below.

What on earth did he say to the woman? Or better yet, what did my husband order? He speaks even less French than I do!

As I calmed myself down, I became aware of the animated banter going on around me. Yes, the locals did acknowledge me; they smiled and nodded their heads. In fact, a few "bonsoirs" were exchanged, but as much as I would have loved to converse, I knew I would have been reduced to awkward hand gestures, head bobbing, or the inevitable shrug. We all knew I was an outsider. All villagers knew when outsiders arrived—and when they left. I remained silent but smiled boldly.

As I finally stepped up to place my order, I, too, marveled at the beautiful child of the Pizza Wagon. As a stranger, I hesitated to reach out to the baby, but instead blurted out, "*Très jolie!*" Not certain if that meant jolly or pretty, I figured I may have covered my bases. I had no clue. Just then, a beatific smile graced the tiny, upturned face as she sat precariously on the counter like a petite princess.

In the meantime, her harried parents whirled about their

small mobile kitchen. They pounded out the dough, spun it into the air, and adroitly slid it onto waiting pans while the child giggled with glee. Local olive oils, cheeses, sausages, and olives were sprinkled and layered onto the crust, then thrust into the oven.

After selecting a pizza, although not certain what I had actually ordered, I stepped back from the line only to see the bar owner's wife trudge back up the hill. Several bottles of wine were now tucked under her arms. I hoped they were not all for us, but then again, my thirst *was* returning. She disappeared into the bistro while I, swooning with savory aromas wafting about me, continued my vigil. Shuffling from one foot to the other, I resumed my post as voyeur. I couldn't help myself. Perhaps my desire to communicate had slipped into visual gear. Not once, not twice, but repeatedly I watched as people physically reached out to one another: the soft touch, the quick kiss, the gentle embrace. Hailing from a culture that keeps clear personal distances, I'd rarely seen such overt intimacies. But to witness a gentleness of spirit within an entire village? Once again, my mind raced back to the books of Marcel Pagnol. Before, I had assumed his delightful characters were fictitious, but could they have sprouted from his own reality? He was born and raised not terribly far from Claviers. Suddenly, I felt the presence of his amicable nature around me. I swayed. I had no words, French or otherwise, to describe the sweetness I felt in that moment.

After a few more minutes of standing on one foot and then the other, waiting, waiting, the villagers finally gathered up their boxes of pizza, bid each other adieu and returned to their homes. I, too, picked up our pizza and moved quickly to the table, as the heat was burning my fingers through the white cardboard box. Hovering over my husband, the bar

owner's wife was serenely pouring a bottle of recently retrieved wine. My husband sampled it, beamed up at her and
nodded his head vigorously because head nodding is the
French dialect he knows best. She turned toward me, smiled
graciously, and filled a wine glass for me. A desire to speak
with her rose in my throat. I wanted her to sit down and talk
for a while. I was feeling intoxicated, but it was no longer the
influence of the pastis. I realized I was high on this little village
of Claviers. Sadly, I knew we didn't share the same language,
so I settled for the language we knew best—a smile.

I slipped back into my seat, opened the box, and found a
medium-sized, delicate, thin-crusted pizza. It was browned to
perfection with hot melted cheese pooling magnificently into
small crevices. The sauce was flavorful with a light touch of
fresh tomatoes, herbs, a subtle splash of olive oil and enhanced
with *piment oiseau*—hot red peppers. And there peeking out
from under the cheese was a layer of *jambon,* thin slices of salty
ham, reminiscent of the sandwich my husband had once ordered for me. And all of which I didn't remember ordering for
our pizza. *Ah, c'est la vie. C'est delicieuse!*

We ate ravenously and swilled down the wine like it was
water. Shortly, we realized we should have ordered more pizza.
Perhaps one or two more. It had been smaller than our appetites
and was, oh, so good! But, by the time we came to our senses,
the Pizza Wagon had folded up and was grinding its way out
of the square. We finished our wine and reluctantly left, calling
our little repast *magnifique.*

As we began to stroll back to the house, my husband
lopped his arm over my shoulder and pulled me close to his
side. I, in turn, wrapped my arm around his back as we walked
in our hip-socking fashion up a slight hill, before turning
down a long cobblestone *allée.*

"'Twas a magical evening, my dear," my husband mumbled softly into my hair.

"That it was, my love," I said. "It was like attending an outdoor theatre—complete with the surprise appearance of the Pizza Wagon Family."

We stopped and stared up at the night sky. The moon had risen high above the campanile at the top of the village where the stars were sprinkled across the heavens in wild disarray. The evening was reveling in crystalline beauty.

My husband quietly took my hand in his and led me down the allée toward home. A funny thing! We didn't feel we were so alone after all!

Chapter Twenty-One

Not in Front of Those I Know!

On the next morning, while sipping coffee and looking out from our balcony to the south, we, once again, could see that the clouds had already lifted on the Mediterranean. Yes, we could see the sea! The Côte d'Azur would be expecting an extra nice day. Over a small scrap of breakfast, the two of us planned our day.

The June morning felt like the first time we had gone to St. Maxime—the air felt thick and heavy with humidity. A puff of onshore wind swept past without hanging around to cool us and I noticed once again the surprising hint of jasmine. The other familiar aromas rose up to greet us, as if they had been awaiting our return. Fried seafood, sausages, pizza, pommes frites, and Coppertone. And as we walked down the steps and onto the beach—so bold we were this time—the techno-music welcomed us with its discordant beat. Somehow, I still caught the sound of the cicadas, and smiled. They were always with us.

This time at the beach, we came as wiser beach goers. We knew what to expect. In fact, wasn't it only a day or two ago, when we were way over there at the Plage Tahiti, when we had become more enlightened? My eyes traced the coastline to the west, sweeping over the crystalline waves to take in the entire Bay of St. Tropez as my mind sifted through some improbable images of Bridgette Bardot.

Yes, this was going to be my "come to Jesus" moment, I decided! Would I join the topless women who were already flipping over to even their tans, or would I continue my prudish posturing and laze about in my buttoned-up mode?

It had only been a few days since my sister, brother-in-law, and friends had flown back to the US, so this would be the first time my husband and I would venture onto the beach alone. Was my day of reckoning finally upon me? Would I? Or wouldn't I? We knew no one on the beach now, so . . . Well, now I decided I *certainly* couldn't go topless! Not now! Not in front of total *strangers*! My mental harangues were becoming something like a Dr. Seuss poem:

Not in front of those I know.
But, strangers, too, I will not go!
I cannot strip in front of him.
And her? I can't because I'm prim . . .

Hour after hot sweaty hour, as I slipped down on my chaise and attempted to read a more licentious mystery while putting Marcel Pagnol aside, I also contemplated the freedom of baring my—soul? It was quite obvious I didn't need to be a curvaceous beauty to flaunt about the beach, for ladies of all sizes and shapes were stretched out on their beach towels, comfortably luxuriating like cats in the warmth of the sun. Women of all ages were expressing their femaleness, and I must admit I was jealous. Not because of their bodies, but because they appeared so comfortable *within* their bodies.

Obviously nervous, I casually quipped to my husband, "If you've seen one, you've seen them both." He chortled, and we both slipped back down behind our books. I realized I was finding this a difficult topic to discuss with him. I saw myself as more than willing to join the ranks. Or was I? I think I had convinced myself I was holding back because of him. I knew that he was more than a tad conservative in his ideas about dress—or undress, in this case. He already had his top off, but the rest was not up for discussion. I imagined his mind whirling about as it took in this dilemma: To delight openly in this available-for-viewing newfound freedom or to suffer silently the pangs of guilt for enjoying what his eyes beheld. But, of his own wife? Egad!

So, on this final beach day, the water was warm and gentle to our touch, the golden sun continued to burnish our bodies, and the aroma of coconut oil permeated each incoming breeze. We reveled in the leisurely pace of reading, having wine and food delivered to our chaises, and swimming in the lulling waves. Thoughts of participating in public nudity (almost) dissipated with the heat of the day.

My husband even bravely ordered sandwiches by himself from the bar.

"*Jambon et beurre pour deux,*" he announced with a flourish.

"Jambon et beurre?" I hooted, once again.

"Yes," he said matter-of-factly. "I just ordered two ham and butter sandwiches—no cheese, no mayonnaise, no mustard—just two dry jambon et beurre sandwiches, like you like them."

I started to protest, then he said, "But ma Cherie, don't you know appetite makes the best sauce?" He was right. A heaping of universal truth was served forth, as we had been famished. Again. And he ordered what he was comfortable in ordering, and believe me, they were excellent jambon et beurre sandwiches.

After déjeuner, we sipped our wine, stretched out once again, and I slipped off to sleep. When I awakened, I noticed two nubile, young women playing paddleball in front of us, almost completely nude—only an illusory filament of dental floss crossed their hips and a cursory figment of one's imagination covered their nether regions. I noticed my husband was hiding behind his book, his color conspicuously brighter red than prior to my nap. He confessed, rather quickly I might add, that one of the young women had hit the ball right over him and it had lodged in the sand—between our two chaises.

"The young woman," he wheezed, "walked nonchalantly over to me, and then leaned w-a-a-a-y down over me to retrieve the ball." A look of panic swept his cheeks as he turned to face me.

"I was terrified you would awaken to find me in a rather compromising position," he blurted out. When I burst into laughter, he seemed almost relieved.

"Confession is known to cleanse one's soul," I said, but confidentially, I wondered what man hadn't had daydreams of this sort? But probably not in such a risqué position, only inches away from his sleeping wife. The best and worst of all scenarios!

After hearing his tale, I again began to loosen the bonds of my own resistance, along with the straps to my top. Just then, a couple speaking in clipped, crisp Germanic sentences plunked their chaises near us. As I picked up my novel, I casually observed over the top of the pages that the woman was not only wearing a full-body swimming suit, but also a high-collared-over blouse. She was buttoned up to the gills and, surely, would not be tempted by nudists. Obviously, they were new in town.

Rats, I thought. *Now that I am beginning to push through my feelings of bodily revelation, how can I possibly break free in front of—THEM?* I must have said something out loud—oh, I sweat in the retelling—as I remember my husband saying, "It is strictly up to you, my love. Do what makes you comfortable. You know I find you beautiful either way."

Did he really mean it? I *was* rather fond of my Rubenesque body, I told myself. Suddenly, with complete reckless abandon, I threw caution to the wind—along with my bathing suit top— and bounded quickly into the water. I heard my husband gasp. I doubt he thought I'd really do this. He must have been stunned, and yet felt the need to do something, anything— cover me up, frolic with me, I doubt that even *he* knew. A moment later, I could hear him pounding quickly into the water behind me.

Keeping my back to him and the beach, I must confess, I was a little shocked at myself as I began to swim out a few yards. But when the coolness of the water enveloped me, ca- ressed me, swooped me up, and embraced me, my anxiety slid down my legs, over my ankles and was swept away with the waves. It was only then I realized this experience was not even a little bit naughty, but simply exhilarating. Most of all I found it freeing. Freeing! This wasn't just the physical act of bounding along the beach and into the water unharnessed that mattered most to me. It was the mental freeing of myself that I loved. It was the blending of the Nebraska girl I was on the inside with the California woman I had become on the outside—if only for a few brief moments—along those waters of the Côte d'Azur.

CHAPTER TWENTY-TWO

Aubagne – Home of Marcel Pagnol

"I was terrified that the wild boar might be attacking my father, and so I prayed to God—if he existed—to protect him and to direct the boar against my uncle instead, who believed in heaven, and therefore was more willing to die."

—MARCEL PAGNOL

The day at the beach in St. Maxime had been a test of bravery and a baptism of water! Winston and I had become even closer with each other—public semi-nudity can do that—but we were more in lockstep because that's what we do best when we travel alone together. It was grand to be us, again! Back in Claviers, we basked in our time together fixing one of our last suppers and staying up late to read. I don't think my husband would be embarrassed if I told you that I woke late that night to his weeping. He had finished Marcel Pagnol's book, *My Father's Glory*, and the hauntingly beautiful descriptions of childhood and family had taken him by surprise and overwhelmed him. Tears splashed down his cheeks and, without words, I understood his feelings.

So, on this second to the last day in Provence, we chose to

take a leisurely drive down to the village of Aubagne, the childhood home of Marcel Pagnol. Maybe we sought to make this journey because we both had finished his book. Or, perhaps, because we felt we understood the Provençal character now. But there was a definite call for us to drive down to the little village where he had spent his summers.

As we motored down the highway, we realized we had passed close to Aubagne several times over the past two weeks. Certainly, when we went to Cassis. And on the way back from Aix-en-Provence? No matter. Winston's confidence level for driving had hit an all-time high and we were riding it.

We circled around an enormous limestone bluff, known as the Garlaban Massif. It was said this abutment could be seen from quite a distance and was once used by sailors from Marseilles to find direction along the Mediterranean. But, like I said, we were focusing on the inland landscape. With the bright sunlight dancing over the fields of grape vines, wheat, sunflowers, and lavender, the land appeared transformed into the fantasy land of Pagnol's own boyhood tales. Yes, the haunting beauty of his book, *My Father's Glory*, was working miracles in our imaginations.

We first attempted to find the *Maison Natale de Marcel Pagnol*, or Pagnol's birthplace, which we assumed was the most important house in his book, *My Mother's Castle*. We honestly didn't have a clue where to look and the road we were on circled through town and then headed back out of the town. It wouldn't be until much later, it dawned on us he grew up in Marseille, but summered in Aubagne. So, we turned around and drove back down the main streets of Aubagne. We located a museum called *Le Petit Monde de Marcel Pagnol,* or The Small World of Marcel Pagnol, which celebrates his characters with little eight- to twelve-inch tall folkloric and religious figurines made of terracotta, dressed up with Provençal fabrics, and created to represent little saints from Marcel Pagnol's movies and books. Yes, both French writer and motion-picture producer-director, he won fame as the master of stage comedy and critical acclaim for his filmmaking.

So, what are *santons?* Originally made to place in *crèches* for Christmas, santons have become a large market in Provence. Each one carries a gift to the Lord Jesus, which usually reveals what is most important to them. There are shepherdesses carrying little lambs, hunters carrying their shotguns, cheese makers carrying baskets of brie, lavender growers carrying sheafs of lavender, laundry women holding laundry . . . why, there are also boules players on a boules court, men playing cards at a small café table, a man carrying the local newspaper *Mistral*, a couple preparing to dance. They are simple characters acting out normal activities in life.

As with the museum, Pagnol's book begins with the phrase: "I was born in the city of Aubagne, under the Garlaban crowned with goats, in the time of the last goatherds." Slowly, we walked through the rooms paying homage to the stories and characters that represented scenes from his movies, such as *Jean de Florette, Manon of the Spring, The Baker's Wife,* and of course, the movie version of his own life. Such a rich excursion of delight and joy which, of course, stirred our own childhood memories. Winston and I have always enjoyed reveling in the stories our grandfathers would tell.

After we stepped out into the heat of the afternoon sun, we realized how hungry we were. We had eaten little breakfast again that morning—French press coffee and croissants—so we were famished. It was well after 1 p.m. so we decided not to leave the town of Aubagne but took our own sweet time having lunch at a nearby bistro. We chose local fare: a crock of eggplant dip, which was their local baba ghanoush, sidled with baguette slices; French onion soup for two; a brochette with lamb and vegetables for me, and entrêcote (small beefsteak) with French fries for Winston. Of course, a carafe of rosé helped to tickle the nose and open the doors to even more childhood memories as we feasted on excellent yet simple food. We were not eager to rush the day.

We returned to Claviers late that afternoon, parked in the car park outside the village as usual, but slowed as we passed to wave at the old gents playing boules. They looked up, smiled, but didn't lose concentration as the metal boule, which had been set off across the court, let out its magical clink. A loud and raucous cheer went up as we threw a thumbs up gesture and turned the corner onto the village square.

Win grabbed my hand and we walked to the wine bar we had sat at a few nights before. The same place we had encountered the Pizza Wagon Family. Could nostalgia be setting in?

"We have no choice but to stop at our favorite wine bar," Win said. I didn't mention it was the only wine bar in town. No point in belaboring such details.

I agreed, as it was our last night. Without words, we both knew we wanted to savor our evening surrounded by the Clavierois, the locals of Claviers. Even though these folks only knew us as the Americans, for some odd reason we felt the need to say adieu and merci to them.

Once our metal chairs scraped across the stone patio as we sat down, the bar owner's wife popped her head out of the door. She smiled in our direction, waved, and disappeared. Very shortly a bowl of nuts, then olives, was set down at our table and there before us stood this same lovely woman from the other night ready to take our order. Again, I yearned to talk with her, to have a casual conversation, and I felt like she, too, wanted to speak to us. But none of us had the language skills to make that leap. Instead, we did what we did best and that was to shrug, smile and order a bottle of local rosé. She returned to the bar to place our order.

I popped a couple of salty nuts into my mouth and contemplated this lost moment. Lost because I had not prepared myself for this trip in knowing adequate French. And I wasn't certain why this woman, in particular, had captured my attention. She was young, in her thirties, had shiny black hair piled on top of her head, had deep brown eyes that twinkled when she smiled, and she wore a stylish but rather tight black sweater over a very tight black skirt. I suppose she was, in polite terms, overweight, but this was why she intrigued me. As we watched her walk back and forth from the bar to her customers, she carried herself with such grace and confidence. For me, that was what was so eye catching about her. She moved like a woman who was completely comfortable in her own skin. Could this be a French thing, I wondered? Certainly, this was not an American thing, as we are more prone to hide our weight. Or so it seemed to me that night.

Of course, this was all an internal dialogue, as I figured it was a woman thing and Winston was engaging with her as she opened the bottle of wine, as if he had a cross-over language. I smiled at them both and relaxed into the moment.

We took our time finishing the bottle of wine—I'm not sure why we thought we needed a full bottle—but when I asked Win, he quipped, "We're in crawling distance, aren't we?" Indeed, we were, although it would be a craggy crawl, at that.

Like a few evenings before, the shadow of the buildings surrounding us blocked out the brightness of the sun as it slid down behind the mountains. We just sat there seemingly numb but actually trying to absorb the voices around us, capture their banter and bottle the essence of the moment. Yes, I know. I'm sounding a bit maudlin. But it was as if we were attempting to capture time in place.

Then, in the distance, past the boules court and down the road toward a high school practice field, we could hear music—both vocal and instrumental accompaniment—echoing through the valley. We had finished our bottle of wine, so we decided to wander (wobble?) down to check out the music. The melodies were familiar, but we couldn't figure out what the merriment was about. Maybe this was a summer play with musical accompaniment? The music stopped, then started up again. The vocalists would begin again and then break into laughter.

Or was the music patriotic? Bastille Day was just around the corner, and we were nearing July fourteenth. We had learned that a number of regions celebrate with great vigor on the thirteenth, leaving the fourtenth for home and family. But, in other regions, the holiday was celebrated much like our July fourth. Posters were already showing up in each of the villages we had passed through.

We made our way down to the school practice field and sidled onto a couple of empty bleachers. We were far enough away that we felt we were not barging in, but we were able to see how much fun these folks were having. No, these were not just high school age but also adults, so this must be the official Claviers band. And once the rousing music from *La Marseillaise* rang out into the night, I wondered if we should stand and put our hands over our hearts. Instead, when they finished playing, we clapped in appreciation. The band and chorus turned, noticing us for the first time, and bowed. Yes, bowed. We felt honored.

Okay, it can't get any better than this, I thought. As I walked past the many houses along the road, I could see into the windows of family homes, through the gauzy white curtains, and into the kitchens, where family were cooking the family meal, the aromas distinctly wafting out to greet us, and the laughter and banter felt so real and so joyous. I couldn't help but wonder what it would be like to live in those houses, along those village roads, in this village of Claviers, and to hear and rejoice in their own family stories. I shrugged my shoulders. Maybe someday!

Winston encouraged me to keep walking as we still needed to pack that night. But an orange marmalade sky lingered just beyond the mountains to the west, so we walked back to the other end of the town and climbed up to the highest point again where the ancient chapel of St. Sylvestre rose above the craggy rocks. Just like the night of the Pizza Wagon family, we sat down on the rocks and watched while the day became night. And I thought about the comment that Dan had made to Melody: "I think you lived here in another age." Perhaps he was right!

CHAPTER TWENTY-THREE

Nice, Menton, and Monaco, Oh My!

*T*he next morning seemed like a blur as we not only had to complete our packing, but to clear out all the remnants of two weeks of frivolity and camaraderie. We would spend years remembering all that we were able to do in this rustic but lovely little house. The card games! The wistful conversations. The sound of the cicadas. The radio station blasting popular music that not only filled the house with music but with laughter. The shared dinners, the planning for the next day's adventures, the swilling of wines each evening . . .

But, for this final day, the housekeeper instructed us to bring the Mercado closer to the house to load the car. In all the time we stayed there, we hiked in from the car park at the edge of town. So, this was quite a nice treat—or so we thought. The road that Winston had to use was a one-way narrow road that circled around the back of town and eased along behind the house. As we figured out, the road was built on top of the rampart wall, so one side was against a stone wall and the other fell sharply to the valley below. It was fairly easy for Winston to drive the car behind our place, but once the car was packed, there appeared no way forward. Ahead of us, the road narrowed even more. Only a chicken feather's breadth separated us from scraping the rock wall on one side and the steep drop off on the other. We were certain we were doomed!

From behind a hidden door, one of our neighbors stepped out to give us assistance. No, no one spoke each other's language, but he began by slamming the side mirrors on our car flat against the car. And, as I watched standing behind the car, he coaxed Winston very slowly down the road. "Come on," we assumed he said as he waved Winston forward while he backed down the path in front of our car. "Come on, come on," he repeated gently. Like a father bird coaxing a reticent baby out of its nest, he sweet-talked us safely out and away. I could have kissed him. And Winston considered it himself.

We were actually a bit teary as we drove out of Claviers early that morning, but we made good time as we wound back down the mountain hairpin turns for the last time. We drove through a *péage* again (pay station), and onto the autoroute to Nice. Our plans were to spend one last night back at the Park Hotel, because our flight was the next morning at 6 a.m. We dropped off our luggage at the hotel, and because we felt the world was ours for the day, we decided to drive east for a change of pace.

So, what adventures could we find? What great seafood could we indulge in? There were so many options. We drove along the coastal highway, which skirts the French Riviera on the right and butts up next to the Maritime Alps on the left. We zipped in and out of Eze, Monaco, Roquebrune-Cap-Martin, and ended up at Menton, which was the last French city before crossing into Italy. We chose a lovely beachside bistro, La Pergola, as is our want to do, and settled into plastic chairs at a white plastic table, with our toes in the sand. The early afternoon was a bit hazy but the breeze off the water seemed to cool everyone nearby. Behind both of us, and along the beach, were chaises with sunbathers enjoying the balmy weather. The waves next to us were a gentling sound, a softening of the disco music that floated through the air from a nearby transistor radio. I was appreciating my view of the coast to the west, as was Winston, who was facing east and the mountains of nearby Italy. It was feeling like each of the last few days were just that . . . the last day here; the last day there; and through osmosis we were soaking up every ounce of our shared Provençal experiences.

We looked at the menu and realized that throughout our entire trip we had succumbed to the Italian influence on the Provençal cuisine. Now, being mere steps away from Italy, the dishes seemed even more solidly Italian: Capri salad, cannellini bean dishes, pizza, prosciutto, fried sardines, calamari, deep-fried shrimp.

In fact, most dishes consisted of local catches off nearby Ventimiglia. We opted to share a large platter of paella, filled with mussels, clams, and slipper lobsters all swimming around in a deep, savory tomato broth with Niçoise black olives. Baskets of fresh bread were available for sopping up the juices and added to the meal. Life is sweet!

But first, a special aperitif! As a salute to our day in Cassis, we opted for the extra-special Kir Royale once again, made with champagne and Crème de Cassis. And of course, we ordered a carafe of rosé.

We had a long, leisurely lunch. We weren't in any hurry! When it was time for the dessert course, we both opted for the *tarte au citron,* or lemon tart, along with a couple of cappuccinos. Sleepiness while driving the winding coastal road back to Nice was not how we wanted to end our vacation.

It was about this point in our lovely repast my dear husband suggested that I trade seats with him, as he had been enjoying the grand view of what I assumed were the beginnings (or endings) of the Maritime Alps. I made the switch to his chair, sat down, and was a bit flabbergasted to see—yes, a couple of lovely, but also voluptuous, and fully topless women spread out only a couple of feet from where I had been sitting. Now, I must tell you that my husband's version was a bit different. He said they had only been there a short time before he switched seats. But he also confessed that he had become paranoid about me turning around to discover those beauties behind me. We'll never know which version was more accurate.

But never mind, I believe we had faced those challenges before and had conquered our queasiness! We were wiser and older now. I shook my head and laughed. Once again, the beach scene had wrought moments of discomfort and wonder. Trepidation and triumph! And, where else, but on the Côte d'Azur?

We returned to our car to head back toward Nice, but first we wanted to take a spin through the streets of Monte Carlo and past the world-famous Place du Casino. Opulence and conspicuous wealth were on display at every corner with palm tree-filled parks, fountains, sculptures, and modern apartment buildings etched with gold leaf. And the yachts in the harbor? The small ones were sixty to one-hundred-feet-long, both sailboats and cruisers, all looking more suitable for a cruise line. We were told that the small yachts had only one helicopter. We laughed. Such preposterous notions were beyond our comprehension! Why, we didn't even own a boat! And the tenders (or small boats that tended to the needs of the larger boats), whirred through the harbor like buzzing bees, going from land to boat ferrying the rich and famous to lifestyles we could only contemplate. Or not. Not our gig!

We drove past the Royal Palace of Monaco, also a part of this same municipality. Because it was late in the afternoon, we simply skirted the area and took in what we could see from the road. We would come back another time. From our guidebook, the Palace was described as an odd composition of multiple architectural styles as it had been originally built in 1191 as a Genoese fortress and suffered an inordinate number of bombardments. Through the years and due to the changes in ownership, the buildings are composed of medieval fortifications to gentile baroque-style architecture. The creamy and elegant front of the castle exuded the same grand designs we had just witnessed in Monte Carlo. Made sense, I thought, as they were within the same city.

We continued back onto the road toward Nice but turned off once again into Villefranche-sur-Mer, a coastal village, noted for its beauty and famous for having one of the deepest harbors in the area. We threaded our way down the steep, winding streets, found parking, and began a walk along the harbor. Like a magnet we were continually drawn to the water, and the pull of the beauty from this charming place directed our steps. We followed along the port, once again enjoying the lift and bob of the boats along with the clang of the halyards against the masts.

We wandered up the stone streets through the old town, reveling in the colorful façades of one home after another— bright orange, next to fuchsia pink, then tangerine, which was next to deep green, then bounding back to a mellow yellow with contrasting shutters throughout. In other areas of the village, wealth and prestige were on display as each stately sandstone building was well-cared for with rich black wrought-iron balconies, exuberant sprays of magenta bougainvillea and subtle but colorful shutters. A complete panoply of color displayed up and down this village and reflected in the shimmering waters far below. It was a glorious day, and a great way to bring our trip to a close.

It was clear we had to return. There was so much to love, to learn about, to enjoy and to embrace. From sumptuous coastal villages like this very Villefranche-sur-Mer to the traditional villages high in the mountains like Claviers, we embraced them all. Yes, we would come back!

SECOND TRIP *to* PROVENCE, April 2000

"If I'm an advocate for anything, it's to move. As far as you can, as much as you can. Across the ocean, or simply across the river. Walk in someone else's shoes or at least eat their food. It's a plus for everybody."

—ANTHONY BOURDAIN

CHAPTER TWENTY-FOUR

Good Morning, Paris –
Good Night, Moustiers

"Travel is about the gorgeous feeling of teetering in the unknown."

—ANTHONY BOURDAIN

Yesterday, we awakened in Paris to another lovely, albeit cloudy, day. My sister, Melody, and I had spent the last two days frolicking around Paris by ourselves—a dream come true. It was due to a promise we had made to each other on our first trip to Provence only three years earlier.

But this time we were on our own. No one to pooh-pooh our whims and fancies, or frown at our choice of tours. No one coaxed us to move along a little more quickly or encouraged us to walk instead of taking a cab. No one to talk us out of a nighttime cruise down the Seine past the glorious Eiffel Tower lit up and bespangled with *Ans 2000*, followed by dinner at Madame Brasserie on the première étage, or first floor. Yes, it was the year 2000! And who would Melody run into but an entire group of folks from her hometown in rural Iowa!

We felt completely cut loose—not that two sisters who grew up in Nebraska knew exactly how to cut loose. But we reasoned that the past two days were solely to acclimate ourselves to France before our first culinary tour together began in Provence. The prospect was joyous!

On the last day in Paris, Melody and I sat and talked the morning away over a petit déjeuner of chocolate croissants and café with hot steamed milk. It's not that we hadn't been talking before, as we had taken a nonstop flight from Chicago into Charles De Gaulle Airport and chattered the entire trip. In fact, every waking moment, we were in full-throttle catchup mode. It had been over forty years since we lived together as sisters, and we had territory to cover.

We walked down the street to purchase a few essentials from the drug store as well as bottled water for our flight to Marseilles. Yes, we had enjoyed our time in Paris, but we were eager to meet up with the other gals who would be joining us on this Provençal adventure.

Now, I had met several of our fellow travelers a few months before while taking a gourmet cooking class in Sunnyvale, California. It was there that Sharon Shipley, a chef and our culinary teacher, offered us the opportunity of a lifetime— a trip to Provence—all in order to learn traditional cooking. She was filling the trip rapidly, so I quickly contacted my sister, Melody, to ask if she could join us. As it turned out, she was just retiring from her job in Iowa City as a city planner and needed a break. Others from our cooking class also jumped at the chance to go to France or Provence for any reason—shopping, drinking wine, eating, shopping . . . maybe some cooking and more shopping. It was all good with them. It was time in France.

The taxi arrived in a timely manner, and we were

whisked through the busy streets of Paris. Being overly anxious, we arrived at the airport a tad early. We strolled through the concourse of the Air France's terminal before lunching on sandwiches of tuna—despite having ordered chicken. "Ah, perhaps, it is chicken of the sea," my sister joked. We waited for our turn to check in.

Shortly, Karen Burnett, one of our travel mates, introduced herself to us as well as the six of the women plus Russ (the only spouse), who would be sharing time with us on our tour. Everyone was excited to finally get together, and we shared a bon voyage drink before walking down to our gate. Nonchalantly, I watched as rain streamed down and over the glass roof tops of the new air terminal and over the planes. We were grateful for being inside while the chilly April rain poured down, even though the song is "April in Paris." I believe we all looked forward to April wrapped in the warmth of the Mediterranean sunshine once we landed.

The flight from Paris to Marseilles was short—only an hour and a half—and was at first comfortable, but then became a bit lumpy. The weather caused the plane to hit air pockets, sending our stomachs into a tumble as we bumped over the interior mountains. Suddenly we landed. Like my first flight into Nice, bright sunshine greeted us as it glanced off the Côte d'Azur near the runway! We were back! Hoorah! Melody and I cheered.

Once our luggage was collected, we were handed glasses of rosé as a special welcome drink. And, like old hands at this Provençal stuff, Melody and I clinked our glasses together, "Tchin-Tchin," we said, then turned to cheer on our tour group. There was Lise, who was our intrepid French guide and good friend; Sharon, our culinary guru; and, of course, take charge Karen. And then there were the rest: sweet Joan and her dear and supportive husband, Russ; coquettish Pam; sophisticated, yet fun Colleen. And then there was dear Chris, who was like a mother to most all this clan, and quiet and unassuming Margie.

Our Provençal journey began as we drove away from Marseilles airport and headed into the foothills. As we cruised along the autoroute in a private van, Timon was at the wheel, and our group started to become acquainted. Voices rose, squeals were heard, and chatter became almost earsplitting. Old friends were meeting new friends, and the camaraderie was vibrant. Could it have been because we had been well supplied with wine? Or thoroughly excited about the culinary tour we were on?

As the mountains spread out before us, Melody and I pinched ourselves. We were heading back to Moustiers! Yes, the same beautiful little village, poised like a mountain goat high on a perch, that we had visited a few years before.

The bright blue sky that had welcomed us when we had flown into Marseilles, was beginning to cloud over. The winds whipped about, but we rejoiced as spring had arrived in southern France. The fields were covered in wildflowers—blood red poppies; dark purple iris; yellow mustard grass; and a profusion of blue buttons. It was too early for the lavender to be in full bloom but the fields of closely cropped grey-green furrows lined the landscape as far as the eye could see. And the grey-green leaves of the olive orchards shimmered with the breeze. The mountains appeared more regal than we remembered from a few years before, and the hills were intensely green and welcoming.

Around 6:00 p.m. we arrived at the Bastide de Moustiers, a lovely country house (or hotel) owned and operated by, yes, the world-famous chef, Alain Ducasse. With instructions to kindly hurry back for dinner, Melody and I were escorted to the Aviary Room, which was an extraordinary suite of rooms furnished in antiques and charming country clutter like old birdcages. Once an aviary, it was now an elegant bedroom. The four-poster king-sized bed with pillows piled high looked all too inviting. We then discovered the extra-large bathroom, which had many additional accoutrements such as large terry cloth robes and slippers, a giant tub for two—not that we would try that—baskets filled with fresh towels, special olive oil bath salts, and wash cloths with gloves . . . Yes, we were receiving royal treatment. A bit different from the house we had rented in Claviers, those few years ago. Ah, but we needed to hurry!

In the brief moments between being shown our room and heading up for dinner, we peeked through the window to spot a quiet little courtyard with an old fountain. Through the French doors, we caught the last glimpses of the sun before it set over the village of Moustiers. A large expanse of green meadows spread up the hill to that perched village above us and was so lovely!

We hastily changed clothes for dinner and were ushered into the dining room. As we joined the table, Sharon, our chef extraordinaire, was already holding court. She was surrounded by Russ and all the other women, but it was quiet and unassuming Lise who became the voice of our tour. She was French; she grew up in Paris; and as a girl she spent summers in the South of France. But most importantly, she knew how to speak French! We quickly learned to lean in close to hear her words and translations.

As Sharon described the upcoming days learning the culinary arts of Provence, the room became electric with anticipation. But first things first, the evening's meal was about to begin, and it promised to be the first of many epicurean adventures we would experience over the next ten days.

The menu provided by Alain Ducasse's most capable staff consisted of three tapenades: eggplant, olive, and anchovy on croustades with bread sticks. The second course, fresh from the garden, was pea soup with croutons, foie gras, and spring garlic. The main course was roast chicken with glazed succulent potatoes and carrots. The cheese course, the servers pointed out, also came to our table from local sources including goat cheese wrapped in grape leaves. The *pièce de resistance* was not one, but two delectable desserts: a nice-sized slice of apple tart plus a sliver of chocolate torte, all served with vintage port and cappuccinos or tea.

The entire meal was orgasmic if I must say so myself. The moans and murmurs of delight throughout our dining experience replaced the chatty banter that had been running non-stop since we met in the Paris airport. Only the intake of food slowed us down.

"Excellent! Excellent!" We all clapped in appreciation. Everything had been created and, of course, delivered in the most excellent manner. Oh, Melody and I quickly succumbed to this beautiful and hospitable Bastide!

CHAPTER TWENTY-FIVE

A Tour of Faïence Factory

"The journey is part of the experience—an expression of the seriousness of one's intent. One doesn't take the A train to Mecca."

—ANTHONY BOURDAIN

*T*he following morning, we awakened to rain—soft and gentle—but a constant thrumming on the tiled rooftop. No, we had not left the rain behind in Paris.

We met again in the dining room for our petite déjeuner, which was specialty cakes with lavender-infused sugars; bowls of café and steamed milk; freshly squeezed blood orange juice; local yogurt and fresh fruits. And baskets of toasted baguette slices were laid out beside tiny pots of jam, which were scattered around the table.

I believe it was at this point we all realized that coffee no longer came in cups for breakfast. No, they arrived in what we had once considered cereal bowls. But there was no questioning it. There were just surprised looks, before we all picked up our bowls and slurped down the dark rich coffee crowned with frothy milk.

Once we finished breakfast, Sharon had scheduled a tour for us to the nearby faïence factory.

"But what is faïence?" Pam asked. We heard the question reverberate through our group. Of course, Melody and I grinned at each other as we had taken a tour of the faïence museum up the hill in Moustiers.

"Faïence is the lovely earthenware," Sharon responded, "or dinnerware that has graced our tables while at the Bastide. The factory makes all hand-painted dinnerware, plus tureens, platters, and the rest."

"So, this is not the same as the faïence museum in town?" I asked.

"No, no, no! We are going to the factory where these beautiful dishes are produced, and hand painted. After completing the tour, perhaps, you will find something to purchase for your own homes."

Murmurs of the possibility of shopping buzzed through the group. We all enthusiastically pulled on our rain gear, were handed umbrellas, and began to hike out in the rain. We walked through the gates of the Bastide and down the road to the nearby faïence factory, Atelier Soleil.

We were warmly welcomed into the factory, where we were first shown finished products as examples, before receiving a short tour of how faïence was made, baked, and painted.

Our guide told us that these highly glazed pieces had been manufactured right there in Moustiers in only four or five factories from 1679 to the 1800s. The guide, thankfully in English, although Lise was nearby, filled us in on more of the history.

"The art flourished because of a little Italian monk who had been visiting the Monastery of the Communauté de Lérins, which is located on the island of Saint-Honorat, near

Cannes. He came up with the secret of white enamel (tinned ceramics) in 1668. Not long after that, Louis XIV ordered all the gold and silver tableware to be melted down to restore the royal treasury in preparation for war. He replaced the dishes with the faïence from Moustiers. It was at that moment Moustiers' earthenware acquired high notoriety all over European courts." It was quite an amazing story and one our group fully appreciated.

"Originally," our guide continued, "the pure white glazed pieces, whether soup tureens, plates, platters, or bowls were hand-painted with figurative scenes, often copied from engravings of hunting scenes, or mythological subjects. In the seventeenth century, a Spanish influence added more color, and the images became more of flora and fauna designs and then whimsical."

We walked through the rooms where the earthen ware was being made. "From rough clay to smooth, sparkling, silky platters," the guide continued, "there are just a few basic ingredients: water, earth, and fire. But for the alchemy to be successful or for the magic to work, a great mastery of an age-old art is required: stamping, turning, biscuit, enameling, drawing, firing . . . We choose to master this art with the most authentic bright and warm earthenware, with both traditional or contemporary shapes and decorations."

We walked from one staging area to the next, oohing and aahing as we watched those craftsmen and women create the beautiful pieces. At this point, Lise, who had been at the ready to help with any translations from French into English, led us into a room where we were able to meet the young women who hand-painted all the pieces. Their work was so beautifully and masterfully wrought; some with the more traditional floral and fauna, but also some with the precocious images of santons that were prevalent in Provence and one of my favorites.

"So, what are santons?" Pam asked.

"Ah," replied Lise, "all these little characters are celebrants of their traditional lifestyle. They represent peasants or everyday man as little saints who carry gifts to the Christ child at Christmas."

We all hovered around oohing and ahhing, and I knew I had no choice but to purchase something to ship back home. Oh, but instead of one piece, like my husband and I had done in Moustiers before, I chose a set of eight salad plates, with a different image of a santon painted on each plate. If you come to my house and you will see the delightful designs I chose: *a la fermière* (farmer's wife); *le vigneron* (winemaker); *le braconnier* (poacher); *la porteuse de pain* (bread carrier); *le chasseur* (hunter); *le paysan* (peasant); *le cantiniere* (cantina operator); *le pecheur* (fisherman). I couldn't wait to get home to display these treasures.

The rain continued as we walked back down the road to have a pique-nique in Joan and Russ' room. As it turned out, they had been given a larger room with a fireplace and had plenty of space for us all. We feasted on fresh ham slices, cheese, olives, marinated hot cherries, breads, pizza, fruits, wine, and hot red radishes. All the products were fresh from the market and purchased by Sharon that very morning, while we were obviously spending our euros on ceramic plates.

We ate contentedly while Melody and I waited for our new room to be ready. Yes, our beautiful aviary was being rented by another couple for the weekend. Rats! Ah, but we would be leaving the next morning for Aix-en-Provence. *Non problème!*

I decided to hike into Moustiers as it would be the only opportunity to see the village. The others had started ahead, but Melody chose to stay behind to write and rest. I began by trudging up the hill—and trudging sounds at a faster clip than I actually moved—as the change in elevation was 3,000-to-5,000 feet. I caught up with Joan as she, too, was slogging along and somehow with our umbrellas and rain hoods obstructing our view, we missed our turn to meet the others at the Museum of Faïence. We continued climbing higher and higher for another thirty minutes before we realized our error, and turned around and eventually found the others. We almost collapsed in a heap in the museum . . . soggy wet, cold, and tired. I was grateful I had been there before, because I certainly didn't have the energy to follow another tour.

The afternoon continued the same confusing spiral, and the rain did not let up. But the village was beautiful, almost ethereal, as the clouds and mist floated around its edges playing with the flowers lined in every flower box along the road. We headed back down the hill—me, without really seeing anything as I was too tired—and headed to our rooms, this time in the Blanche Chambre—for a much-needed nap.

I did glance around the Blanche Room before crashing, which was also lovely and substantial in size. One would consider the bathroom as extra-large, with a bathtub hidden behind white draperies. The tiled walls were painted with lovely blue flowers . . . oh, my, the nap was calling my name!

That evening we returned to the dining room for our final formal repast at this memorable bastide, the Bastide de Moustiers! The menu was like the previous evening's meal, always with a finger on the season. We were told that the philosophy of the kitchen was this:

"Every morning, our gardener picks up produce from the vegetable garden and then places his filled crates under the kitchen windows. The vegetables, fine herbs, and fruits then spend a short time in the hands of the chef. And then, still in their very freshness and barely processed, they invite themselves onto the plates of the guests. This is always a magical surprise that happens in the imagination of the chef each and every day."

CHAPTER TWENTY-SIX

Aix-en-Provence

*B*right and early the next morning, our tour bus rolled away from the grand grounds of Bastide de Moustiers, Timon at the helm, with rays of sunshine glancing off the ancient city of Moustiers; our first glimpse of sun since our arrival. The spring rains had cleansed the air leaving it bitingly crisp, the sky brilliantly blue, and the flowers and bushes along the roadside standing up to draw our attention. Red poppies, lavender-colored wisteria, and bright yellow broom waved us on our way. Fruit trees were in full bloom with pale pink apple blossoms, and delicate, white petals on cherry trees opening with the promise of a bounty of fruit.

We, the merry group of gourmet travelers, bumped along the mountain roads that skirted Lac de Sainte Croix, the lake mirroring the beauty surrounding us. We breezed through one village after another, then entered the village of St. Maximin la Sainte Baume. Lise turned in her seat and spoke in her soft, French-accented voice. We cocked our ears forward in order not to miss a single word. Hers was the voice we were training to tune in for instruction and enlightenment.

"We are passing through the city known as the burial place

of Mary Magdalene." We all gasped, and our eyes scanned the surroundings as if proof would present itself at curbside.

"Oui, following her years as a recluse high in these mountains, upon dying she was buried in a crypt right in the basilica here."

"Mary Magdalene? Why?" we asked, astounded. "How did she find her way high into the hills of Provence from Palestine?"

"Wasn't she the one who not only witnessed the crucifixion of Christ but also discovered His resurrection?" someone asked. We were all aghast. Maybe we were not all that religious, but we knew our Bible.

"Oh, the stories you will hear in this area of Provence," she said tossing her hands into the air. "They will amaze you. Not just Mary Magdalene, but of the three Marys. Yes, that is what they are called here, and their stories are sprinkled far and wide as it turns out."

"Three Marys?" we blurted out.

"Yes," Lise nodded. "The three Marys were known as Mary Magdalene, Mary Salomé, and Mary of Clopas, who were ushered out of Palestine by the Romans due to death threats. They fled to Alexandria, crossed the Mediterranean Sea, got lost and drifted onto the shores of the Côte d'Azur at the mouth of the Rhône River. In the Camargue, south of Arles. You will hear all about these stories when we visit Arles for one of your first cooking classes. Just in a day or two."

We made our way into the regal city of Aix-en-Provence along the famous boulevard, Cours Mirabeau. The boulevard, known for being the center or heart of the city—and its name meant beautiful heart—was one of the most popular and liveliest streets in Aix. With wide sidewalks and double rows of plane trees it was a welcome sight for all who congregate under the trees or near the many fountains or at the famous cafés and bistros along the route. I smiled at the memory of drinking a cappuccino at Les Deux Garçons only a few years before and loved the thought that it had been a frequent watering hole for French cultural figures such as Paul Cézanne, Émile Zola, and Albert Camus.

Sharon and Lise scurried us out of the tour bus. Our tour guide was waiting! We had to reach the flower market during morning hours and the clock was ticking.

"The flower market?" we all asked. "Aren't we here for the food market?"

"Today," Sharon explained, "you will be immersed in the Provençal culture and history of Aix-en-Provence."

Lise picked up the story as she led us quickly through the alleys (narrow cobbled streets) to the meeting place of our guide. "The architectural, artistic, and historical elements literally seep out of every corner of each street," she said, with a sweep of her hand. "This was once an ancient Roman city founded in 123 BC and named after a local spring." She stopped to emphasize a point: "As it turns out, every Roman city that has Aix in the name tells you the purpose and importance of the city. It refers to a most important commodity necessary for human habitation—water!"

"Makes sense, Melody," I whispered to her as we once again picked up the pace and one fountain larger than the last was sending up sprays of water into the morning sun. The sound of the waters echoed off the buildings as we scooted past.

Melody and I had wandered through Le Marché aux Fleurs, or the Flower Market, in Nice those few years back. But this was the first time we would have a guided tour. We clattered through the streets and up to the Place de Hotel de Ville where Isabelle, our guide, awaited us.

Isabelle was a petite young Frenchwoman with dark brown hair swept back with a clip to reveal her lovely face. And she was a student at the local university studying the arts and history. She spoke English flawlessly

Standing in the Place, the historic backdrop to her tour, Isabelle began by describing the square where we were standing. "The Hôtel de Ville, or the City Hall, was built in 1655 in grand Italianate Baroque style. The Gothic clock tower stands to the right of the Hall and was erected in 1616 on top of white limestone foundation that had been linked to the city in the time of the Roman occupation of Sextius."

She pointed to the clock tower again and said, "This clock was installed in the 1300s, but that astronomical clock was mounted in 1661. It has four wooden statues representing the four seasons."

We leaned back and forth trying to see the statue of springtime as it was April, but it was unfortunately tucked inside and below the astronomical clock at the height of a three-story building. We would take her word for it.

"The statues," Isabelle continued, "are rotated manually as the seasons change and among the statues is a blindfolded cherub that reminds us that love is blind." An audible, "Aaaahhh" went up from our little group.

"The tower's interior has a wrought-iron cage with a bell that rings the hours of the day. The bell was originally set up to notify the town of any dangers approaching the borders."

I do believe she mentioned within the history of Aix that all through the Middle Ages and even now, the city of Aix was known as the Paris of the South. I wanted to ask her more questions, but she then led us across the square and into the flower market itself. And the stories of the kings and queens who had walked along those same streets were left far behind.

The flowers beckoned us forward. If a rainbow had sprung a leak, there couldn't be more color spread before us. As far as we could see across the Plaza and beyond, containers of flowers erupted on flower carts surrounding us. Yes, indeed, there were our friends, the blood-red poppies; plus, bright-cheeked pansies with yellow, white, and purple faces; regal stands of mustard yellow sunflowers; and carnations in pale pinks, peaches, and purples, oh my! Geraniums boasted their lush red blooms; clutches of baby roses were fanned out in every color imaginable; sprays of daisies showed off their crisp white petals and did I mention peonies, poppies, and wisteria? The kaleidoscope of color could only be enhanced by the floral aroma, which seemed to crescendo in strength as we passed through the stalls. It seemed a shame not to buy armfuls of flowers, but we still had a full day of touring ahead of us, the day was getting hot, and we had nowhere to put them.

With all our senses fully engaged, we trotted through the streets following Isabelle as she led us on yet another historic journey. "Yes, this was the city of the artist Paul Cézanne," she said. "He was the child of the country, the father of modern art and was born and raised right here in Aix."

We were led up the stairs and entered the Musée de Granet where we were able to view some of Cézanne's most famous pieces.

"The fact that he chose *this* museum to host his works makes this place seem even more intimate and special," Isabelle told us. "He also had a workshop, farther north in town, and if you have extra time, it would be worth a visit.

We stepped outside the museum as Isabelle told us more about Cézanne. "Cézanne was born in this city of Aix in 1839 and was the son of a wealthy banker. Which is something because Aix was an exceptionally wealthy city to begin with. His boyhood friend was Émile Zola, who later gained fame as a novelist and an academic. As did Zola, Cezanne developed artistic pursuits at an early age, but chose different outlets for their interests. As is the case with so many parents, their desires and wishes for their son, Cézanne, were thwarted. Sound familiar, parents?" We laughed; yes, it was all too familiar." Yes, teenage rebellion is never far away in any generation." We all tittered, possibly because our teens were already grown. Possibly out of relief!

"Eventually," Isabelle continued, "he was sent to study in Paris where Zola had already moved. From the very start, Cézanne was drawn to the more radical elements of the Parisian art world. And he was influenced by Camille Pissarro, Claude Monet, and August Renoir. Much to his father's chagrin, he made his own mark in the art world."

We strolled back across the streets as the clock in the clock tower rang out that it was noon. I was beginning to feel a little peckish even though lunch was not for another hour. As we passed the stores, we all were drawn to the windows of the patisseries that were filled with jewel-like pastries, tarts, cakes, éclairs, and a traditional local sweet named *calisson*.

"Could you tell us about this *calisson?*" Pam asked. The fact that it was displayed in every color in most shops along our route indicated it was clearly a local specialty.

"Calissons are a type of *confiserie* or candy and are made from melon and almond paste and delicately frosted. They're quite sweet. The history goes back to the middle of the fifteenth century and the stories of Good King René. Are you familiar with him?"

We all shook our heads, and Isabelle said, "Good King René became a cult figure, hailed as a wise and just king who remained calm in the face of adversity. Once he moved to

Provence, he learned he could literally cultivate his garden and lead the life of a country gentleman. It was said to be an age when justice ruled in Anjou and Provence; a time before the rapacious kings of France laid hands on these territories. The cult of René gained new force in nineteenth-century France; statues of him were erected in Angers and here at Aix-en-Provence, and he won praise for his justice and liberality, which were qualities recent regimes had ignored."

"So, what does this have to do with the candy, calisson?" we asked.

"Mais oui!" she laughed. "The candies were created on the King's wedding day. He had requested that these sweets be made in the shape of the new queen's lips. She was quite a beauty, it was said."

She beamed after completing this story and took a bow. We all followed her into a shop where each of us bought a box of these sweet little lips; these calissons.

We still had one more stop before our lunch, and the noontime heat was beginning to build. It was difficult to believe that just yesterday we were hunkering down due to cold rain. Isabelle led us inside the Aix Cathedral where the cool of the sanctuary provided instant relief.

"This is rather a unique cathedral," she began again, "in that it was built on the site of the first century Roman forum of Aix." She led us into the baptistry that stood tall with Roman columns as well as parts of a sixth century Christian church.

She swept both hands around her, encompassing the entirety of the edifice. "This building was built and rebuilt over the centuries in Romanesque, Gothic, and Neo-Gothic architecture and now is considered a national monument. Originally, it was located on the route of the Roman road, Via Aurelia, and the original church was said to have been built on top of a Roman temple dedicated to Apollo. According to the Christian tradition, the first church on this site was founded by Saint Maximinus of Aix, who arrived in Provence from Bethany, a village near Jerusalem, accompanied by Mary Magdalene on a boat belonging to Lazarus. Maximin built a modest chapel on this very site and dedicated it to the Holy Savior . . ."

With Mary Magdalene's name mentioned twice within a few hours of each other . . . Why, it brought gasps from all of us. We heard Lise's story that morning about Mary Magdalene, but thought it was myth. At this point we felt we had no choice but to take the information more seriously. I spun around to look at Lise, and a smile and a twinkle in her eye told the story. Mythology or not, it is considered the accepted truth in all Provence.

Sharon, who had not followed on this entire tour, popped her head into the baptistry and said, "Soups on!" And, even though there was much more to see, we were ready.

We bid adieu to dear Isabelle, who had become like a daughter to all of us, and we plodded off behind Sharon, who had a nose for the best of culinary delights. We were fortunate to be seated at outside tables at Entre Midi et Deux, which was comfortable in the shade of the plane trees. And, because the time was 1:30 p.m., if I translated the name of the bistro correctly, it meant between noon and two, so I was assuming we squeaked in just before their daily closing hour.

The food was delicious, seasonal, and came with a plethora of fresh fruits and vegetables. We were learning early on this trip that if tomatoes or eggplant were fresh in the garden, we would surely find them popping up on every menu.

CHAPTER TWENTY-SEVEN

Bonjour Bonnieux

$\mathcal{W}$e headed west out of Aix-en-Provence, then up into the mountains where we spotted a church tower at the top of a charming, perched village known as Bonnieux. We pulled up to Le Clois de Buis, a delightful looking stone guest house, or hotel with potted geraniums welcoming us. We all were looking forward to settling into one place, so this appeared ideal. As we deboarded the bus, I peeked over the boxwood hedge to catch sight of a swimming pool and beyond a view of Mount Ventoux, the Luberon Valley, and the surrounding villages as the guest house was clinging to the mountainsides.

The manager kindly invited us inside and gave us a tour of our new abode. She told us this building had once been a bakery, a grocery store, and a family home, but she said quite proudly, renovation had taken place only a few years earlier when the entire dwelling had been made anew.

"What does the name of the guest house, Le Clois de Buis, mean?" one of my cohort asked.

The manager smiled and said the owners had named the hotel after the century-old boxwood trees in the garden.

The eleven (or ten plus Russ) of us were to be the only

occupants of the hotel for the week, which suited us well. The living room was tastefully appointed with plenty of comfortable chairs around a fireplace and a grand piano that was perfect for comfortable yet casual living. The spacious dining room held a large wooden table covered with a bright yellow Provençal-print tablecloth. Places were set for eleven. A large sunroom with expansive windows looked out at the village and down in the valley. Tea, a light breakfast, and wine would be served here, we were told. And there was a kitchen for just our needs. *Cooking classes?* I wondered. I looked around for clues to the past bakery but was hard pressed to find an inkling. The kitchen was as modern as any I'd seen. But in the early hours of the morning, couldn't a waft of freshly baked croissants drift up the stairs from ovens past? I drooled at the thought.

Because this was to be our home away from home for the next week, we all clamored up the narrow staircase to check out the bedrooms. Of course, Melody and I had chosen to share a room, and were privileged to have a nicely appointed room with Provençal printed fabrics covering both bed and curtains. We had our own modern bathroom and had a window that we threw open to catch a view.

Below us was the swimming pool and gardens that were surrounded with boxwood trees for privacy. And where the valley fell away below us, we could make out the nearest village, known as Lacoste. As we were later informed, Lacoste was best known for its most notorious resident, the Marquis de Sade, who in the eighteenth century lived in the castle Château de Lacoste that was visible from our window.

Again, we busied ourselves with unpacking as our group would be meeting in the main dining room shortly. I don't know why I didn't notice this before while in Paris, but my sister—yes, my sister had packed a full-size iron. What was she thinking?

"Melody," I asked, "why did you bring that heavy iron all the way over here in your suitcase? Wasn't it heavy enough?"

She tossed her chin in the air, and said, "I don't like to appear wrinkled!"

I looked at her and then looked at my wadded-up clothes, which I had thought had rolled perfectly well for packing. But, as I took my clothes out of the suitcase, unrolled them, and shook them out, I could see that, yes, I would be a bit more casual, as they say. Ah, well! I suppose this speaks volumes for our two personalities! And did she use the iron on the trip? Yes, every single day! I digress!

We then headed down to the main dining room that immediately became our meeting place for many great meals, classes, and camaraderie. My sister and I had gotten to know the other gals and Russ over the past two days as they exuded a party ambiance wherever they went. As it turned out, most of them had been long-time friends, so, when they stepped forth to join the culinary tour, it was en group as it was met with spontaneous joie *de vivre!* This, I believed, can only happen if you were well acquainted. Plus, they traveled with a case of champagne, which was one clue, we found, to be a great traveling companion.

Around the fireplace that night, we settled in for glasses of wine, savory canapés, and small talk. The large lunch in Aix had diminished our appetites. Sharon and Lise, our fearless leaders, brought us up to date on the next week's happenings, including cooking classes. I was thinking everyone was as excited about the classes as I was, but no . . . not as much! For some of our group this trip was a means to spend time with friends and shop while in France. Ah, well! I'm good with that!

The next day was one of exploration! We would be discovering this area beginning with this ancient village of Bonnieux with Lise as our tour guide.

"This region," she announced the next morning as we sat at breakfast, "is said to have been occupied since neolithic times with monuments dating from Roman times scattered throughout the Luberon Mountains." In fact, we were promised we would not only drive over the Pont Julien, or the Julian Bridge that was built in 3 BC, but we might picnic near there. I perked up as I always looked forward to sandwiching in vestiges of ancient history on my trips.

After our breakfast of standard bowls of café with steamed milk, freshly baked croissants (did I smell them baking that morning?), fresh fruit, cheese, yogurt, and granola, we were ready to hike. And hiking was what you did in a perched village. All streets were cobbled with few flat spaces to be found. Yes, we had experienced this on the streets in Ste. Marie de Moustiers, but once again going into a full-court press with a bad back and knees, I was not looking forward to this trial. Sharon, I noticed, stayed behind. I tried not to whimper.

We headed out of Clois de Buis, which was in the central part of the village. Thankfully, we wouldn't have to walk all the way to the bottom and start anew. We walked across the street and up a narrow allée, where Lise began our tour:

"The architecture of Bonnieux, which was a papal town for about 500 years, testifies to the prestige of its inhabitants over the centuries: ecclesiastical dignitaries, counts, lords . . . up until the modern times of the nineteenth century. In fact, during the Middle Ages, the Knights Templar were stationed in this village and in other locations close by such as at the ancient monastery known as St. Hilaire near Ménerbes. Why were they staying here, you may ask? They were traversing back and forth from the Crusades."

We walked under and through ancient Romanesque arches and viewed some superb residences dating back to the sixteenth, seventeenth, and eighteenth centuries. Lise told us Bonnieux had once been a wealthy village when the region had belonged to the Popes. All the buildings were constructed of the same light beige rock or stone that had been honed from the nearby mountainside. The combination of enormous blocks of rock, smaller chiseled stones, and smooth river rocks were all interwoven into the tapestry and composition of walls built over half a millennium of time.

"The village," Lise said, "has kept all its authenticity, including its steep sloping streets, fountains and washhouses, its old church and upper church, and all which is a mix of both Romanesque and Gothic. Plus, the view is worth it all."

I asked if we would be climbing all the way to the top of this hill, as my knees were already acting up.

"Yes," she said, "we will be climbing to the church, which is at the top as the view, you'll agree, is stunning."

In the meantime, I focused on the weathered and slippery stones embedded in the roads. Fortunately, the roads that zigzagged back and forth up the steep incline, were not wide enough for cars, just donkey carts. We were relieved that we saw no donkeys on this trek and were not forced to the side of the road because of vehicles.

We stopped en route at the Bakery Museum that was set up in a seventeenth century building around an old bread oven. I wondered if the bakery at Le Clos de Buis had been laid out like this. I knew many villages had more than one bakery to serve the needs of their residents, plus specialty pastry shops, known as patisseries. But this shop appeared to have done the work of baking the heartiest of breads and baguettes.

"Often times," the guide within the museum said, "the locals were allowed to bring their own casseroles to the bakery after the baker was done for the day. Because the ovens held the heat for many hours into the day, and oven ownership was a rare commodity, this became an important community service." We nodded in acknowledgment.

We continued our walk up the steep hillside to Église Haute (High Church), also known as Vieille Église (the Old Church), which dated to the twelfth century and was a mix of both Gothic and Romanesque architecture.

"I'm surprised I didn't think of this before," I said to Lise, "but does the word 'Romanesque' refer to Roman times?"

"I believe it relates to an architecture style that existed in Europe from 900-1200 AD, although it sometimes refers to the end of the Roman Empire in the 5th century."

"Ah," we all said in unison and nodded as we ambled along.

After climbing all the way to the Vieille Église, we found it closed. Rats! We made our way over to a bench near the edge of the hill to sit. From there we were able to see through a stand of old cedars that framed a beautiful view of snow-covered Mont Ventoux. The mountain range of the Vaucluse was also visible, as well as the vast green valleys far below planted with lavender, olive trees, and grape vines. A short distance away stood the charming villages of Gordes and Roussillon, which we hoped were on our agenda to visit.

We were beginning to get a little peckish as we slowly made our way back down the steep decline. We were to meet Sharon at the restaurant for lunch, in the village below. Not surprisingly, we found her holding court at a lovely old restaurant, Le Fournil, which was marked by a large fountain, obelisk, and an outdoor terrace.

"So, what does Le Fournil mean?" I asked Lise as I was seated next to Melody at a long outdoor table. White table-cloths and crystal glasses had been set out for the lunch crowd and we were ready.

Lise scooted closer and said, "It means bakery! Do you think we could get a job in this town as bakers?" We laughed. It did seem like there was a plethora of such businesses.

When I went inside to use the facilities, I looked around as I passed the kitchen. Rough interior walls on the back of the restaurant indicated the bakery had originally been built into a cave or against a cliff. Walls close to the woodburning ovens were blackened with soot that eked up the walls and across the ceiling. No, it wasn't close to where the food was being pre-pared. But I found it amazing to see how innovative the owners had been to create this lovely old restaurant from an ancient boulangerie.

The food was traditional, local, and fresh, as was expected at every restaurant and bistro in Provence. Superb plates of duck confit or local brook trout terrine, bowls of crisp lettuce supporting lamb ribs, and pasta options were prepared in an *haute cuisine* manner. I was hoping for something I might be able to attempt at home—perhaps, more traditional—but that would come in time. In the meantime, the food was delectable, and we had worked up an appetite.

For the evening, we were invited by a local couple, Denis and Solange Brihat, for a light dinner and a private art show-ing. The Brihat home, which was located up an almost vertical driveway at the top of a nearby hill, commanded a view from their front yard of the surrounding Luberon Mountains. Quite extraordinary!

The Brihats threw open their door and welcomed us into their home. Lise, an old friend of Solange's, embraced her and the French banter began to flow. . . as did the wine as bottles of champagne were immediately brought out, along with a tray of crystal glasses for each one of the eleven of us. We were in for a treat.

Denis, a dapper man well into his seventies, was wearing a white shirt, black vest, and pants. He sported pure white hair, a beard and mustache, and immediately posed by the fireplace with his unlit pipe clenched tightly in his teeth. Yes, we would take photos of his best side, as we were there to see him.

His wife, Solange, a bit younger, spunky, with a short blonde bob and sparkling blue eyes, was clearly his greatest supporter. She spun in and out of the kitchen and dining room bringing out hors d'oeuvres, nuts, and olives to accompany our wine and the private art showing.

Denis, an internationally known photographer of still life, seemed eager to show us prints of some of his most famous works; the originals, we were told, resided in galleries around the world, especially in New York and Paris.

How can I describe four-foot-high photographs of the inside of onions? Or voluptuous pale green pears, or sumptuous blood red poppies the size of a man? There were prints his camera had captured of whorls of mauve-tinted rose petals intertwined across a five-foot canvas. And lascivious-looking black iris that brought sexy negligees to mind. Even a simple kiwi half—so beautiful—exuded sexual overtones. His work, obviously, was beyond extraordinary. And there was no way to describe the pride he exuded because we were there to enjoy his fine prints. Would we care to purchase one?

But first, Solange called us into the kitchen for a short cooking demonstration. She knew we had come to Provence on a cooking tour. So, she adeptly showed us a traditional recipe she had created from common ingredients. "These ingredients," she said, "can be found in any Provençal kitchen." She prepared two different but equally delectable quiches, made with eggs, cream, and garden-fresh vegetables, such as mushrooms, asparagus, spinach, spices, and a home-made dough. They were all traditional, all regional, and all made with local products.

This conversation and demonstration struck me as something I had come all the way from California to find: a connection to the people and the land through their food. Standing in Solange's kitchen, I was surprised at how this experience affected me.

The evening swam by as we sampled delicious bites of savory hot quiche and sipped more champagne as glasses were often refilled. Conversations ebbed and flowed throughout the room, but I stood back to watch as Melody, Karen, and Marge contemplated purchasing prints. The others were enjoying friendly conversation with Lise and Sharon, but I stood aside thinking about the family recipe we had just been privileged to learn.

As we prepared to leave, we each thanked the Brihats for the lovely evening. We acknowledged the extraordinary gift we had been given to meet them in their own home; it was a special privilege. When I thanked Solange, I told her how much it meant to me to be shown her own family recipe. I told her of my interest in collecting traditional family recipes from her region. I wondered if she would be open to being inter-viewed. To talk about her family. She seemed pleased to be asked and said she would get back to me. I thanked her, and we left.

All in all, it was a lovely and full day!

CHAPTER TWENTY-EIGHT

Market Day at Isle-Sur-la-Sorgue

*T*he next morning was Sunday. Antique market day! It was a bright day with the sun high in the sky as we took off in our minibus for an adventure. Antique market? Culinary? What exactly did Sharon have in store for us? When were we going to be taking these cooking classes?

We rolled through the valley, over one mountain, around another, then discovered a unique village known as Isle-sur-la-Sorgue—one of the most picturesque villages to be found in all Provence. We tumbled out of the van and made our way across a street that was abuzz with activity. Sharon headed in one direction, while Lise, once again, led us in another. We intrepid souls padded along quickly behind her hoping to hear all that she was conveying about this lively city.

"Sometimes called the Venice of France," Lise said, stopping her march along a river, "the Sorgue River circles around and through the village creating an island in the middle of town with craft shops overflowing into intertwining streets, a farmers market, and restaurants and cafés all vying for attention in this very small space."

Plane trees lined the riverbanks and provided shade over

the water, which we could see was a blessing during the heat of the day for picnickers and those strolling to and from the markets. Flower boxes with bright red and magenta geraniums, yellow pansies and purple petunias seemed to pop up everywhere—along the water's edge, on the bridges, in the markets, and near the immense old water wheels. Plum and cherry trees, in full bloom, bowed down close to the clear stream only to drop their blossoms gently on the water. Although it was April, summer felt like it had arrived.

"The history of this village," Lise continued, "embodies the importance of living with and near the Sorgue River. Fourteen waterwheels remain," she said, pointing up and down the river, "and some continue to be functional. At one time—during the fourteenth century, in fact—there were over forty water wheels churning up the waters as corn, wool, paper, or silk were milled or created." We walked down to a large black metal wheel and posed for photos.

"The Sorgue also served as a big food source. In fact, be sure to remind me to point out the names of some streets around here as years ago they were named for the abundance of certain species of fish, such as Écrivisse (Crayfish) Street or Anguille (Eel) Street. I'm told one could always know where to catch a bit of dinner just by following the signs." We all grinned and nodded. Made perfect sense! We continued behind Lise, like ducks in a row, as she chose our path beneath the shade of the plane trees.

"Of course, as you were told, we are here for the antiques market." We all circled around to hear her. "As you can see, booths of all shapes and sizes line the main roads along the river."

Yes, we had noticed. At least a thousand or so people had arrived before us. It was like a cloud of locusts had descended as shopping carts and bags were swooped up and filled with newly discovered prized possessions. Folks were dragging away fine furniture, old ceramic pots, odd assortments of china, plus ancient willow baskets. As Lise led us past the booths, a bit of haggling was kindly enacted as a special price for a new-found treasure was obviously being decided. This was not a bull ring; these people were polite and proper. Yet, a circus-like frenzy filled the air with obvious high-price stakes at hand.

"This is one of the most elite of all the antique fairs in the entire region," Lise stated. "Country homeowners, *relais* and guest house operators, plus those with bed and breakfasts, and tourists—all are bidding for a purchase of a lifetime." She stepped back and smiled.

But what were we doing there? I wondered. We continued to amble along single-file but didn't take much time to look. We had no interest in purchasing items that would need to be shipped home at an exorbitant price.

Ah, but this was one of the many places where Sharon shined! And there she was! Her sun bonnet bobbed as she bartered away. Her ruddy face grew even more intense. She didn't know French, but she did know what she wanted. Why, she had spotted a prime copper pot from a few booths away. She brushed an errant hair from her face and said, "I can use this in my teaching kitchen back home."

"Ahhh," we all echoed.

"And those blue stoneware water jugs will be handy, plus the immense platters here." Yes, we could see she could use these to serve at least fourteen pheasants at a single sitting. She was an ingenious caterer. Won best caterer of North America one year from the IACP (International Association of Culinary Professionals). We began to see shopping in a whole new light.

And speaking of seeing things, just at that moment I saw a

table with bolts and bolts of Provençal fabrics. The calicos in bright blues, yellows, reds called out to me, and I was giddy but with indecision. Unlike Sharon, I have a propensity for seeing something I love, but have no earthly idea of how to justify its use later.

"Oh, surely you could come up with ways to decorate your home—napkins, place mats, curtains," Sharon said to me.

I knew Sharon was right as, after my last trip to Provence, I had arrived home with all kinds of Provençal products to lay claim to being French. Even my sister couldn't find a trace of our own Swedish heritage in my house. I had become a Provença-holic!

Suddenly our stalwart bus driver, Timon, appeared, and swept all of Sharon's purchases away and hauled them out of sight. I turned to chat with my sister but realized she had disappeared into the crowd. How is it possible that at barely five feet tall and almost sixty years of age, I must track my sister down?

The last I saw of her was the top of her little white cloche (sun hat) as she disappeared into the crowd. I dashed after her, now beginning to panic—silly, I know—but after a few frantic minutes I finally discovered her staring up at a mural that had been painted on the height and breadth of a three-story building. In *trompe d'oeil*, (the art form used to deceive the eye with 3D images) was the likeness of a man facing away but tossing into the air hundreds of sheets of paper. He was releasing them to the world; setting them adrift, so to speak. I knew immediately this spoke to my sister as she had just retired from a frenzied position as a city planner. The image must have sung to her heart. She turned toward me and smiled as if she knew I would find her. She handed me her camera and asked if I would take her photo. Why not?

We were in front of a chance expression of freeing oneself from paperwork, work. It was my pleasure. We then made our way quickly back to find our own group.

We met up with them and crossed a bridge over the Sorgue and onto the Isle, as were finally on to culinary things. The food! Now, this was what I had been hoping for all along! To me, there is nothing more colorful, exuberant, joyful, aesthetically pleasing, or sensually evocative than a Provençal market! Yes, I have been to several on my past trips, and I found it far more fun than a circus.

A bounty of goodies filled multicolored booths, which were strewn side-by-side, filling every square inch of space skirting along the streets, the river, the squares and fronting bustling restaurants and mercados or stores. Tables laden with baskets filled with twenty different kinds and colors of olives—tiny black olives from Nice, cracked olives flavored with fennel, enormous green olives from Greece, plus those stuffed with almonds, anchovies, or roasted red peppers. Stalwart bottles of glistening golden olive oils with olive soaps; bright, fresh sunflowers four feet high; lavender in all its forms—sachets, wands, bundles, packets, in culinary mixes, or stuffed next to little lavender spice grinders.

The sausage booth exhibited meat products from the local areas, including many found along the Rhône, the Ardeche, the Var, and the Vaucluse regions. Pork was prominent in the rich display of sausages mixed with fennel, black peppercorns, herbs de Provence, and other spices. Salamis, hams, pâtés, and rillettes (little pots of duck meat, truffle, or pork spread), all were displayed like an avalanche of enticements across the table. And then there was the Merguez: a specialty sausage from North Africa, made with uncooked lamb, beef, or a mixture and heavily spiced with cumin, chili pepper or harissa that gave it a rich red color. In Provence, the local foods are always kissed by the flavors of the exotic!

And fromage! Did I forget to mention the array of cheeses calling out suggestively to us? Locally made goat and cows' milk, all were distinctively flavored with local herbs and spices including lavender, rosemary, black pepper, bay leaves, or with *eau de vie* or brandy. Some are chosen to be served with figs and nuts. Others are creamy and mild and served with fruit. Then there were the aged cheeses, some aged for a short amount of time, while others for many months.

A lusty-looking character with dark, flashing eyes, a heavy beard, and big grin captured our attention as he was hawking tins of *pâté de foie gras.* Of course, I scooped up a bunch of those. (They were small, and I loved it!) And then there was the vegetable booth that took pride of place with bunches of bright red radishes, local Cavaillon melons, voluptuous red and black tomatoes, sumptuous eggplants, red and green bell peppers, and then there were the strawberries, which stole the show. Big and bright with promise! Yes, all these beauties were seasonal favorites and would be part and parcel of the variety of ingredients we would find in every meal.

With packages of olives secreted away, tins of foie gras, sausages and cheeses wrapped against the heat, plus a baguette from a boulangerie, we were set for a picnic anytime, anywhere! Ah, but off we went for lunch!

We popped back into the van, where Timon had awaited our return. We headed along a route lined with Mediterranean pines, cypress, and olive trees, and pulled into a driveway near Gordes. Our reservation for déjeuner was at an excellent restaurant named l'Estellan, a posh hotel named Mas de la Senancole. The maître d' escorted our group to a long table that was pleasurably out in the garden. We were surrounded by the beauty of red poppies, yellow broom and purple, pink Centranthus, along with the aromas of wild roses, jasmine, rosemary, and wild thyme.

After our market tour, we were famished and immediately dived into appetizers of duck pâté, olive tapenade, slices of grilled vegetables, such as *courgettes* (zucchini), *aubergine* (eggplant), and tomatoes with basil dressing.

This course was followed by either roasted salmon or trout, or a choice of grilled duck, lamb, or veal. All were served with delicate sauces with fresh herbs and served on beds of fresh greens or creamy risotto. And the meal was followed with fresh strawberries drizzled with mint oil. A refreshing ending.

Following cappuccinos, we piled back into the van and headed home, but not before we stopped for photos around Gordes. Evening was quiet around the pool, where we soaked up the ambiance and rinsed the tiredness out of our bones.

CHAPTER TWENTY-NINE

An Arlesienne Holiday:
La Fête des Gardians

*W*e arrived in Arles in the dappled light of early morning as the sunlight streamed like molten gold through the leaves of the plane trees. It was the first day of our traditional foods culinary tour in Provence when we were promised our first hands-on cooking class. But again, this was to be no ordinary lesson. No. No. We were in the ancient city of Arles, which held fast to its history of over three thousand years. So, this class was to include both ancient and medieval recipes. I was ecstatic! And to top it off, the class was to be conducted in a converted Roman stable. I couldn't envision it, and I also couldn't wait. But first our tour guide, Lise, told us it would help if we understood some of the local culture. So, we showed up early for the celebration of May Day, a national holiday, and in the city of Arles, La Fête des Gardians.

From the moment the twelve of us stepped off the bus, my sister Melody and I were swept up a hill with a multitude of festivalgoers. Many wore nineteenth-century costumes, but, at that point, I didn't know why. Glancing around me, I searched the sea of backs for my sister and for Lise. Suddenly, I felt like we had become part of the running of the bulls which, I'd been told, did happen in this town. I needed to stay vigilant.

Everyone was pressing us up the hill toward the church, Église Notre-Dame de la Major, where the Blessing of the Gardians was to take place. It must have been close to the time of the blessing as we were herded quickly up the narrow cobblestone streets. I had no time to take note of what we were passing as the crowd was much too thick, and I was just trying to stay upright. But as we rounded a curve before the Roman arena, I caught sight of men on horseback. The Gardians, or the herdsmen of the nearby Camargue region, sat regally seated atop their pure white horses. Dressed in black woolen jackets, with bolo ties, black felt hats, and black and white polka-dotted shirts, they held their heads high. In one hand they clutched the reins of their horse; in the other hand each carried the traditional *ferre,* a silver-pronged trident. This instrument was used to corral their herds of horses and black long-horned bulls—yes, the same bulls used in bull fights. I know this because I sidled up to Lise to catch her explanations over the din of the crowd.

"For many generations," Lise said, "the Gardians—these cowboys of the Camargue—have traditionally worked the land and managed their herds near where the Rhône River flows to the Méditerranée." She waved her hand pointing in a direction over our heads and invisible to us. She continued, "The Camargue is not far downstream from Arles and the Gardians are very much a part of the Arlesienne culture." Lise, as I've mentioned before, is French by birth, and I leaned in closer to catch the nuances of her explanation.

Behind her I could see women sitting primly on horses in sidesaddle fashion. I surmised them to be the wives of the Gardians, as they, too, were dressed in vintage costumes. They wore long, satin dresses, rich in tones of burgundy, green, or black and their skirts draped gracefully down the sides of the horses. As other women paraded about, their skirts caught the shimmering light from the morning sun. Lise said, "Do you see the woman closest to us?" We all nodded our heads. "Do you see the lace shawl covering her shoulders and the white lace cap covering her hair?" Again, we nodded and sidled closer.

"The very style of her cap and shawl," Lise whispered in more subtle tones, "indicates the region she is from, along with the wealth of the woman. And, as you see, the antique lace handkerchief, white lace parasol, and her broad smile complete her attire." As if on cue, the woman on horseback turned as if she understood what Lise had said and flashed a dazzling smile over us. A blessing of sorts!

Aware of our need for upward and onward movement, Lise coaxed us farther up the hill. I saw little along the way—being short-of-leg had its continued drawbacks. As we cleared another corner, I suddenly heard a cacophony reverberating off the city walls: Laughter, music from a band as it warmed up, children calling to their mothers, men greeting old friends, and the swishing of long skirts and crinolines from other Arlesienne women as they moved quickly along the cobblestoned streets. I turned slightly when I heard the call, *Muguets à vendre*. A flower vendor was selling small bouquets of lilies-of-the-valley.

"Why are they selling lilies-of-the-valley today?" I asked Lise.

"Ah, ma Chere, it is a May Day tradition. You must buy them for those you love," she said with a twinkle in her eye. "You will bring them good luck."

"Oh, Melody, that's like our May baskets," I said to my

sister. "Remember?" I turned toward her only to catch sight of her cloche, or her little hat bobbing away once again through the crowd. "She has this uncanny knack of disappearing like that," I mumbled to myself, as I had gone through this with her yesterday. It can be so unnerving watching over an older sister.

But just when I was about to get upset, she quietly nudged up to my side and pressed a small *muguet* into my hands. It was such an unexpected gesture that I pressed the small clutch of white, bell-shaped flowers to my breast. They were simply lovely as was their unforgettable perfume.

I was suddenly sorry for all the grief I had ever given Melody as her nasty, nail polish-stealing little sister of years gone by. I wrapped my arms around her and gave her a hug.

Suddenly, we were being jostled from behind and the sound of horses' hooves on cobblestones grew louder. I leaped onto a step and out of the way as the streets swelled with an increasing number of horses with men and women on horseback. From this vantage point, I could finally see along the route. And there above me I caught sight of enormous bouquets of sunflowers and wild iris that had been tied to the Roman columns and lamp posts along the streets. I could also see the homes, which sat above the street level shops. They were festooned with bright red and orange geraniums in window boxes, while yellow jonquils brightened flowerpots in kitchen windows. A springtime celebration sprang from every colorful corner.

Just then the church bells rang out from the Église de Nôtre Dame de la Major, the patron church of the Gardians. Young acolytes, followed by the monsignor, all dressed in their vestments of the season, emerged from the front doors of the church. Then, barely audible above the noise of the crowd, came the slow, even cadence of chanting. Above them all, the deep sonorous voice of the monsignor began his blessing of the men, their families, their work, and commended them to yet another year of fruitful work.

The moment the blessing concluded, cheers erupted, and the band began to play. The Gardians swung back into their saddles, and as the band began its slow descent down the city allées, the men, too, began to move down through the crowd. With a cocky grin and a touch to the hat, each man (on horse) sauntered through the crowd. Each wife, still holding tightly to her man, beamed as the two of them passed through the cheering crowd.

With our backs pressed against the ancient Roman columns as the parade flowed past, Lise again attempted to fill us in on some of the local history and customs. Through the din, I could hear her say, "This whole region is called the Bouche du Rhône, which means 'the mouth of the Rhône River.' It is one of the oldest regions in Provence—France, for that matter. The Rhône River was once the gateway to the interior of France, long before Julius Caesar made his way up the river to claim territory for Rome. Before the Romans, it was the Phoenicians who sailed here from today's Lebanon, bringing the flavors and spices from the Arab world. After them, the Greeks came who, together with the Romans, continue to influence today's Provençal cuisine. We will get to experience those flavors in our cooking class later on today."

I quivered with excitement. I couldn't wait to get my hands around some unsuspecting tomato or eggplant. We turned to follow the parade down through the streets, and passed the Roman amphitheater, Les Arenes, which, we were told, had been the centerpiece of Arles activity since 80 AD.

"The Arenes is one of the largest amphitheaters in all of

Roman Gaul," Lise continued, "and the twentieth largest in the entire ancient Roman world. Massive in size, this elliptically shaped arena was once three stories high. Now, only two of the floors remain, along with two watch towers that were added during the medieval times when the arena was used as a fortress against the barbarians."

"The barbarians? Oh, I love this kind of information," I burbled to my sister. "Don't you?" She nodded her assent but held a finger to her lips. I had interrupted Lise once again.

". . . is really impressive," Lise said, "to know that the arena once seated 23,000 spectators who came to watch the gladiators fight for the pleasure of the Romans. This took place during the reign of Caesar Augustus. The Romans mostly fought wild animals, I am told, and they brought them in from Tunisia. This arena continues to be the heartbeat of Provençal activity. Beginning with today's annual festival and continuing throughout the summer months, the Arenes will host scores of horse shows and, of course, bullfights."

"Bullfights?" Our words echoed as we edged in closer. We had heard this tale before, but really?

"Fortunately, no bulls are killed here anymore." Our tour group slumped with relief.

"The tradition now is called, 'Courses Camarguaises,' in which competitors snatch a rosette from between the horns of a bull. *Dangereuse, oui! Ensanglanté, non!*"

Lise looked at our horrified faces and quickly translated, "Dangerous, yes! Bloody, no!"

Again, a collective breath hissed forth, and our group laughed with ease.

"Now, across from the amphitheater," Lise said as she turned us in that direction, "is what must have been the loveliest building of all—the Roman theatre. It is still used for concerts and plays throughout the year and it appears to be set up for some event today."

Before I realized it, the morning had turned to noon, and the sun above this May Day was beginning to simmer. The heat had already begun to radiate off the cobblestones under our feet and off the old buildings along the cavernous streets. I noticed for the first time, the gift shops and stores had closed for déjeuner. So, as we ambled along, we took our time ogling the numerous window displays of offers to rid our cellulite with one fell swoop. Each of us made noises of disbelief, but I noticed that some women in our group took note of the shop's location for future reference. We headed over to the left side of the street where our tour director, Sharon—our Earth Mother of all things culinary—stood in the shade. We swarmed about her for directions to the bistrô she had arranged for our lunch. Our petit déjeuner that morning had been just that— *petit*—and we were becoming gnawingly hungry.

"I am sorry group. The restaurant is not ready for us. Not for another hour. Remember, you are in France." Her voice lifted shrilly. "They don't always eat at the crack of noon around here."

She put on her best smile and shoved some errant strand of hair back into her topknot. Grumbles and laments went up, as an hour seemed an interminable length of time as we had already been standing out in the hot sun for several hours. And, as we had just ascertained, all the shops were closed for lunch, and we had some hardy shoppers amongst us. But we slowed our pace and ambled off in opposite directions.

As Melody and I rounded the corner, we both recognized the famous hotel, the Grand Hôtel Nord-Pinus. We had been there before, but it had been a couple of years since we had come to Provence with our husbands. Back then we had noticed there were so many things we hadn't had time to do. Without thinking, I stopped to touch the marble on the Roman column, which was embedded in the southwest corner of the Grand Hôtel Nord-Pinus.

My sister nudged me to a nearby table, where I sank down into one of the chairs. I realized I was fraying around my edges and needed a rest. Melody went in search of something cool for us to drink.

"Would you care for a Coca-Light?" she asked me. Without waiting for my answer, she strode off in search of a Diet Coke for each of us. I couldn't move. Even though this may have been a table for a nearby café, I was too tired to be bothered. As I looked around, it dawned on me that I was in the Place du Forum—the very spot where the ancients had walked and shopped. And I was across from the restaurant where a few years before Melody and I had eaten, Le Café de la Nuit. This was the restaurant Van Gogh made famous with his painting. I so wanted to stay put and soak up this memory.

From my chair, I had a great view of the hotel, which, now that I thought about it, didn't appear to be so grand. It was no longer a *grande dame* or anything like that, but more like a ma-tronly aunt in shoddy finery. Beyond the Roman column to the left, the hotel itself was decidedly of the 19th century with its stone face the color of light ochre. The upper floors were set off by dark green shutters and black wrought-iron balconies. My eyes glazed over.

Yes, this was what I needed. To simply sit back and take all of this in right there in the Forum, under the canopy of plane trees. And, if Melody didn't hurry back, I knew enough French that I could order a nice, cool glass of rosé, or a pastis. In the meantime, I could contemplate the myriad of people who had frequented this place in years past—Van Gogh, like I mentioned, Gaugain, Cézanne, Picasso, and Cocteau . . . And there before me—I don't know how I missed it before—was a larger-than-life statue of Frédéric Mistral, the pride of all Provence. Yes, here was the poet who had harkened back to the ancient language of his ancestors and encouraged all Provence to hold tight to their culture and traditions. I looked about me. This fête was also a celebration of Mistral. The Arlesiennes were dressed from the same period of his writings; from the 1800s.

"Yes, this is what I love about being here," I said to my sister when she came back empty-handed. She scowled. She looked at me like I had lost my mind. Clearly, the heat was taking its toll on her too. Forgetting to point out the restaurant where we had eaten before, I pointed to the statue of Mistral as an explanation for my comment.

"I'm beginning to understand the role Mistral played for Arlesiennes . . . for all that is Provençal . . . I believe he is the key to the traditional and cultural values held here." My sister nodded her head and started to sit, but just then we heard Lise calling us.

"*Qu'est-ce que ce?* What? *Mais oui, Madame,*" we responded in our best French. Yes, we had picked up some French, especially when we'd been called to déjeuner. We walked a block or two from the hotel to find Sharon holding court, as she was wont to do. She had found the only comfortable chair and, being a heavy-set woman, she was already ensconced at the head of a long table at the outdoor café, Le Galoubet. All those around her were dripping with perspiration but her full face remained serene and without a hint of discomfort. Only the same sprig of hair escaped her tightly wound bun. Over the course of this tour, I found Sharon to be a marvel. I don't know how to explain it other than she knew magic. There were times when she appeared to be completely disorganized;

then, in the blink of an eye, and without seeming to have lifted a hand, all things were complete, with everything in their place. We witnessed this phenomenon often in our cooking classes in the States. And, like I said, it had to be magic.

The waiter brought buckets of chilled wine and my sister and I wriggled into our seats, that backed up to an already overcrowded street. The table itself was almost hidden under a thicket of vines on a trellis overhead and the blossoms dipped down into our hair and faces as we talked and drank, but it felt cool—cooler than just a few inches farther into the street—where the sun continued to beat down. And much cooler than where we had been earlier that morning.

Our déjeuner was delightful. Once the waiter poured the wine, we lifted our glasses in a toast. "Tchin-tchin," we all said as we began to quench our thirst. Baskets of bread, along with dishes of black and green olives, were scattered along the table. The food, of course, was delectable: first, an *aubergine* terrine, followed by chicken roasted with spring vegetables, and then the cheese course. We finished with fresh strawberries with ice cream and almond cookies. And, of course, wine, wine, and more wine. Oh, I could hear a nice long nap calling my name about then. Actually, I felt the need to curl up like a cat and sleep under the table in the cool of the shade and in the soft dust. Mais, non!

We got up from the table feeling drowsy but sated and again began wandering the streets. The heat had reduced our energy levels to almost zero and, as the church bells chimed three o'clock, we realized we still had two hours more before our cooking class was to begin.

"Oh, Lordy," I whined to Melody. "We will only be limp rags of our former selves by the time we actually get to cook." Melody, who was not one to complain much, said, "Well, my dear, until then we have nowhere to go and two hours to get there."

She was so astute. So up the streets we trudged, attempting to avoid places that were filled to the brim with festivalgoers. We headed for the infamous yellow house, le jaune maison, where Van Gogh was said to have lived. We stopped someone on the street to verify our facts. After a feeble attempt at bad French, the passerby told us in clear English, "Nope, you'll not find it here. That house disappeared during the air raids of WWII. That house before you is yellow, oui! But it is not the right one, I'm afraid."

Despondent, we slogged further up the hill, and finally wound our way toward the green of trees where we found a respite in a beautiful little park—Parc l'Été, the Summer Park, to be exact. It was a bower filled with trees and flowers, just on the other side of the Roman amphitheater. Red tulips, yellow and white pansies, purple violets crowded together under the coolness of the majestic willow trees. Darting through the stippled light were costumed children playing in and around their full-skirted mothers. And I thought I was hot in my summer attire. Their laughter was infectious, and as we attempted to jettison from the Greek/Roman era beyond the gates, to the nineteenth century of these children, I experienced jetlag of sorts, just as an empty park bench presented itself. The rest of our tour group was flagging, too, so I didn't feel so alone in my need to sit down.

I must have dozed off, for suddenly I was roused from my reverie when bursts of gunfire roared from the streets to the north of the Roman theatre. Like a starter's gun, everyone rushed out of the park and up the street as the festivalgoers were once again on the move. The air was thick with dust and the smell of gunpowder as a feeling of electricity vibrated through the crowd. Everyone stood on the corner with great expectancy, craning their necks to see through the crowd and down the hill. I looked around for Lise to give us an explanation when suddenly, there was a sharp staccato of snare drums that reverberated between the buildings as the shrill pitch of fifes could be heard. More guns were fired as the drum and fife team neared us, and then, without further ado, they led the unruly throng over the hill and straight into the Arenes (arena).

"Bullfights?" we asked with exuberance. "Are they having bull fights now?"

"No," we were told by another passerby, "the Gardians are putting on a horse show."

"Thank goodness someone fills in our blanks," I muttered to my sister. And as we stood there watching, another parade of costumed people filed past us and out of sight. Our lowly culinary tour group was left all alone, blinking into the late afternoon sun. Just then, laughter, cheering, and a mighty roar could be heard from the raucous crowd from within the Arenes.

Melody turned to me and asked, "Do you feel like the human race just passed by—and passed us by in the process?"

"Actually, yes," I said, "I feel as if I've been invited to the prom, but not to the dance."

At that moment, the cathedral bells began to ring, and we realized it was 4:45 p.m. In fifteen minutes, our cooking lesson would finally begin. We clattered down through the streets with arms a-flapping. The event that we had looked forward to all day was about to begin.

CHAPTER THIRTY

Cooking Among the Ancients

"In France, cooking is a serious art form and a national sport."

—JULIA CHILD

*W*e were all feeling logy by this time, but once we entered the home of Erick and Madeleine Vedel, our spirits rose. Their house, a converted Roman stable dating from the first century AD, was now a building several stories high. Obviously, the building had been reconfigured many times over during the past centuries. It held many apartments, but not in the manner that you might think: one apartment could be comprised of two large rooms on the first floor, three rooms on the second floor, and two more on the third floor. And the rooms were not necessarily connected on the inside, either. *Most unusual,* I thought.

The walls of their apartment were more than two feet thick and held the coolness of the morning late into the day. For us, the cool air felt like a blessing as we had wilted from the sun and knew few places in this city had air conditioning. This establishment was no different. We also noticed that mere electricity was an issue.

"With walls so thick, there is no way to break through them to encase the electrical wires," laughed Madeleine, one-half of the culinary team. "But, somehow, we manage." She smiled kindly.

As she showed me through their house to the bathroom, I noticed the wires—like an electrical spider web of sorts—were strung up the walls, across ceilings, then snaked outside through the windows, and I assumed into upper stories. Even as I stepped into the bathroom itself, I lifted several sets of cords just to pass beneath.

When I came back out, I found Madeleine telling our group that she had come from Boston originally but was now married and living full time in Arles with her Arlesienne husband, Erick, and their two-year-old son. She had teamed up as translator and marketing director for her husband's cooking school and was now a very essential part of their team. We were more than grateful, as she was there to help us understand the nuances of her husband's instruction. We were all novices in French, and he spoke little English.

Willowy of build and movement, Madeleine glided ahead of us. She was in her late thirties, had dark brown hair with reddish highlights, and as she stood next to her husband to introduce him, we could see he was the shorter of the two, probably one full head shorter and older, by approximately fifteen to twenty years. As Madeleine spoke, their son was slung over Madeleine's hip. He made no sound, but simply blinked his big black eyes at us, before being whisked away by their nanny.

Erick continued the tour through the rest of the house, his balding pate gleaming in the fractured light. I noticed that his body type was the polar opposite of his young wife's and visions of Danny Devito ran through my mind.

We passed through a long but narrow room, which was described as the family's living and dining room. The middle of the room was dominated by a lengthy dining table. I paused for a moment as I could easily imagine exotic dinners for twelve or twenty people seated at this table. Everyone would be laughing, talking, and lolling over the courses they had just prepared. Of course, wine pairings would go late into the night. *This is my kind of place,* I thought, and hoped we would be dining there shortly.

Instead of stopping there, we followed Erick through a tiny kitchen, again ducking through loops and hoops of wire, and on to the back of the house. We headed down a couple of steps into a larger room still, which served as the classroom/demonstration area. This was the lowest level in the house, and as we looked around us, we realized we were actually in the ancient stable of twenty centuries past. We were in awe.

Thankfully, the room had been changed, for there were no recognizable stalls, but you could tell the room had served many purposes. Arched doorways had been blocked and stuccoed over and were covered with hooks and a variety of pots and pans. At the opposite end of the room, an outline of a once massive fireplace had been replaced by a doorway leading to some distant pantry or storage.

Down the center of the room, a couple of long tables stretched with a stove apparatus on one and a workstation on the other. More electrical wires crisscrossed back and forth across the floor. Another, much larger table was set back with chairs scattered about. Once the twelve of us flooded into the room, we filled the space and the room no longer felt large, or cool. No windows or ventilation had been built into this stable.

Erick began to set up his many *tians*, which were Provence-traditional red terra cotta baking dishes. Like magic, fresh vegetables began to appear on the counter, such as varying sizes of eggplant, zucchini, brightly colored peppers, and voluptuous tomatoes. Fat round onions lay side-by-side along rows of garlic cloves. Local bottles of luminous green olive oil stood like soldiers awaiting duty while bottles of wine were now being poured for those of us who were lolling on chairs awaiting instruction.

Erick had created a hefty menu for us to learn that night, and we were anxious to get started. We pulled on our virginal aprons, unscathed or marred by any spot or stain, as Madeleine set about translating and stating her husband's philosophy of cooking. She was proud to announce that he had done considerable research on his own to gather recipes from, oh, about a thousand years ago. He nodded his head in acknowledgment and smiled. A twinkle lit his eyes.

"We are now ready to fully engage in the serious business of ancient and medieval cuisine," Madeleine began. "As you know, Arles is situated on the Rhône River and is one of the first ports-of-call on the inland highway into France." We all nodded our heads in acknowledgment and turned toward Lise with grins. She had thoroughly prepared us.

"This began long before France was named Gaul by the Romans. In fact, there are records of well over three thousand years of commerce flowing through our city. You see, food and recipes have always transcended the need for a common language, and as the mariners would stop at our port, they would share their recipes, spices, and stories from their homelands. And tonight, you will experience first-hand some of the recipes that passed through here hundreds of years ago.

"Our first recipe is called *Paquets d'Aubergine*, or Eggplant Packets," said Madeleine. We all wrote notes feverishly, but once again grins broke out throughout our group. Exactly how often had we had eggplant on this tour? Along with fresh strawberries, it had become a staple in our diets.

Erick was busy slicing a thin eggplant into quarter-inch lengths and sweating them with salt. He set them aside. Then he demonstrated how to prepare the stuffing. He adeptly scooped up some chopped onion and tossed it into olive oil to simmer. He chopped about a half cup of eggplant discards and added it to the pan, then splashed in a half cup of water to let it simmer and reduce. Then came the thyme, chopped ham, an addition of stale bread (soaked in water and squeezed out), and when I was busy writing, he must have dropped in a raw egg. He mixed it well before taking the pan off the stove, then set it aside.

After the eggplant slices had completed their sweat, he rinsed and tapped them dry. With a tablespoon of stuffing placed at one end, he carefully rolled up the eggplant and placed a nice strip of bacon—yes, that's an old French word—around it and pinned it shut with a toothpick. Voilà!

We leaned forward to try our hands at the procedure, but Madeleine told us, "No. No. Not yet. You'll be able to complete this task later, after Erick has shown you all of his recipes. Not to worry. Soon," she promised us, waving her index finger in the air, "you will be able to fill the *tians* with lovely little rolls and pop them into the oven. Is it 380 degrees, dear?" she asked Erick over her shoulder as her husband calculated centigrade to Fahrenheit.

"Exactly 380 degrees Fahrenheit?" I asked. "Not 375 or 400?" That seemed like an odd temperature.

She turned to us and said, "Mais oui. It is clearly 380 degrees Fahrenheit." She threw her hands in the air as if that's the way it was. Period. "And, after forty-five minutes time," she continued, "those sumptuous little *paquets* will be served as our appetizer. It can also be served as a side dish . . . hmm, say a pork roast, or a nice salad along with a crusty baguette."

I don't know why it mattered to me, but I looked around for Sharon, our culinary director, as she was our fearless leader in this field. I always struggled when there were conversions from Celsius, or centigrade, to Fahrenheit. Did she have any input on this issue? She looked up and smiled pleasantly at me from her seat on the sidelines with a glass of wine in hand. *Nope. I guess not,* I thought. Having taught cooking for years in the Silicon Valley, it was probably good for her to take a break and simply observe. She was enjoying herself. I wrote down 380° F.

"The second recipe," Madeleine continued, "is *Le Tian Provençal,* which is a mélange of succulent summer vegetables." Once again, we huddled around the table with pens poised over our note pads but some of us were anxious to get our hands on some knives or cooking utensils.

Erick began cutting two fat—what? Eggplants, again?—into slices. Giggles ebbed through our group. Once again, he salted the eggplant to begin the sweating process. We could relate. The heat was rising in the room, and we were beginning to strip off our excess clothing—sweaters, over-blouses, T-shirts . . . (No, not really!). He sliced the zucchini and tomatoes and set them aside. He poured several tablespoons of local olive oil into a pan and began sautéing sliced bell peppers and onions until they were caramelized. He layered them into a clay tian, then sautéed the zucchini rounds. Once the eggplant had been sweated, rinsed, and dried, it was time to layer the vegetables.

"Place the eggplant on top of the peppers and onions, then layer with the raw tomatoes, a bit of chopped garlic, crumbled bay leaf, a little salt, and finish with the zucchini rounds," said Madeleine. "Then start again until all the vegetables are used up. Sprinkle the top with grated Gruyere cheese and bake in the oven for thirty minutes at about the same temperature as the paquets. Any questions?" she asked. I took a quick swig of wine and got ready to roll up what sleeves I had left.

"And the third recipe is a most unique recipe that came from the medieval period of Provençal history. It's called *Les Cailles à'Hydringus et Zinziberine,"* Madeleine said. "This is quail with *Hydringus* root and fresh ginger. This recipe uses the double-cooking method of the medieval period by which meat and game are cooked twice. First the quail is poached in broth and then it is deep-fried in lard. The little birds are then served with a relish or *confiture,* which was first noted by Nostradamus in the sixteenth century, and who lived only a few miles to the north of us in St. Remy. This sauce is an example of sweet and spicy flavors coming together."

As Madeleine spoke, Erick began the unique preparation of this medieval recipe. Again, we put down our wine glasses and scrambled around to grab our pens as we watched him prepare the quail and the confiture.

"Zinziberine is the medieval word for ginger," I overheard Madeleine saying, "while *Hydringus* is the medieval name given to a rare root vegetable known in Provence as *panicaut.* I believe it is in the artichoke family, but Erick chooses to use carrots in place of the hydringus as they are more readily available and the flavors work well together," Madeleine said. I watched carefully as I feared this was a complicated recipe. Fortunately, it was only the medieval terms that threw me. I breathed a sigh of relief.

Finally, it was our turn to try our hands at the recipes we had been shown. My sister wandered off to work with a couple of gals on Le Tian Provençal, while others made those sumptuous looking little paquets. But I chose to work with a team on the *cailles,* or quail. My own childhood came into play as I recalled helping my dad and brothers prepare pheasant and quail. Don't ask me why Melody wasn't interested, but I was fascinated with the idea of learning this ancient recipe.

If truth be told, my imagination took wing when I thought of how these recipes had been handed down by boatmen a millennium ago. I could envision the whole setting: light and olive-skinned Phoenicians, wearing filthy blousons and pantaloons with brightly colored scarves wrapped about their dark heads. Grimy locks of hair falling into sweat-soaked faces as roughened hands dipped into steaming pots. I was certain I could hear a concertina playing in the background as men laughed raucously while singing around a roaring fire. And I could also hear knives chopping and whacking at fish, meats, and vegetables, while greasy hands sprinkled spices and herbs from faraway lands over the food, before dropping them into the sizzling cauldrons before them. Of course, I imagined all this taking place along the banks of the Rhône River. Perhaps, I've seen too many pirate movies. Or maybe I've read too much about the childhoods of Frédéric Mistral or Marcel Pagnol, my favorite authors from Provence.

I began by wrapping my hands around those lovely little quail just to experience what others had done before me. I ignored the titters of laughter and the lively banter about me as the rest of our group worked feverishly. On occasion, I heard my sister's laughter and I, too, swiped at a flopping tendril of hair as I leaned over the pot of simmering broth to drop in the tiny featherless carcasses. I would like to say that, out of the corner of my eye, I looked to see what I was missing with the other food preparations. But the truth was, I had found my passion: preparing traditional and ancient recipes for tiny birds in an ancient Roman stable.

Once the dishes were finally prepared, it was well after

nine o'clock. We were all dripping with perspiration and drooping due to hunger. Once again! Throughout the hours, the room had held tight to the heat, and, of course, without windows to fling open, some found themselves swooning with lightheadedness. I tried to keep in mind the adage that, appetite makes the best sauce, but who was I kidding? I was starving! I helped myself to a little more sauce of a different source: wine. Then I stuffed my mouth with some roasted almonds, which had magically appeared when I wasn't looking.

I joined my sister as we pushed the worktables back toward the wall and made room for a long dining table. In short order, the room was transformed into a formal setting, with a clean tablecloth, new wine glasses, plates, and more. Sliding into our places, we lifted our glasses in salute to Madeleine and Erick as they presented us with our own masterpieces of culinary art.

The succulent aromas of olive oil laced vegetables filled the air as the cheese-encrusted tians were set on the table. Long platters with aubergine paquets sizzled in our midst. And the pièce de résistance, Les Cailles à l'Hyringus et Zinziberine, was placed in the center of the table. And there, staring up at us from the largest of platters, were fifteen pairs of eyes from the displayed—or splayed—golden-brown bodies of the quail. Some of my cohort, including my sister, withdrew from the prospect of eating those little creatures, but I found them quite delectable. All was consumed, including the crunchy little heads. And why not? Where else could we experience such delicious and sumptuous recipes shared from over a thousand years ago along the Rhône River? And just a touch more of that Provençal rosé from the Côte de Rhône, *sil vous plaît.*

LES CAILLES À L'HYRINGUS ET ZINZIBERINE

Recipe created by Erick Vedel of
Association et Cuisine et Tradition, Arles, France
Serves 5 persons.

CONFITURE D'HYDRINGUS

1 1/2 cups of carrots (or *Hydringus*), peeled and cubed
1 1/2 cups fresh ginger root, peeled and cubed
1 1/2 cups sugar
2 cups of water

PREPARATION

First, peel, chop and cube the carrots and fresh ginger root and placed them in a pot with two cups of water to boil. After about 45 minutes time, remove the vegetables, drain them, but reserve the broth. Next, prepare the syrup by adding the sugar to the same pot with 1/2 liter of water and boil for about five minutes then return the drained carrots and ginger. Continue to simmer on a very low heat for another hour. (This sweet and spicy *confiture* can be served with the lard-fried quail or with plain yogurt or vanilla ice cream; even with *foie gras.*)

Next, prepare the quail. After plucking the birds (one per person) of their feathers and removing the giblets, boil them in the cooking broth drained from the carrots and ginger for about seven minutes. Then remove the birds from the broth and tap them dry with a clean cloth. Roll them in cornstarch and deep fry them in lard. Fry until golden brown, for around twenty minutes. Serve with about 1/4 cup of the *confiture d'hydringus* on the side.

CHAPTER THIRTY-ONE

La Riboto de Taven-Les Baux

*W*e returned to Bonnieux late in the evening from Arles, full of memories of the Gardiens and the unforgettable cooking class in the Roman stable. And I felt full to the brim with the exceptional food we were privileged to help prepare. This event was a life-changing one for me. I kept thinking about *where* those recipes had come from. And, also, about how the migration of peoples across the world changed not only our culture and traditions, but our foods and flavors. What a gift of awareness to have come to know this!

But, the next morning, when it was time to arise for our next cooking class, we were all dragging. "Two days in a row," some were complaining. They were hoping for some shopping. But I pushed out of bed eager to add to my coffers of culinary knowledge. When would I get this chance again?

Following our usual breakfast, we were back on the bus with Timon, the driver, who was alert and smiling like always. Most of our troop dragged paper cups of coffee to stave off the need for sleep, as we were once again bouncing along the roads. Today, we were to visit the unusual city of Les Baux.

Careening down the narrow and winding byways of the Luberon Mountains, circling through villages such as Cavaillon (as there are at least a thousand roundabouts), then along plane-tree lined streets of St. Remy (yes, we would return), we headed up into what was known as the Alpilles, or the Little Alps. Zipping through forested lands of scrub pine and a mix of garrigue scrubland, limestone outcroppings rose in the most unusual shapes and rocky contortions. Only artists such as Van Gogh could capture this unique natural landscape in paintings, such as his *Olive Trees* study. Suddenly, we dropped down into a massive lush, green valley, where olive trees reigned supreme, alongside vast swaths of vineyards. Totally pastoral. Until we turned to the right.

"What the . . . ?" everyone exclaimed in unison.

Rising 750 feet out of the middle of the flat valley floor was an enormous white limestone outcropping or spur.

Lise told us, "The name of the village and this area are known as Les Baux, which came from the term for the mineral, bauxite. Because the promontory rises so high, it was quickly utilized as a lookout for warring hordes and has been occupied since before 6,000 BC. The soft white stone was easily carved into caves or homes and the town of Les Baux has been inhabited since. One of the most intriguing periods of history is the medieval period (thirteenth to fourteenth centuries) when the castle, built on the top of the promontory, was renowned for its highly cultivated court and chivalrous conduct. The estate finally came to an end in the fifteenth century after the death of the last princess of Baux. But the period of the bard and the ballad regaling the chivalric knights in search of romantic love was said to have been born here."

"Really," we all gasped.

"I don't know about you," I said to Melody, "but I find this amazing." I had taken classes on this form of literature, which was a type of prose and narrative that was developed and shared in the noble courts.

I looked up to the top of the hill, and even though I could not see the castle, my imagination was already in full tilt.

"I read that the beginning of the adventures of the knights on quests emphasized love and courtly manners. This must have embodied what we know as heroic qualities today," I said.

"This must have been the beginning of the literature," Melody chimed in, "that continues today of heroes winning their damsels in distress. And romance must have been re-worked into the legends, fairy tales, and history to suit the readers' and hearers' tastes."

Lise laughed and said, "Wait until you hear the stories of witchcraft surrounding the caves of La Riboto de Taven!" This news came as a bit of a surprise. At that point, I don't think we were sure what to expect.

The tour bus climbed up the steep incline to the village of Les Baux, then continued past it, and circled down the backside of the promontory. We were a little bewildered that we had passed the village by, but the driver then pulled into a driveway of a property, which was tucked into the shadow of the mountain of Les Baux. The craggy cliffs, which we thought we had left behind, surrounded us, and dark, foreboding caves appeared at all levels of altitude up and down the cliffs. We inched down the stone driveway, which was lined with cypress trees, and pulled up to a large two-story limestone *mas*, or farmhouse. As we started to get out of the van, the scent of jasmine filled the air. The sun was just beginning to peek from behind Les Baux, and the heat of the day was fol-lowing us. Was that the noise of cicadas I heard?

Fortunately, large parasol pines and a myriad of gnarled olive trees provided much needed shade—over the house/restaurant and a lovely patio area that was set with bistro tables and chairs. A hand-hewn rock fountain burbled a lively greeting, as red, yellow, and pink rose bushes splashed color throughout the grounds. This place was called La Riboto de Taven, a starred bastide and restaurant of great repute.

We were welcomed into the main house by the owners, Christine and Philippe Théme, and Christine's brother, Jean-Pierre Novi. Graciousness radiated from each of them. Genuine smiles and convivial banter set each of us at ease. Christine, who was the manager of all things outside the kitchen, gave us a short tour of the reception area and led us into the dining room. Although constructed with the same large angular rocks of limestone as the outside of the hotel, the room felt refined. Small stained-glass windows were interspersed along the outer walls allowing a sprinkling of light. And a French country classic antique bread safe, or *panetiere,* fit in between. Elegant yellow Provençal-style draperies separated one room from the next and a massive table that could easily seat our entire troupe took center stage. Soft lamp light made the room glow.

Philippe and Jean-Pierre ushered us into the kitchen to begin the class. In contrast to the class we had taken the day before in the renovated Roman stable, this kitchen was large, with many modern steel working tables with lines of copper pots hanging overhead. And all electrical wires were—well, hidden. This was a completely up-to-date facility.

The kitchen was filled with herbs and vegetables, which had just been plucked from the kitchen garden. The walk-in refrigerators were packed with the freshest of meats, cheeses, eggs, and olives while the counters were lined with the essentials: bottled olive oils and spices including Herbs de Provence, black and red peppercorns, and sea salts from the Camargue. Large hanging baskets held garlic cloves, globes of both red and white onions, while the smaller baskets were filled with bouquets of fresh herbs: thyme, lavender, basil, and oregano. A set of terra cotta bowls, which lined one of the counters, held tomatoes, mushrooms, eggplant, and sleek green zucchini—all at the ready for our class.

Both Philippe and Jean-Pierre were top chefs and had been working together at this location for many years. Their movements through the kitchen were representative of the dance they must have created throughout the years. And so, we decided to catch up with their energy. We were given clean white aprons and once we washed our hands and strapped on our aprons, we were ready.

Our group was divided up into three units: One unit over-saw making the dessert, which was an apple tart with fresh pastry, apples, spices, and fresh thyme; another unit created magic out of stuffed zucchini blossoms with a mélange of goat cheese, chopped vegetables, and fresh herbs. As part of the third unit, I dived back into my usual position of grabbing up an unwitting but dead duck to learn the fine art of cutting up duck into appropriate portions.

The duck leg and breast were then marinated for half an hour with plenty of fresh herbs, spices, olive oils, and sea salt, before we roasted them until golden brown. The kitchen filled with savory aromas as the meat roasted, the tarts baked, and the vegetables sung in their olive oil-based baths.

Because both men spoke impeccable English, they answered our questions quickly and thoroughly. I always have too many questions. I felt a bit more relaxed in their company, not that they were any more efficient or knowledgeable than Erick, from the night before, but they were simply more approachable.

Once everything was prepared, the chefs led us back into the dining room, where the table was set with fine, white linen and crystal wine and water glasses that captured the light from the center candles. Jean-Pierre entered the room with a bottle of Chateau-Neuf-de-Pape and had Lise sample it. Of course, it was a perfect choice of deep red with silky elegance. I elbowed Melody when we heard the name of the wine region as several years before, we had ventured into those very wineries ourselves. Originally developed for the Pope of Avignon's use in the 1300s, the quality of the grapes and vintages had only increased with depth of flavor. But the image of us (along with our husbands) climbing down into those deep, dark, dusty, yet dank wine caves came immediately to mind. It was there we discovered hundreds of dust-laden bottles from a hundred years before.

"When it comes to wines, we have never been the same since," I announced after we had extolled the virtues of our earlier trip.

Shortly, our carefully prepared courses were placed before us. Each course was presented with such flair as to make us think they were fit for a king. Or queen. Ah, but we did recognize our hand in these dishes. The roast duck was served with au jus, alongside stuffed zucchini-blossoms with goat cheese and sautéed vegetables. A sprig of fresh thyme graced each plate.

The overt expression of groans, *oohs*, *aahs*, and *mmmhs* echoed forth from all our group as we relished each and every morsel. And let's not forget the fresh fruit tart with homemade lavender ice cream. And more of that delectable Chateau Neuf de Pape wine, please! Truly heavenly!

Following our luncheon, we were led into the garden to stretch our legs and relax with a café. A nap would have been good about then, but we still had adventures to enjoy in Les Baux.

Lise came out with Christine and while they were sitting among us, I asked, "What is the story about the witches of this place? Where did the name come from?"

Christine leaned forward and began, "The name Le Riboto de Taven means the Feast of the Friendly Mountain Witch."

"Really," we all said, leaning in closer to Christine to catch her story.

"Oh, mais oui! There is quite a bit to the Provençal history of this name, but it all goes back to a special poem written by Fréderic Mistral in the Provençal language. Have you heard of him?"

I nodded my head and we all mentioned that we had just seen his statue in Arles the day before.

"For those of you who are unfamiliar with Mistral's work, he was both an epic and a lyrical poet. His work is determined by this special region of Provence, not only in language, but in content and feeling. In fact, Provence is the true hero of all his poems. But his first great success was *Miréio* in 1859, a story of two star-crossed lovers."

We nodded our heads but were still trying to track where this story was leading us.

"Oh, it is such a shame that you will not be able to see an actual performance of *Miréio*. It is often performed during the summer months in the Antique Theatre in Arles. You see, *Miréio* has been made into an opera by Charles Gounod and it is all the story of Taven, the witch, Mireille, and Vincent."

"So, the word taven means witch?" I asked.

Christine nodded. She had been raised in Provence, knew all of Mistral's stories, so she had great fun sharing this with those who came to their bastide.

"So, what is the story of *Miriéo?*" we asked in unison. We were hooked.

"This is the love story between Mireille and Vincent," Christine continued, "which is a story of two lovers, much like Shakespeare's story of Romeo and Juliet. Mistral put a witch between the two lovers and that witch's name was—yes, Taven. And the name of the caves in the rock wall right there are called Taven." She pointed over her shoulder, and we all swiveled to see exactly where she indicated. The white, massive rock walls that rose all around us were pockmarked with caves of all sizes and sorts, so we were keen to find out exactly which cave she thought this all transpired in.

"So," she continued, "Taven tried to help the young lovers get married because the parents of the couple were not of the same status. Yes, it was Taven who put them together. But, because Mireille was a beautiful young lady, she also had many lovers and one of her lovers was called Ourrias. He was a Gardien, which is a horseman, and a bull trainer, who rides horses from the Camargue . . ."

We whooped into the conversation at full tilt as we still had the whiff of horse dust left in our nostrils from the Festival of the Gardiens from the day before. We definitely knew who the Gardiens were!

"Ah, well, then you know how dashing and handsome they can be!" Christine said. "And one day, Vincent, who was very jealous, was injured by one of Murielle's lovers, and Taven finds him and takes him into her cave—right here in Les Baux to make him well." Our eyes were practically popping out of our heads!

"When Mireille finds out that he has been hurt," Christine continued, "it was summertime, and very, very hot. She was desperate to find him, so she began to walk a long, distance across the Camargue, which was much like a desert, to the church in the St. Maries. Yes, it was Ste Marie de la Mer. Because the sun was so very hot it gave her sun stroke, and she died. Oh yes, always in an opera someone must die, is that not right? It is not fair! But that's just how it is!" She threw her hands into the air as if that was all that could be said.

"Did you know you can reserve a room right there in one of those caves?" Lise asked us.

We all physically whirled around and stared in the direction of the cliffs.

"Yes," Christine said, "and I would love to take you on a tour, but those rooms are rented right now. Although," she said as she stood up, "I can show you our brochure, which has photos of the cave interiors, as well as those rooms available in the bastide."

She excused herself and we all got up, stretched our legs, and walked through the gardens and around the fountain. Some crept closer to where the cave rooms were supposed to be, but then grew timid and returned. There had been witches here, hadn't there? Melody and I peeked into the swimming pool area, where the cooling of the blue waters called out to us. Yes, we said to ourselves. We will return when we can.

CHAPTER THIRTY-TWO

St. Remy to Fontvielle

The following day, we trundled out to the van as if by rote! We were getting this routine down pat! Early morning, we threw open the window to greet the day, then grabbed a bit of breakfast and camaraderie and hit the road. But Sharon was even more excited about our day's excursions as we were not going to go through St. Remy like in days past, but rather stop to enjoy St. Remy. This town held her favorite of all-time food markets so this would be a most auspicious destination.

Before we left the hotel, Tìmon, always ready as our tour driver, lined us up by the van to take our pictures. I was not certain why, after all these days, that he would choose this day, but he knew something . . . No, it was not my place to reason why! We lined up like good little soldiers and beamed into the sunlight, before we climbed aboard.

I did enjoy the journey, although familiar, especially as we drove through the valleys filled with fields of sunflowers, lavender, and olive orchards. We circled through the round-about twice to see the large ten-foot-tall metal cantaloupe in Cavaillon, as Sharon told us the village was world-famous for its melons.

But there is nothing quite like driving down the roads that lead into St. Remy, as they, too, are world famous for their beauty. Lined along either side of the narrow roadway are the famous plane trees, which arch over the road creating a magical tunnel of diffused light.

We continued into town and turned into the parking lot nearest the downtown square. We scurried out of the van as Sharon was in full-tilt mode to pick up the best bargains. Once again, we found the farmers market crowded and in full swing.

"Didn't we just see these same vendors on our trip to Isle-sur-la-Sorgue?" I heard a rumble through the crowd. Yes, indeed. But, somehow, it was even more glorious with the array of tables covered in brightly colored Provençal tablecloths with at least a hundred varieties of olives, radishes, carrots, sweet peas, peppers, and strawberries as big as a house. We cast our eyes over the fresh local cheeses, yogurts, and eggs. We peered at selections of jumbo shrimp, anchovies, clams, cockles, and mussels showcased on ice from nearby Méditerranée. I was certain there were at least a thousand varieties of local olive oils and vinegars that called my name. We picked up (and fondled) little jars of tapenade and tins of paté, including paté de foie gras (my favorite). And then we spotted a display of artichokes of all shapes and sizes to make even us Californians envious. I supposed after having taken a couple of local cooking classes (one in Arles and the other in Les Baux), we were seeing the abundance of fruits and vegetables in a whole new light, knowing new ways in which to prepare them once home. And I was considering the purchase of one of those burnt-orange ceramic tians to take home as there would be no way my newly discovered cuisine would taste as good in my old pots. Right?

Instead of purchasing the heavy bowl, Melody and I focused on little items for gifts to take home: lavender sachets, miniature spice grinders, Provençal-styled hot pads, miniature paintings, and cellophane bags of herbs de Provence. Then I spotted the spice tables, which were something to behold: two tables filled with more than twenty-one hemp bags splayed open with fresh spices. The air around the vendor's table was more erotically intoxicating than most as the aromas of saffron, cinnamon, cumin, coriander, ginger, allspice, and cloves commingled and lifted into the air.

"Would you look at this?" Melody said to me. A colorful array of peppercorns—yes, peppercorns—in pink, white, black, red, and green colors were sending us into a spice coma. Oh, and then there was my favorite! Little round boxes of sea salt from the Camargue called *Fleur de Sel.*

"Have you tried this?" Lise asked us. "The name means 'little flowers of salt,' and when you bite down on it, the salt crystals give you a burst of flavor. I still use this daily." Yes, we had to purchase these little treasures.

Before we could even make all our decisions, Sharon swept us up the street and around the bend to make our way to a boulangerie/patisserie. And then as a special treat, to a candy maker's shop. Or a chocolatier's shop! Joel Durand is a one-of-a-kind chocolate maker. Once inside his small establishment, we were given a quick tour through the kitchen and helped to make some of the chocolates that were coming out on a tray. So, what was Durand's specialty? It was called the *Carte of Numeros,* or the Numbers Card, which has thirty-two different chocolates from which you can choose. Some had Earl Grey tea in them, or coffee, or salted butter, or almonds, pralines, hazelnuts, cloves, lemons and, of course, lavender that was made with milk chocolate and lavender blossoms! Yes, we had to indulge! Each of us bought several boxes of these numbered treasures.

The next stop on our hit parade was Chateau d'Estoublon, the massive 1489 chateau, which was well-known for following in the Roman tradition of making their own olive oils and wines. We had come to taste olive oils, so our group was led into a large, vaulted tasting room. A long table had been placed in the middle of the room with thimble-sized glasses, water glasses, and pitchers of cool fresh water. We all took our places and once we settled in, we were privileged to learn the fine art of olive oil tasting.

A dapper young man came into the room with a flourish. He immediately introduced himself as Laurent and told us his job was oleologist. "It's similar to the job of a wine sommelier, but instead of being an expert in wine, I am an expert in the study of olive oils. What does that include? Why, it includes olive oil education, like now where I am teaching you about the oils. Plus, I'm involved in taste testing, recipe development and other research." We were duly impressed. At that moment, a door flew open and two young women arrived with an array of olive oil varietals on a tray.

Laurent continued "Take a look at the bottles of olive oil and you will see on the label the place, season, or date of its production. Unlike wine, there is no year of production as there is no aging done here. Olive oil is best as soon as its pressed."

Pam leaned back with her eyes open wide. "Really?"

Laurent asked, "Does that surprise you?"

"Yes," said Sharon, "most all of the olive oils purchased in grocery stores back home are probably already old or have gone bad." Our faces blanched. "Yes, be sure to purchase the newly pressed olives in the fall. That way the oil is fresh!"

Laurent continued his talk: "You will find that we choose clear glass bottles for our olive oil, so you can see the color of the oil. Many olive oil companies that ship their products overseas choose dark bottles for bottling as they need to keep the product in the dark as much as possible."

At this point, Laurent took up one of the bottles of olive oil and began pouring the warm, lemony-yellow liquid into small glasses—like little communion glasses—and we were instructed in the art of olive oil tasting.

"One must not sip as we do with wines. We need to suck in just a little bit." He made a *slishing* sound with his mouth as he sucked in a few drops of oil. "Let it slide straight back across your tongue and hold it there. How does it taste? Is it spicy? Mellow? Does it have a bit of a bite? Our olives have a very mellow, buttery taste, yet they are not heavy on the palate. It is light yellow as you see here, but olive oils from Florence, for instance, are light green in color, as they are produced with some of the leaves. This also gives it more of a significant bite. Oils from Liguria are light and oils from Sicily are heavier in flavor. It is all up to you and your palate as to what is pleasing to your taste. The same goes for wines!"

He began to give us several tastes of the variety of oils produced on their land. We *oohed* and *aahed*, then bought bottles to take with us, as we were once again ushered out the door and into the van. We had another appointment to make, and we were late: lunch at La Régalido Auberge in Fontvieille.

While in the bus, Lise asked us if we were familiar with Fréderic Mistral. We all enjoyed Christine's stories about Mistral, and we all raised our hands.

"Yes," we all said, "we know who Fréderic Mistral was."

"Bon! I would like to introduce you to another local author, who made Fontvielle famous." Just then, we made a turn to the left and rolled off the highway and into the village of Fontvielle.

"This is the very village where Alphonse Daudet wrote his

famous *Lettres de Mon Moulin,* which means letters from my windmill. The actual windmill lies just south of town on a hilltop covered in olive and pine trees. It was up there where he dreamed up the characters in his books. It was while listening to the shepherds and the inhabitants of the Montauban chateau, which is quite a massive home on a nearby hill. Both buildings are now museums so you can learn more about Daudet, but his books are filled with characters more in keeping with the real Provence, much like Frédric Mistral.

"Like Marcel Pagnol's characters?" I asked.

"I think many who grew up in Provence find Daudet equally authentic. You'll have to decide for yourself." Just then she pointed at a sign on a restaurant, which as it turned out was where we were heading, La Régalido.

Spending the morning basking in the glories of local produce and products can make a gal extremely hungry! We were famished and sat with a thump into our assigned seats in the garden/patio at this delightful traditional restaurant. It was a perfect lunch, albeit a bit heavy as we were to finish our dessert, don our aprons, and head into the kitchen. So, what was it we ate and would be replicating?

Well, of course, we began with cool glasses of rosé to go with the hors d'oeuvres that were small platters of flash-fried anchovies. I know! It may sound a little off-putting, but these were delicious, crispy, and tasty little guys, and we gobbled them up as if they were potato chips. Or like we had grown up with them.

For the next course, we were served individual plates of sautéed rolls of paper-thin slices of eggplant stuffed with fresh tomatoes and garlic drenched in golden olive oil sprinkled with cracked red and green peppercorns. It was served warm, was light and quite delectable.

The main course was called *Jambonnette de Volaille aux Olives Cassées,* which translated to the ham of a chicken, or the quarter of a chicken with a cracked black olive sauce and served with *Riz de Camargue aux Raisins* or rice from the Camargue region with raisins. Yes, all things were made with local products in celebration of the bounties of Provence.

But the pièce de resistance was the dessert: *Millefeuille Croustillant aux Fruits Rouges.* This, my dear friend, translates to a thousand layers of thin puff pastry with bright red strawberries and raspberries, layered whipped cream, custard, and raspberry coulis, or sauce.

As you can imagine, we were dragging after a morning's tromp through a farmers market, a chocolatier's class, and an olive oil tasting. Then we were seduced by a marvelous, but very filling lunch plus wine. But it was time to put on another set of whites, and this time with white netted hats. Fortunately, we were given an entire culinary show, wherein two chefs (including the owner of the Régalido) demonstrated all the dishes we had been fortunate to eat beforehand. Again, the most difficult and most dramatic to assemble was the dessert, which brought about a performance with red hot rods that touched lightly onto the custard to produce a caramelized sugar topping! No, don't try this at home—even with a curling iron!

Once again, we were entertained by two skillful chefs who had learned to dance the light fantastic around each other in the kitchen and with *joie de* vivre that was delightful to witness! If we learned anything at all, it was to love what you do every day and to celebrate that love with gratitude for the rest of your life.

CHAPTER THIRTY-THREE

Abbaye Notre Dame de Senanque
and a Special Evening with the Brihats

*A*s you can tell, we had been on a full tilt run since we first arrived in Provence, so on the following day, it was a great relief that Sharon opted to have a more low-key adventure. We would begin the morning with a trip only a short distance away to visit the famous Abbaye Notre Dame de Senanque. We were thrilled with the idea as our bodies had reached the point of exhaustion and were pleased that our begging for a break worked.

Timon once again loaded us into the van to take us back over the hills through Gordes and on for a few miles beyond to the Abbaye. We passed by numerous odd-shaped stone structures that resembled beehives.

"What are those?" came a voice from the back of the van. Lise turned in her front seat to face us, and in her best tour guide-speak, answered, "These buildings are known as *bories*. They are frameless assemblages of flat stones with corbelled vaulted ceilings." (Wow! Now, that was precise. She was ready for us!)

We *oohed* and *aahed* as we passed by one after another of

the six-foot-tall beehive-shaped buildings, which appeared to be markers in the middle of lavender fields.

"How old are they?" came another question. "When were they built?"

"They are actually not certain," Lise responded, "but supposedly in the 1600s. It is said that they were once shelters for road weary travelers. Then, they became barns or stables for local farmers."

We drove swiftly past them and around a bend where we caught sight of a cluster of many bories together that suggested a village of sorts. "It's interesting," Lise continued, "that they can only be found on the north side of a mountain, which might speak to the need for keeping cool in the summer months. Now, it appears, they seem to serve as storage for the lavender farmers."

We rounded another curve and dropped down into a narrow, verdant valley surrounded by a forest. This was the home of the Abbaye de Sénanque, a Cistercian monastery founded in 1148. Again, Lise turned around to enlighten us as our van zipped through the switchback turns to the bottom of the valley.

"It is said that the Cistercian monks always searched for a location to set up their monastery within a narrow valley, for easier access to water from mountain streams. They sought out a place that would provide land for cultivation for their own needs, but also a remote valley to give them the peace to further the purposes of their work toward humility. A development of virtues, so to speak," Lise said.

A large pastoral expanse of purple lavender separated the forest from the ancient buildings. We easily recognized this field in front of the Abbaye as one of the most photographed in all of France. Once out of the van, we took turns capturing nature that sidled up to this austere church.

"Yes," Lise said as she herded us toward the abbey with a guidebook in hand, "the architecture of this haven of peace and tranquility was highly ranked among the masterpieces of Romanesque monastic life. In contrast to Benedictine abbeys, Cistercian architecture was distinguished by austerity revealed through the reduction of the size of the buildings and the height of the roofs, spires, and towers. Modesty of spirit was also exposed through the stark grey stone walls of the exterior and barren grey walls within the interior. No frescoes, no sculptures, and no colorful ornamentation—including stained glass windows—were found embellishing this Order's buildings. The goal of the aesthete was to stick to the philosophy of Christ's purpose within the monastic way of life."

We made our way up the long walk and into what was the gift shop and the beginnings of a tour of the Abbaye. Melody, who I think in another lifetime must have been a monastic or a nun seeking the quieter side of life, became more serene with each step of the guided tour. The monks were attending services, so we were directed around those sections of the monastery. We did manage to weave in and out of the spartan church, the dimly lit Chapter House, and the dormitory before breaking out into the sunlight once again in the cloister. I do think the cloister was my favorite as the buildings surrounded a beautiful garden with the sunlight streaming down from a bright blue sky. Benches, which clustered around geometric-shaped bushes, were where the monks were known to pray, meditate, and work. It gave me pause as it was the only place I felt I could take a breath—literally. I realized the starkness of the rest of the abbey had closed in on me to the point I knew I could never be a candidate. But Melody? She resonated with her surroundings, and not long afterward, decided to become a deacon in the Episcopal church. Meditation, for her, was grace itself.

On our return to Bonnieux, Timon pulled off to the side of the road and the edge of a field. What was this about? He popped out of the van to open the doors for us and took out a couple of baskets and some blankets. What was happening?

"As a special treat today," Sharon said as she clamored off the van, "we will have a picnic at the site of the Roman ruin—the Julien Bridge." We shouldn't have wondered why Sharon had not joined us at the abbey. She was forever sneaking off, but when she returned, she always had a culinary delight to share with us. This was no exception.

We all piled out of the van and helped to lay out the blankets and the baskets. Sharon eased herself down onto a rock to pull out a platter with cheese and meat-filled baguettes. Special glass jugs of iced tea and apple juice were set beside the glasses. Real plates, silverware, and napkins were also provided. No paper plates for us! And a bowl of fresh fruit, including enormous strawberries and grapes, were laid out for our pleasure.

As we ate on separate blankets or rocks at the base of Pont Julien, the Gallo-Roman bridge, Lise pulled out her guidebook and told us about the bridge named after Julius Caesar. "This more than-200-foot stone bridge, which was built over the now-dry Calavon River, linked up the Milan–to–Arles route across the Alps. Imagine that!"

I love information like this as I tried to imagine what life must have been like during Roman occupation of this remote field far from the view of the Alps, much less Arles. I needed a map!

"This bridge" she quoted, "is without a doubt one of the finest and best-preserved Gallo-Roman bridges to be found in this province." Hmm! We had to check that out!

Despite the afternoon heat, some of us took turns walking down through the wild brush and jumping from one rock to another like young frogs, instead of the sedate matronly broads who had just toured a monastery. I suppose little changes! We all see life through our childhood lens!

Once we returned to our hotel, Le Clos de Buis, it was late in the afternoon, and we all raced up the stairs to our rooms to get into swimming suits and then back down to the pool. A note had been left on the desk for me from the Brihats. It seemed my questions about families and traditions with Solange the other night compelled her to reach out to me. Could Melody and I come over for a short chat that evening after dinner? Mais oui!

Solange picked us up after 8:30 p.m. and drove us to their home. Denis was once again in rare form and awaiting our return. He effusively invited us in and had us sit in the living room in front of the fireplace. As, on the occasion of our last visit, he leaned up against the fireplace as if in a pose. He had one finger extended out, as he was pointing out a work of art . . . a photograph that he said had been taken. No, no, he had not taken it. A twinkle flitted through his eyes, and he shifted his glasses further down his nose.

"Do you know what this is?" he asked. The photograph he was referring to appeared to be a piece of abstract art of— white paint splashed on beige. We knew that he was a world-renown photographer of nature, so my mind tumbled back in time as I attempted to recollect having seen the image before. And then he began to tell us.

"This is something that you see as you walk along the sands . . . like when you walk along the sea." We looked at the photograph, then looked back at him. We were perplexed.

"It is what you might call, 'pigeon sheet,' I believe!" He

threw his head back and laughed. And we knew we were in for another rare interview.

Solange bustled into the room with a tray of champagne flutes, then returned with bowls of olives and nuts. She handed Denis a bottle of champagne, and as he popped the cork with a grand gesture, he said, "This is what we always do for guests." We remembered, as he said the same thing when we were visiting a few days back. But we were tickled to be sharing this time with them again.

"Carole," Solange began as she settled in a side chair near us, "you mentioned the other night that you want to know about the local Provençal traditions—the ones we celebrate and have celebrated in our families. I would love to answer your questions."

"Thank you," I said. "I have an interest in learning what traditions bind families together, mainly through their foods and holidays. After I retired as a family therapist, I began interviewing families in both France and Italy about their favorite holidays, their favorite foods as a child, and asked them what brought their families together at the table. I'm thinking of writing a book about that topic and I wanted your perspective."

"Sounds like an amazing project!" Solange said, shifting into a more comfortable position, and nodding affirmation to Denis. "Where would you like to start?"

"First of all, are you open to my recording our interview?" I asked. She nodded her head.

"Well, then," I said as I clicked the recorder on, "we recently celebrated Easter, so let's start there. How does your family celebrate Easter?"

Denis, who had taken another side chair, leaned forward with interest although he understood few words of English.

"For Easter," Solange began, "we join the whole family together around the table. We do this for the children, or grandchildren. In any case, when we hear the church bells ring, some distract the kids, while the rest of us put the eggs and chocolate into the garden along with small gifts for the children to find. We most often have rabbits made of chocolate. Once the children search for the chocolate, they quickly return to the table. And we begin to eat—oh, this is definitely an Easter tradition—we eat Easter salad, known as the *Salade Pascal*. Are you familiar with that?"

Both Melody and I shook our heads no. Solange explained in English, then French for Denis' benefit.

"First of all, Pascal means Easter in French, so that should help." We nodded our heads with understanding.

"We use the first romaine lettuces, along with the first tomatoes and the freshest of vegetables of the season, plus hard-boiled eggs. We eat this Salade Pascale with the Gigot Pascal (lamb). The family is used to following these fêtes and traditions even if we are not religious. Mais oui! This is a religious holiday. We try to celebrate the holidays of the year, such as Christmas, Easter, and their birthdays, which are on saints' days. Some are Provençal traditions, and some are not.

"For Pascal, the family is used to helping prepare the lamb on the spit." She pointed to the fireplace behind Denis. At that point, Denis stood up and loudly described to Melody and me how to use the fireplace spit. We got up to see what he was saying, as English wasn't his best language and French was not great for us either. He was pointing at an interesting conveyance attached to the fireplace. Again, Solange came to the rescue by translating, although Denis gave it quite the go!

"There are two brass strings (or chains) that hang down to connect the spit," he said, "and, therefore, the *gigot* or the leg of lamb is connected to the metal rod. You can adjust the lamb up and down to place the meat closer or farther away from the fire," he said, as he indicated by waving his hand up and down.

"And," he continued, "the lamb turns around and around over the fire. And every five minutes, it *flump, flump, flumps* over, and then the cooking continues." Here Denis described, with the accompaniment of sound effects and the flailing of arms, the noise the spit made when the lamb became lopsided. The meat was hanging closest to the fire, yet inching, inching, inching up and over as the spit turned.

"The spit," he continued, "is set up on a mechanical pulley system of sorts. We place a tray below the gigot (lamb), which is filled with garlic cloves, and as the meat cooks slowly, the meat juices drip into the pan. Awwwww, the aroma!" he exclaimed as he kissed his fingertips. "And then, you take the lamb off the spit, throw it away, and eat the garlic!" He smacked his lips again for effect and laughed uproariously at his own joke.

We rocked back in surprise but also with laughter as his banter and the scene he described was delightful. I noticed that he, like us, resorted to acting everything out, especially when accurate words eluded us.

Melody and I enjoyed every moment of his demonstration while dear Solange smiled patiently and patted his chair to sit back down. We, too, returned to our seats.

Solange said, "Last week, after you left our home, I phoned my daughter, Anne. Her name is Anne Brihat Jourdan, and she lives in Aix-en-Provence. I asked her if she was interested in sharing some of her own childhood memories with us." I was pleased that Solange had taken my questions to heart.

She picked up a letter she had received from her daughter and began reading: "On the twenty-fourth of December, in the afternoon before the Christmas Eve celebration, my grandmother who was Italian, spent the afternoon finishing up the chocolate truffles. This was part of the traditional Thirteen Desserts, which is a Provençal tradition. My mother and aunt finished the preparation of the meat that was usually a large capon, chicken, or duck. We kids were supposed to finish this job, while my father, when he was here, would prepare the fireplace with wood, and we would prepare the most wonderful part in the fireplace."

I wondered what Solange's daughter was referring to here—about the wonderful part of the fireplace—as I'm assuming she meant the roasting of meats, or perhaps, the hanging of stockings. But Solange was fully engrossed in reading the letter.

"My cousin always prepared the traditional *aperitif,* a specialty drink, and he also made a terrible tapenade! He put in way too much garlic!" Solange giggled as she read this part, and I could feel a whole new story bubbling forth.

". . . And my brother's job was to look for music. In the meantime, the young parents would try to calm down their children who were very excited because of the coming of Santa Claus."

"But the most important thing, and the most traditional, was the preparation of the Thirteen Desserts. This was how each family prepared for the Three Kings who were obviously coming to the celebration, too! In Provence, you use fruits and nuts that are available at that time of year. This should include an orange, an apple, quince paste, dry grapes or plums, melons, almonds, the figs. All in all, you have a tray of only thirteen desserts.

"In Provence you also have nougat, which is a soft candy, either dark or light. And we make the *fougasse* or *pompe de Noel a l'huile d'olive* (cake). This cake, which is always made with olive oil, is *only* made in the South of France. This is a light-textured cake made from yeast and egg dough, then sweetened with sugar, flavored with grated orange and lemon zest, and sprinkled with orange flower water. Bakers in Provence traditionally used to give these cakes as gift to their regular customers during this festive season, and the wine merchant would also give everyone the *vin cuit* to drink with it."

"Sorry, Solange," I said, needing an explanation there.

"Ah," she answered, "the name of the drink literally means 'cooked wine' and is a naturally sweet wine. And the *pompe*, or cake is never sliced but is always broken apart with the hands. It's just part of our tradition," Solange said with a lift of her hand. She continued reading.

"So, we make thirteen desserts, and at the end of the dinner, each family member has to try to taste each one of these thirteen desserts. It was always a race to see who could finish first. My grandmother said that the celebration of Christmas could not finish on the twenty-fifth of December without this traditional preparation, and the finishing of all these desserts."

"That's a powerful statement now, isn't it?" Melody chimed in.

"Oh, my yes!" Solange responded. Our mothers and grandmothers are very, very important in carrying out the traditions within the family." She continued reading Anne's letter.

"There is always a very large dinner known as *le gros souper*, and it begins with *aïgo boulido*, which means boiled water, and is eaten to aid as a *digestif*. In Provence, the light soup was prepared as a first course to aid in digestion as there are many courses to follow. My mother would prepare it, which was difficult for her, because my brother-in-law would always say, 'Ah, this is very light! Not much for the dinner here!'" Solange nodded, laughed, as did Denis, and she continued to read on.

"It was always a joke! But the soup is made with garlic, sage, water, and one or two small potatoes. When you serve it, drizzle a little olive oil over the soup. It is delicately aromatic and is believed to have powerful curative properties.

"My grandmother, who was also a wonderful cook, gave us some recipes. The one I most often use is the one in which we boil the fish—court bouillon."

"But my favorite moment of Christmas begins on the fourth of December, which is St. Barbara's Day. You begin by taking some wet cotton and planting some seeds into the wet cotton. They begin to grow and then they are placed on the table on the twenty-fourth of December as part of the Christmas celebration. This, we believe, symbolizes prosperity for the family."

Solange stopped reading and said, "Anne is very attached to the traditions, even more so than I am or my mother. But Anne continues to carry on the traditions with her own small family. This way we share with each other, and we give life to the traditions of Provence and our families."

"This is so lovely," Melody said.

"I agree," I said, "and I can't wait to hear what else was served at the gros souper, but she has given me so much more than I expected. Please tell her how much I appreciate her gift of memory!"

Solange and Denis beamed at each other.

I looked at the clock and realized the time had flown. It was already after 10 p.m. and we were scheduled for an early morning start the next day.

"Solange, would you mind if we came back one more time to finish this interview?"

"Oh, mais oui! But, of course," she said, jumping to her feet. She seemed amenable to the idea, and as she drove us back to the hotel, she clicked off other memories and foods she wanted to share with me. "I haven't begun to tell you about my own mother!" she said. "Now, that's a story worth sharing!"

CHAPTER THIRTY-FOUR

Avignon: In the Kitchen of the Popes
Soupe de Fraises
(Strawberry Soup)

My love of strawberries began the summer of my third year. Sneaking out of the basement apartment of my grandparents' home, I would head down the darkened garden path, past the lilac bushes, through the back gate and into the warm, morning sun of Mrs. Nelson's strawberry patch. There, I would swoop down with a vengeance onto the brightest red berries my chubby fingers could wrest free, brush away the dirt and leaves and quickly, quickly before my mother would wail, "Calamity Jane, are you at it again?" I would sink my teeth into one of those sweet, juicy, yet tangy red strawberries. In that moment, I would experience summertime exploding in my mouth, oozing down my chin, and then I could get on with the business of being a three-year-old.

So it was with great joy that I found myself the following day the giddy participant of a Provençal cooking tour in Avignon, France at the grand five-star hotel, La Mirande. This elegant seven-hundred-year-old renovated Cardinal's palace, tucked deftly behind the magnificent yet austere former Palace of the Popes, was built in 1309. And our cooking group would have the distinction of learning how to cook on one of their mighty nineteenth century wood-fired stoves. Ah, but that would be the challenge!

We were running a tad late, so Timon raced through the eastern portal or gates of this great walled city, bumped along the narrow cobblestone streets, past the *Palais de Papes,* or the Palace of the Pope, and down what seemed to be a back alley behind the Palais to find the hotel. The beautiful seventeenth century façade of the Mirande Hotel suggested images from scenes of *Dangerous Liaisons.* We had been introduced to elegant hotels and restaurants on this trip, but this place appeared to be a standout. We were met at the front door by none other than Michael Hanhardt, the owner/manager. He greeted us warmly, told us to call him Michael and seemed especially excited to have our culinary travel group attend one of their cooking classes.

"To be able to learn new traditional culinary techniques along with Provençal recipes in one of the oldest kitchens in France will be a unique experience for you," he said kindly.

Before heading to the kitchen, he gave us a quick tour of the elegant lobby, the *salle de manger* (dining room), and the sitting areas, which were filled with both eighteenth and nineteenth century antiques.

"The interior features," Michael began to tell us, "embraced the Age of Enlightenment in the revival of an eighteenth century nobleman's townhouse. Each salon or room is adorned with the regal air of both Baroque- and Rococo-designed furniture." Ornate gold framed floor-to-ceiling mirrors were interspersed throughout the rooms, reflecting a shimmering light from the expansive crystal chandeliers.

"The wallcoverings reveal the romance of the century of Enchantment, with its Anglo-Chinese Garden designs in the Toile de Jouey-style, which reveled in the pleasures of love and nature." A corresponding design was replicated in matching cotton and silk fabrics, which swathed the chairs, pillows, draperies, valances, settees, and lounge chairs. In the larger salons, tapestries stretched across the breadth of the walls, telling their own stories of another time, another place.

"These tapestries remind me of our tour inside the Palace of the Popes a few years back," I whispered to Melody. "I wonder if that is where these are from?"

Melody nodded her head and beamed, but put her finger to her lips to shush me. But Michael was beginning to speak as he was moving through the hotel, and we wanted to keep up.

"La Mirande has always been a private home, and it stands as a guardian to the glory and era of the Palace of the Popes. It all began in 1309 when the Popes took up residence in Avignon. One of the cardinals accompanying Pope Clement V was his nephew, Cardinal de Pellegrue, who built this *livrée*, as Cardinals' palaces were called. It was built right here in the privileged neighborhood adjoining the Popes' Palace. The property remained in the hands of the cardinals until the siege of the Palace in 1410 when the palace was partly destroyed. Ah, but fortunately, this *livrée* remained."

Michael led us to one of the front windows that faced the eastern wall of the Palace. He parted one of the elegant draperies also made of Toile de Jouey design as we stared across the street.

"Have any of you visited the Popes' Palace before?" he asked. Melody and I raised our hands. "Well, then you have an understanding of the historical background during the papacy here in Avignon." He turned to the group.

"That façade of the Popes' Palace is visible from almost

every room here in the hotel, as well as from our lovely garden. I will take you out to the gardens during a break from your class." He led us back through the lobby.

"Can you tell us a bit more about this refined hotel?" Lise asked, encouraging Michael to continue.

He smiled, and said, "The ownership of this building changed hands many times throughout the centuries and the name was changed. Then in 1653, our building was sold to a man of law, Claude de Vervins, and his son Pierre, who was the Marquis de Bédouin. It was the Marquis who built the typically classical façade that we see today," he said, waving his arm about.

"His architectural statement was one of a nobleman's residence, or *hotel particulier* as they are called in French. One can only imagine the long span of years and of the life lived by a bourgeoisie close to people like Napoleon III." We all nodded but truly had no idea.

"Where did the name La Mirande come from?" asked Sharon.

"La Mirande was named after a famous room in the Popes' Palace. It was in this room that representatives of the Popes received the city's notables as well as the highest of dignitaries who were visiting town. We like to think we do the same today."

We again nodded our heads in agreement.

At this point, Michael led us to the rear of the hotel and down the back stairs to the basement level. Yes, this was where the kitchen could be found. We entered a large but surprisingly well-lit room. It was clear that this kitchen had once been the hub of the household for hundreds of years.

Answering our questions before we even asked them, Michael said, "We no longer use this kitchen for the hotel, but instead hold our cooking classes here because this is a place where chefs of Provence love to teach their most auspicious dishes—right here in this historical kitchen."

He turned to us and pointed across the room, "How often can it be said that you have cooked on an old nineteenth century wood stove?"

Our eyes rested on the opposite wall where an immense black iron stove had been inserted into what must have been an enormous fireplace. White ceramic tiles lined the insert around the stove and acted as a backsplash to all the culinary activities that had taken place there. In the center of the room was a long wooden table with ten chairs pulled up in place before the stove. But it was obvious that the stove was the high altar of this exalted kitchen. And was already radiating with heat in preparation for our class.

Looking around the room, I noticed the walls were lined with open shelves holding crocks, pots, wine glasses, tureens, platters, plates, and simple cups. One whole row of shelves held large white ceramic jugs, for what I wasn't sure. Another shelf held a collection of regional ceramics from all over France—Brittany, Burgundy, the Alsace. Even Provence. And brightly shined copper pots hung wherever a wall hook was present. I breathed in deeply. I did love this so! I simply loved the energy that bubbled forward when new culinary creations were brought to life!

A side door led outside to a private glass-enclosed herb garden, where Sharon was checking out the herbs.

"Ah," she said, "take a look! Here they have chervil, tarragon, chives, and parsley. Perfect! These are the herbs that make up what is known as the Fine Herbs in French cooking. They are the ones most called for in French *haute cuisine*. They are employed in seasoning delicate dishes, such as chicken, fish, and eggs, and may also be used in a beurre blanc sauce for seasoning such dishes. And look here," she said as she leaned over the raised plot of plants.

"Here are the more traditional herbs that are found in Provence, especially within the herbs de Provence blend. These include thyme, oregano, summer savory, and rosemary. Oh, and they have plants of culinary lavender here! My favorite!"

"So, you know all our fresh herbs, *n'est-ce pas?*" came a low voice from behind us. We turned and looked up into the face of a tall, very handsome young man. He had swarthy good looks, dark cropped hair, and dark brown eyes that twinkled as he smiled at us from the door.

"Yes, I learned at the Cordon Bleu," Sharon said, standing up and adjusting herself. "And you must be our chef of the day?" He nodded and gave a slight bow.

Just then, Michael called us into the kitchen as our lesson was about to begin. We bustled in and found seats as Michael officially introduced Daniél.

"I am pleased to present to you the instructor of the hour, Daniél Hebét. He is a young chef but one of great sophistication, yet has a humble approach to his cuisine." He told us that Daniél spoke only a modicum of English, so he would be by his side to assist. We didn't care. We could tell his charming manner spoke volumes.

Pam leaned over to me and said, "I'm pretty sure that any handsome French chef who doesn't speak English could be reading a Jeep manual and everyone would be spellbound." We giggled, just as Lise was being introduced to help with the translations.

So, we were ready to go! Aprons, utensils, and technical sheets were laid out for us, and we hurried to suit up.

The menu for our cooking lessons began with a creamy yet delicate artichoke soup, infused with Spanish ham (only acorn-eating ham, at that, Daniél pointed out). That course was followed by a succulent roasted red snapper stuffed with a uniquely prepared ratatouille with a saffron sauce. But for me, the piece de resistance was a marvelous dessert, wild strawberry soup with herbs, spices, zests, and a house made lemon-basil sorbet. Did I mention strawberries? Wild strawberries?

After a bit of theatrics stoking the fire within the stove, Michael and Daniél washed their hands and returned to begin the demonstration of preparations. Daniél rolled out a cart with an entire leg of air-cured jamón poised on a rack. He explained that this was a Spanish culinary specialty known as *Jamon Iberico Bellota*. I believe he said the Spanish name translated to the word acorn and no, not all ingredients had to hail from Provence to make them Provençale.

"Oui, and *Jamon puro de bellota* is the best ham you can find. Bellota ham *must* be from Black Iberian pigs, which are 100 percent pure Iberian breed. This means they have been fed only with acorns in pasture areas during the final three or four months of mass-feeding."

"It is exceedingly expensive," Michael added, "but then it is a Spanish culinary icon and a true pleasure for the taste buds. That is why our chefs choose to use it."

"How expensive would it be to purchase a leg of ham that size?" one of our cohort asked.

"Oh, I imagine," Michael responded, "that this eight kilogram, or eighteen pound, leg would cost over $1,200, depending on the market."

"Plus," Daniél said, wielding an enormous knife high in the air, "how else could I become an expert *cortador*—a ham carver?" Why did I immediately conjure up the image of a toreador?

With that he carefully began the elegant work of carving paper-thin slices of meat from the ham. This was to be one of the ingredients for the artichoke soup, which was then simmered on the stove to create a velvety smooth texture.

He then began enlisting us to help make the ratatouille to stuff the red snapper. He roasted the red peppers and eggplant with a small butane torch before we began to chop up the vegetables. When asked if he prepared his ratatouille the same way as his mother, he replied with a twinkle in his eye, "I am a good son. I do not contradict my mother."

We each took turns preparing mise en place, which literally meant to 'put into place'. This process involved the chopping of fine herbs directly from the herb garden, as well as shallots, roasted artichokes, red peppers, onions, spices, zests, strawberries . . . all as preparation before the actual cooking process. We marched around the room with our clean white aprons on, moving from one station to the next; why, we became a force to be reckoned with. Those who had been squeamish with cooking before took to these techniques like ducks to water. Or, perhaps, to Daniél, as he was a wonder to behold.

At one point we were offered a break, and we all were led back up the stairs to the garden. Glasses of rosé were served, along with hors d'oeuvres to tide us over until our déjeuner. The morning had turned into early afternoon, with the sun high in the sky, but we were grateful we were tucked behind the palace and under the fruit trees blossoming in the garden, as they provided a modicum of coolness within the shade. It was here that we could take a break and wipe away the perspiration from our heavy workload. Whew!

White tablecloth-covered round tables and wrought-iron chairs beckoned me to sag down to rest after a morning on my feet. Ah, but I was not the only one. We all clustered about and with the camaraderie of Daniél and Michael, it felt like an ongoing party.

Once we started down the stairs to the kitchen, marvelous aromas wafted up to greet us. The prep table had been
converted into a dining table with, again, white tablecloths,
wine glasses, as well as dinner service set for ten. The serious
cooking was almost completed; we just needed to finish the
main dishes. The copper pots simmered with ratatouille and
artichoke soup while the ice cream maker was loaded with
the ingredients for the lemon-basil sorbet. The red snapper
was prepped and stuffed with the ratatouille, as others created
the saffron sauce and finished puréeing the strawberries for
the dessert.

In due time, we were ready for lunch. As you can tell, it
was more than eating a most delectable déjeuner, it was a feast
for the senses! Every element of each dish had been carefully
created by Daniél. Pure genius! And like little mother hens
over dear Daniél, we confirmed to him that he had a very
bright future in the culinary world going forth.

So, then the piece de resistance was masterfully served.
The strawberry soup was delivered to us in wide-rimmed soup
bowls with a scoop of lemon-basil sorbet floating in the center.
Then a tray with an array of spices, herbs, and zests were offered to each of us. Fresh herbs such as basil, coriander leaves,
tarragon, lemon grass. Spices such as ground vanilla, ginger,
cinnamon and/or cardamon. Zests such as sweetened lemon,
grapefruit, ginger, orange, and limes.

Now, how do we eat this? Once you sprinkle the chosen
spices, herbs, or zests onto the wide rim of the bowl, you lift
your spoon, glide it across one of each of the groups, then into
the strawberry soup itself, ending in the cooling sorbet in the
center. Every single bite was an extraordinary explosion of
flavors not to be found anywhere else—unless it was in the
backyard of your childhood.

SOUPE DE FRAISES

(Strawberry Soup)

2 pts. fresh strawberries
1/2 cup of sugar

Group 1: Fresh Herbs—2 Tablespoons each-finely chopped basil, coriander leaves, tarragon, and lemongrass.
Group 2: Spices—ground vanilla, ginger, cinnamon, and cardamom
Group 3: Zests (sweetened)—lemon, grapefruit, ginger, orange, and lime zests
(Sweetened with 1 qt. water and 2 cups of sugar)
Lemon juice
Gaseous spring water/mineral water

Blend the strawberries in a blender with 1/2 cup of sugar. Set aside in the refrigerator. Mix each of the groups separately. When ready to serve, mix a small amount of lemon juice and mineral water into the strawberries. Pour the strawberry mixture into individual bowls with broad rims. Place one scoop of lemon-basil sorbet in the middle of each bowl. Then, sprinkle small portions of each one of the groups consecutively along the outside rim of the bowl.

CHAPTER THIRTY-FIVE

An Escape into Traditions

*O*ur culinary tour *extraordinaire* with Sharon ended abruptly the following day, as she informed us she had been called home a day early. No, no one else was aware of this beforehand, and we all, most of all Lise, were caught off-guard.

As it turned out, it took three of us—Melody, Lise, and me—to accompany her along with Timon, of course, to the airport in Marseille. Plus, Melody and I decided to accompany Lise to pick up a rental car at the airport. This would afford us the opportunity to spend a few more precious days in beautiful Provence.

The following morning, after bidding adieu to our dear friends and the folks we had come to know at Le Clos de Buis, Melody and I had been given directions to a hotel known as Chateau des Alpilles in St. Remy. Both Sharon and Lise had recommended this place and knew we would not be disappointed.

But, first, we had arranged to see the Brihats one last time before we left the area. We took them to lunch at Le Fournil, the restaurant in Bonnieux that we had enjoyed on our first days in town. Denis was in his usual rare form, making jokes about being escorted by—count them—three beautiful blondes—and introducing us to their hometown friends. After we returned to the Brihats home, I flipped on the recorder, Denis ascended to his loft for a snooze, and we began our final interview.

"The last time we were here," I said to Solange, "you mentioned your mother, her cooking, and how your daughter had embraced many of her methods. Could you tell me more about their relationship?"

"Oh, mais oui!" Solange began. We were seated in our designated seats in the living room but without Denis commanding a position of power at the mantle.

"Let me pull open her letter again," she said. The letter had been lying on the coffee table ready for our discussion. She began reading immediately:

"One of the recipes I love was taught to me by my Grandmaman. The dish is called *Hachis parmentier.* It's easy enough to prepare as you begin with mashed or puréed potatoes, cheese, and minced boiled meat, and then place them in layers—a type of shepherd's pie."

"Actually," Solange said, interrupting the reading, "the way my mother used to cook was to be very economical and she had many, many good ideas for using leftover meats. This dish was one of them. But this is a French preparation she would use, not necessarily a Provençale method." She looked down at the letter from her daughter:

"I remember seeing my grandmother preparing the fish in court bouillon and she also prepared the bouillabaisse. To make the court bouillon, you use water, fennel, carrots, onions, garlic, and mirepoix (a sachet of herbs), boil the vegetables, then use this water to poach the fish."

Solange took her glasses off and gazed off into space. She

then said, "My mother learned to cook from her aunt, but my mother started to work very early in her years, at the age of thirteen or fourteen years of age. She was raised in the Aubagne area near Marseille. She began work in a restaurant, and she learned many things there. And she learned many things by herself. She invented a very good sauce for the less expensive beef dishes—to extend the meat for other meals for our family.

"The sauce was made with olive oil, butter, parsley, and garlic and it is used to put over the *hachis* (which is like our hash), but she ended the preparation with a splash of vinegar. I don't know why she did this, but it was delicious, and I prepare it that same way today."

Solange got up and handed us a plate of cookies that she had made the day before and served them with cups of coffee. I was grateful as I was beginning to get sleepy after another heavy meal.

"So, I was talking about learning cooking from my mother as she was a most unique cook. When she fried or grilled beef tournedos (like filet mignon), she would finish off the dish by putting a nob of butter and a splash of white vinegar. Yes, she put this sauce on the beef."

"Mmm, sounds delicious, and your mother's use of vinegar is interesting, too," I said. "Our family used to use vinegar on certain meats, vegetables, and in ham and bean soup. It adds a real piquant but pleasurable flavor."

"I also think," I said, "people used it for centuries before, just in case the meat was not good."

Solange nodded. "I'm sure that was what happened especially before we had good refrigeration."

"Aren't we lucky?" Melody said. She was a lover of our mother's bean soups but was a real carnivore of the family.

"And all this time I thought it was because our mother's side of the family came from Kentucky." I nodded in acknowledgment of our family's tale.

Denis let out an occasional snore from the loft that burst forth every now and again and startled us. We grinned. He was content.

"I'm enjoying hearing about your mother. So, what did your mother most enjoy cooking?" I asked.

"She used to prepare for Mardi Gras a small cake which is called the *Merveille* in Paris, but here in Provence, it is called *d'Oreillette,* which means ear-shaped fritter."

"How interesting," Melody said as we nodded our heads in earnest.

"You see, it is made with simple ingredients such as flour, eggs . . . I don't know how now, but she showed me." She laughed.

"My mother is still alive but very, very tired. Sometimes when she is feeling good, she will say, 'I will do today a cous-cous!' And that will suffice. She is still living in Marseilles. Oui, my mother, my sister, and my daughter carry on the traditions. I don't quite as much! But some holidays, I can't help but be swept up in it with the children."

I stood up and signaled for us to end the conversation as Solange also seemed a bit tired. We also had a drive ahead of us, so after hugs and gratitude, Melody and I headed out the door.

The stories I collected were absolute treasures to me. In fact, they became the basis for me writing my *Savoring the Olde Ways* stories based on the interviews I had completed in people's homes with their own family recipes and traditions.

CHAPTER THIRTY-SIX

The Magical Draw of St. Remy

*H*aving left Bonnieux behind, we drove through the afternoon sun to St. Remy, and to a hotel that had been highly recommended by Lise: Chateau des Alpilles. As we entered through the prominent entry gates and continued up the lengthy drive, one-hundred-year-old plane trees arched over the road, creating a breathtaking canopy of chartreuse green leaves and shimmering sunlight. Yes, an iconic drive within St. Remy, if ever there was one. We pulled up in front of a palatial, albeit five-star hotel, and I felt as if we were royalty coming home. Before us was a grand three-story, ivory-colored manor house with perfect neoclassical proportions. It was breathtaking!

Just as I was thinking these regal thoughts while climbing out of the car, I caught Melody walking through a myriad of round tables with café chairs sprinkled around the entrance, where patrons were leisurely sipping glasses of pastis. She boldly walked through the front door . . . without me! I dashed to keep up.

Melody was already chatting with the receptionist and

arranging for a bell hop to get our bags. I looked around me to find the finely restored period décor along with some contemporary furnishings, gave the public rooms a look of comfort as well as Old World charm.

"So, what do you think?" I asked Melody once she turned to me with our keys. Just then a charming host, Danielle, joined us. Elegant in attire and manner, she began showing us around and explaining some of the history and mystery of this magnificent chateau. She led us to a side room off the lobby and began, "The history of this property spans several centuries, and legend has it that this rural land once belonged to a thirteenth century knight. Although nothing certain can be found to confirm this myth, a cypress tree several hundred years old found on this land attests to the fact that this domain dates to medieval times. Now this building," she said, sweeping her arm about, "was originally built in the mid-1800s by a wealthy family from Arles. It became a rendezvous for famous writers and politicians alike. Great week-long retreats were carried out here with the rich and famous vying for attention with poetry readings, and discussions of every discipline imaginable under the trees in the garden. This was a popular resort for the Romantics." She paused. We sighed appropriately.

"Long after the mansion and gardens fell into disrepair, a mother and daughter team purchased the house in 1979, refurbished it, and turned it into this elegant fifteen room estate, with two outer buildings including a family chapel, a large outdoor swimming pool, tennis courts, and a sauna as some of the amenities carried over from the past. This five-star hotel promises you quiet sophistication."

I mentioned to Danielle that we were here for a culinary tour through Provence.

"Ah," Danielle said, flipping her lovely dark hair over her shoulder, "springtime is particularly an enchanting time here as there's something about dining under the plane trees when it is warm enough, or simply taking a dip in the pool—as it sets the scene for total relaxation and a great atmosphere. We have three dining areas. One is a formal dining room," she said as she led us to the doorway that revealed an elegant room with sweeping floor-to-ceiling draperies, tapestries, full length mirrors in Baroque frames, and a bar at the ready. "We serve meals three times per day, reservations needed for the evening. And in the late spring and summer months, we offer meals outside at the café tables in the front, or at poolside. Our chefs have been with us for many years, and they tend to extoll the culinary wisdom of Provence. So, you will have much to appreciate here."

We walked back into the foyer, and I looked up at a lovely old wooden staircase. It swirled three stories up from the center of the lobby and I immediately realized we would be making a long climb. Ah, but it was worth it.

Our shared room up one flight of stairs was quite large with a couple of twelve-foot-high windows overlooking the gardens. Classic navy-blue Provençal-print draperies graced the windows, and the wallpaper. A large oak table with chairs provided space for in-the-room meals or note taking, and if the spring weather turned cold, a stately white fireplace was the center focus of the far wall. Yes, we felt we had arrived . . . if only for a few fun-packed days.

After the bell hop settled our bags in the room, we ventured out into the park to explore. I was recalling the history we had just been told and was thinking that séances or fairy parties must have taken place under those trees. (Possibly poetry readings would be more accurate.) Indeed, we stumbled across heavy stone benches laid out in a circle, which would have been perfect for performing an ancient ritual.

"This reminds me of the rock garden in the park near our house when we were growing up," I said, excitedly, to Melody. The public park, which was only one block away from our house, had provided our family of seven with hours and hours of enjoyment.

"Exactly! Harmon Park! The stone benches are very similar, and I remember us clambering over the large rocks to find our secret hiding places or racing up the steps of the rock hewn lighthouse."

"Do you remember the streams that ran through the lily ponds, then through the rock that made a perfect sink for washing fairy dishes?" I asked. She nodded her head. Instead of imagining the follies that had happened here several hundred years before with famous authors and poets, we had our own fairy images to apply here. Yes, it was a fit!

We returned to our room, where I caught a quick nap, and Melody wrote notes home, before we dressed for dinner. We had experienced so many lovely dinners on this trip—consumed so many extraordinary foods—would this be any different? I believed Melody would have settled for a bowl of soup in our room, but Lise had arranged our dinner reservation, so we complied. I know; it was difficult!

As advertised in the brochure, the chateau's nighttime menu was both romantic and elegant, not that we needed either. The tables were covered in crisp white linens, with crystal glassware glowing in the candlelight. Speaking of glowing, Melody faced me across the table, and she absolutely glowed— was that from the joy of this vacation together, or because it was about to end? She had entered this tour after a difficult exit from her career, and still was reeling from some of the fall out. It had been good to get away, but I knew she was feeling more than ready to go back and collect her life once again.

The waiters carried trays loaded with exotic-looking cocktails. Others zipped in bearing platters of the most amazing-looking food. Our eyes followed every plate that bypassed us.

"They told us at the front desk that the chateau's cuisine comes from the Mediterranean and Provence, but I wonder how this would be different from other restaurants in the area?" I asked.

Our waiter, named Henri, replied, "As it turns out, we all must stick to the same philosophy about serving the freshest of ingredients in the prime of their season, so many of our choices are literally plucked from the kitchen garden, or brought in from the sea or local butcheries, on a daily basis. Always, olive oils are locally produced, as are wines and olives. You are in the land of plenty, especially during the spring and summer seasons when many of these culinary delights are plentiful."

He took our order for aperitifs and sparkling water, and then came back to describe from the menu what we could not translate on our own.

"The appetizers are unique. We have a Sarasin tartelette filled with violet artichokes and served with a poached egg on top; or green asparagus sautéed with fresh herbs. You could consider roasted shrimp in a Parmesan sauce or even lightly batter-fried zucchini blossoms stuffed with goat cheese; and then there is a real local dish: a mesclun salad mixed with red rice from the Camargue—yes, all local."

Melody and I looked at each other and smiled. We knew what he was talking about—Sarasin tartelettes, roasted shrimp, zucchini blossoms stuffed with goat cheese, and were certain we had become acquainted with the red rice from the nearby Camargue. Oh, we knew our stuff!

Henri continued, "For our seafood lovers among you, sea bass is grilled and served with sautéed vegetables; the monk-fish is baked, with creamed carrots, and roasted fennel-filled gnocchi. For you meat lovers, a marvelous savory pork from Mt. Ventoux is roasted and glazed with honey and rosemary and served with pear confit and asparagus and creamed corn. The beef filet comes to us from Charolais beef, which is one of the best breeds in all of France. It is served with potatoes, onions, and mushroom confit. Are you starving by now?" he asked with a smile. Melody had heard the magic word *boeuf*, and she set her mind on getting back to her Midwest roots.

Surprisingly, we felt as if we were starving—had it been so many hours ago? So we made different choices, so we could share. I was most interested in what the violet artichokes were, so I asked. Henri informed me that they are just like green artichokes except purple. As it turned out, the purple-colored artichokes were called Violet de Provence in France, and Violetta di Provenza in Italy. Some say they have more of a nutty flavor than the green artichokes, and I must agree. But then I live in California and have more of an opportunity to know the subtle differences.

"And the other lovely thing about being a carnivore in Provence," Henri said as he enlightened us, "is that no matter what you order, you get plenty of marvelous vegetables on the side. Our meals are savory, sumptuous, and well balanced."

Oh, Henri was good, we decided. He certainly knew where to capture our interests. And it was through good food. And for me, good wine. With Henri's help, I had fun choosing the wines on my own. Was this the first time?

Sometimes, you dream of sitting in a place as beautiful as the one we were at, and eating foods that would bring memories for years to come. We had been most fortunate, as we had been able to travel together on this culinary extravaganza, so we were rich for just having come back to Provence.

The next morning, we woke up to bright sunshine streaming in through our windows. The desire to jump up and close the draperies so we could sleep in was very tempting. But, once again, we had places to go and people to see.

After a typical Provençal breakfast of bowls of coffee, croissants, jelly, and fresh fruit, we ambled through the vast gardens before finding our car in the car park. The morning was delicious, with birdsong accompanying us as we walked. We then popped into our car and drove back into St. Remy, then turned south toward Les Baux. About a mile or so outside of town and off on the right side of the road we spotted a non-descript gravel parking lot. A small sign indicating The Antiques, an ancient group of structures consisting of a massive stone arch and a mausoleum, sat forlornly in the middle of this well-worn patch. Were these the only visible remnants of the Roman past? We spotted a sign on the other side of the road, which was slightly hidden from sight by bushes and weeds. It was an arrow that led into a steep narrow canyon which, as it turned out, was the entrance to the once-forgotten town of Glanum. We crossed the street and followed a path that led us to a visitors' center and museum. Hurrah! I loved surprises like this! All around us were remnants of a village much older than the Roman structures across the street. We bought a map and guidebook and began climbing through the stones, which led back through time.

I sat down on a stone step to read over some of the history: "The original settlement grew up in the seventh and eight centuries BC around a water source, or a natural spring. Water must have been difficult to find as the Mediterranean lay over fifty-five miles to the south. Inland, like the basalt rocks of the

Alpilles surrounding Les Baux, water was a blessing. As was the tradition, a shrine had been set at that spot by the Glanic people, who worshiped the god, Glan. It was known as the Nymphea!"

Whoa! I thought. "What could that have been like," I said aloud. I looked up to realize Melody had wandered off, and I caught sight of her as she disappeared out of sight. Had she discovered the water source, and the shrine?

I called out to her and heard her voice echo from down in a hole of sorts and discovered her standing next to the water on the bottom step of the Nymphea. *That little Dickens,* I thought. But I scrambled down the worn and uneven steps to join her.

From the photos in the guidebook, we could tell we were standing in the Shrine, which was also part of the temple where religious rites had been performed. No, it was not for washing oneself, or for getting a fresh drink of water. That was a good thing, as the water was brackish. But this was a place that had been used by the Celts, then turned into a monument by the Greeks long before the Romans.

Melody and I sat down on the steps, although they were damp from condensation. "Can you imagine what it was like, Carole? Living in this era, in this place?" I looked at the rough workmanship of the stone walls and steps that surrounded us and considered how tedious it must have been to construct such a place. And to celebrate water—ah, but not to drink it!

Again, I referred to the guidebook. "They were known as a war-like culture that commingled with the Celt-Ligurian peoples who also retained Greek (Phocaeans) influences. Prosperity helped the Glanic people develop the area during the second and first centuries BC. This captured the attention of the Romans who immediately laid claim to the valley and all the infrastructure therein."

All my tiny little brain cells were clicking along contemplating the nature of the Celts, much less the Greeks or the Romans. I had taken some special classes at Stanford about this culture and had always felt the Celts did not receive their just due. Water, for them, was a life force, but didn't the Celts also believe in entering water—as if to enter an otherworld—before coming back again? Oh, my! More than two thousand years of culture lay at our feet, and me with only a scintilla of understanding. I sighed. Melody reached over and patted my knee, then stood up and headed back into the sunlight. Ah, but the sun had disappeared. Clouds were hovering over us, and rain threatened.

Near the fountain were three fragments of columns, this time remains of a Roman temple. An inscription on one of the column parts said that the temple was dedicated to Queen Valetudo, meaning the Queen of Health in Latin. On another block of stone, an inscription mentioned who had this Temple built and, as it turns out, he was the minister of the first Roman Emperor, Augustus. I began to read again.

"Over the next two to three hundred years, the Romans did what they always do: they added to the city with their own brand of architecture—sometimes over the top of those who had come before and sometimes next to it. Another temple was dedicated to the goddess of health by Agrippa and two other temples were dedicated to the ruling family. There was a basilica, plus a room to the right of the sacred spring that was devoted to the cult of Hercules . . . There were swimming pools, hot and cold running baths, a downtown section, and a housing section—all carefully laid out in grid formation." But the historic center represented a society that had long passed. A heavy pall seemed to hang overall.

"Are you keeping up with this, Melody?" Again, I stood up

after completing my nose-to-stone examination. Again, she had escaped to seek out more Roman temples, the forum, and the basilica.

To be honest, it may have been because the day had become grey and drizzly. We were grateful we had remembered our coats. But we would have given our kingdom for a colorful umbrella. Yes, the mood of the valley seemed gloomy, indeed. Then, as we passed one of the smaller swimming pools en route to the cantina, we came to a surprising sight: at least four to five dozen bright silver helium-filled balloons, in all different sizes, lay at the bottom of the empty pool. Why were they there? It was as if they were awaiting a prescheduled pool party!

Over lunch at the cantina, we asked one of the servers about the silver balls, and he laughed. "This was part of the celebration for the year 2000! Year 2000!" He thought there were ongoing celebrations for this occasion as it marked more than the year but an acknowledgment of how old Glanum was.

After cups of hot tea and warming bowls of soup, we headed back down the path toward the car. Ah! But we got waylaid when we saw signs pointing across an adjacent field. No, there were no paths! But that didn't hold Melody back! She began tramping across the weeds in the field, as if she had done this dozens of times. But there was some other bee in her bonnet! She had determined that through the field was a special museum of sorts, and she was bound and determined to discover it.

When we finally stepped out of the bramble field, we found ourselves on a well-trodden road lined with olive and pine trees. Yellow fields of sunflowers peeked out from the back and side of an austere-looking building. The rains, which had finally stopped, sent a cleansing, yet woodsy fragrance into the air. Was that a greeting? Yet I feared we had trespassed.

Melody, on the other hand, walked past a sign that announced what she had suspected: this was the famous asylum, Maison de Sante St. Paul, or the Monastery of Saint-Paul de Mausole. Yes, the very asylum where Van Gogh had spent a year or more after attempting to cut off his own ear.

The massive building was a twelfth century monastery, which had been established by the Franciscan monks and later converted into a psychiatric asylum in 1605. We walked up the steps, entered between the columns and through the arched doorway, where we were warmly received by the nuns. I didn't know what I expected as I had just traipsed through several millennia of history before crossing that field, and who knew what this place could possibly contain?

Having been given a map of the grounds and a bit of the history, they handed us an English-only guide and pointed us in the direction of the cloister. Hadn't we just spent time in another cloister? Ah, yes, the day before yesterday at the Abbaye de Senanque. We were allowed to take the tour on our own, including the rooms of those who had been patients. We climbed the steep uneven steps to the very room where Van Gogh had spent a year healing and painting.

The rooms were stark. And some appeared to be quite grim, especially when we understood what medical procedures had taken place there. But Van Gogh was self-admitted, so his stay at the facility had not been mandatory. I stepped over to the window near the single metal bed (also one of his famous paintings) and peered out to see what his view must have been. It was then that I finally understood his artistic style, and why Melody had been such an admirer of his work.

You know those simplistic-looking lines in his paintings, those splashes of paint that might remind you of the paintings of a child? Well, as it turned out those mountains—the

Alpilles—outside his window looked exactly like that, and you could see this rendition in his painting called *Olive Trees*. During his stay he was very productive and created many paintings, including *The Starry Night over the Rhône, Saint-Paul Asylum, Saint-Rémy*, the *Iris* series, and some paintings from nearby fields.

We continued our tour through the rooms of the second-floor museum, while reading notes on the years of care. There were lists and photos of specific treatments, along with lists of doctors who had worked at the facility.

"Why, is that Albert Schweitzer's name on this list of resident doctors?" Melody asked me.

"Do you mean the same Albert Schweitzer who worked as a missionary in Africa?" I asked. My face squinched up with skepticism. I looked around for someone to ask, but then most of them spoke little English, so I would continue to wonder. But, as it turned out, yes, he interned in that facility to become a doctor during the Great War.

Melody and I made our way back down the steps to the open gardens in the cloister. The drizzle had continued to fall, and crystalline droplets had formed on the petals of the climbing roses. The cloister garden was shaped in the same manner as the one at Abbaye de Senanque, so we understood that this area had been a place of meditation and prayer—since the eleventh century. I couldn't help but consider all the people who frequented these now-soaked benches over the years. And I hoped their prayers had been answered.

Goodness! What a day! Beginning in the fairy gardens of Chateau des Alpilles, then roaming through the ancient Celts and Romans in Glanum, then finding traces of Van Gogh's life left us a bit gloomy. We headed into the village of St. Remy to have an early dinner. We supped at Restaurant La Cassolette, not because it was recommended, but because it was close to where we parked. But the food was good and hearty and not so much on the gourmet side of French food. We had eaten so many star-rated meals, we just wanted something simple, like steak and frites! Like I said, we're carnivores from Nebraska; what else can you expect?

We drove back to the hotel to enjoy a glass of wine in the lounge. Then headed up the steps early to snuggle down and enjoy our room and to read. Something we had had little time to do on this trip. But no matter how much time Melody and I had together, we always found something to talk about. So, the books were set aside for our long flights home, and we talked late into the night. Some things never change between sisters!

CHAPTER THIRTY-SEVEN

Marseilles and Beyond

"Aioli intoxicates gently, fills the body with warmth, and
the soul with enthusiasm. In its essence it concentrates the
strength, the gaiety of Provence: sunshine."
—FREDERIC MISTRALE

The following morning, we dillydallied through
breakfast, which was served in the garden. Then, after
we had packed up our room and were waiting for our car to be
brought around, we walked past the family chapel and through
the forest for one last time. The word "touchstone" came to
mind as I recalled touching an aged-old tree stump, the hun-
dred-year-old stone wall, the hefty stone bench, and even the
lacy fronds of Queen Anne's Lace in the fairy garden as a
farewell. *I'll be back,* I said to myself. *I'll be back.*

It was late morning when we finally began our drive to
Marseilles, with me back at the wheel. We would be staying
one last night at the airport hotel after dropping off our car,
but until then we still longed to see the sights of Provence. It
must have been as we drove through the center of the village
of Mouriès that we were stopped in the middle of the street.

Husky men were racing around hefting and heaving a large banner up and over our heads. The white banner, once in place, stretched from one side of the roadway to the other and high above the traffic. I eased the car forward as Melody and I attempted to read the French words on the sign. Obviously, we struggled. Something about *Cours de Taureau*, which had the image of a large black bull charging down the street.

"What do you think that means?" I asked Melody, as the traffic eased beneath the sign. Melody swiveled in her seat and whirled back around again.

"Step on it!" she shrilled. "I believe the sign says something about the running of the bulls. And I don't know when that is to take place!" Without further ado, we roared out of town, daring not to look back!

Marseilles is a Mediterranean port city with an immense history that reached back farther than the Greek settlers from Phocaea around 600 BC. It was known for being the oldest city in France and one of Europe's oldest continuously inhabited settlements. Known by the ancient Greeks as Massalia and the Romans as Massilia, the history speaks of the wonder of the Mediterranean and how people from distant lands learned to navigate those waters so many centuries ago.

Of course, my love of the Rhône River, which was one of the only highways into Gaul long ago, also gave us a clear picture of how not only people, but traditions and cultural foods became part of the Provençal palette. And Marseilles played a part in all this wonder.

Melody and I dropped off our luggage at the airport hotel and headed into the city. Yes, it was immense, busy, and we were not used to the car, much less the directions on the map. We found our way to the center of town near the old port, or Vieux-Port, where the fish mongers were busy selling the daily catch and the fishing boats and sailboats competed for dock space. I pulled into a parking garage like I knew what I was doing, and Melody and I quickly walked over and joined a line for one of our favorite modes of transportation, Le Petit Train. This would be a great way for us to tour the major sights of this fair city.

"I don't know if you remember," I said as we stood in our queue, "but when I was in high school, I was able to take a correspondence course in French from the University of Nebraska. The high school arranged for this special course, even though the high school only offered Spanish. Even back then, I wanted to learn French." Again, Melody smiled.

"Yes, I do remember. I think your love of all things French came from our cousins who lived in Paris, right?" This time I grinned. She was right.

"But my point is, the high school also arranged for a French tutor, Gabrielle Cogswell, or Gaby, to work with me in her home every week. She was a French World War I war bride and a complete delight. Anyway, she grew up here in Marseilles. So, as I look around these neighborhoods, I can't help but think of her. I can almost envision her playing ball with her brothers and zipping out of the way of the few cars or trams on the road at that time. I remember her telling me of her good childhood and her love of Marseilles, even though, when given the opportunity, she quickly married a US soldier and went home with him to Nebraska."

"I think I remember her," Melody said to me. "She was very sweet; a gentle person, and, as I recall, very short like me!"

I laughed, "Yes, I don't think she made it to five feet tall, but her heart was big. You know, I remember taking my weekly lessons at her kitchen table. There I would sit with my sack lunch as dinner and we would work together through the con-

ADVENTURES by LAND and SEA

jugation of French verbs and the study of a language of the
people I would, decades later, write about with great admira-
tion and joy. I loved it! I felt empowered!"

Melody was patient with my recollections. She knew Gaby
had been important to me, even though she had been far away
at college at the time.

"I remember some of the stories she told of Marseilles," I
said, "of being a teenager herself during World War I and of
having been swept off her feet by an American GI. As I mentioned, after the war, he brought her to his hometown of
Central City, Nebraska where she made her new husband
proud by painstakingly learning English and embracing the
town he loved.

"I remember asking her how she managed to live in a
town where no one spoke French. She told me she had a great
incentive: to please her husband whom she adored. Anyway, I
also asked her what differences she found between the two
cultures, especially at the time the US was racing to prepare for
World War II.

"'I recall one incident in particular,' Gaby had answered,
'that struck me as a significant difference.' She paused to shove
her little glasses onto her nose. 'The US had just been attacked
at Pearl Harbor, but this country had never had war on its
shores like in France. Because the Allies had been the same in
both our World Wars, I expected the preparation to have been
like what I remembered from Marseilles.'

"I recall she sat back in her chair, with her finger pressing
gently on the handle of her coffee cup. As her wrinkled finger
traveled around and around the loop of the cup handle, I was
reminded of our Swedish grandmother who often did her best
thinking in this manner." Melody smiled.

"Gaby then spoke: 'I was happening through the Central

City town square one day in 1944, I believe, when locals began arriving with armloads of books—books that were either written about Germany or written in German. They were collected from their homes, their personal libraries, and from the schools.' She described a determined but wild-eyed frenzy exhibited by the people she had come to know as friends. As soon as a pile of books was amassed, the books were set on fire. All semblance of German culture was systematically erased. Even those locals who were of German heritage felt the pressure to burn their own books. Bibles that had been so cherished from their families in Germany were placed on the pyre. And she sadly shook her head, from side to side.'

"'Did this surprise you?' I asked her. I remember not being clear about the message she was sharing. 'Wasn't this something all countries did as they prepared to face their enemy?' I had asked.

"*Mon Dieu, non*! Absolutely not! In France, that was the time we were taught to draw those books to us, and to learn, learn, learn! We were told to absorb everything we could to better understand our enemy: how they thought and what their beliefs, culture and history were. We learned early, you should never fight a people or a culture without understanding their ultimate goals. That's one of the reasons I teach French,' she said to me as she reached out for my hand.

"'Carole,' she said, 'remember, one of the most important gifts of learning a new language is not just to speak the words fluently, but to gain an appreciation and understanding of other people.'"

Melody said, "I do remember her and I think I met her during one of your lessons. But thanks for telling me her story, especially as we are here to enjoy her city." She took her turn to climb into the little train, with me clamoring in behind. The train wound blithely through the city streets before climbing up to the top of the steepest hill known as the Garde. Again, my thoughts were on Gaby. Sadly, I didn't do as she asked; I didn't learn the French language well. My shoulders slumped.

The Basilique Notre-Dame-de-la-Garde, which crowned the hill, was easily recognized by all the people of Marseilles and can be seen from any location within their fair city: From the Vieux-Port to the surrounding islands of Frioul; from the Tower of the Fort Saint Jean to the hills of Aubagne; and even while sailing along the Mediterranean.

The familiar shape of the basilica, known as the Bonne Mère or Good Mother, was built in the Romanesque-Byzantine style made up of a lower church with an arched vault, and a higher church that included the sanctuary consecrated to the Virgin Mary. The black and white striped pillars, domes, and stone polychrome golds were topped with a golden statue of Mary, Mother of God, holding her Son as she showed Him to the world from their lofty position.

We climbed out of the train to take in the panoramic view. As one could imagine, it was breathtaking. Why, we could *almost* see the roads that led back up to the hills and villages of Provence.

Suddenly, we were bustled into the sanctuary with a large tour group. But we found it was hot, stifling even, with all those bodies in such close proximity. We realized we had visited a great many churches on this trip and, frankly, we must have been toured out. We couldn't stand still one moment longer in the heat, even to appreciate one more religious relic.

We made our way back out of the church and onto the waiting train and headed back down the long hill. Despite bouncing over cobblestones in the streets, it was just relaxing as the cooling breeze wrapped around us, which felt oh, so marvelous.

We made our way back to the Vieux Port for lunch and if there was ever a call for lunch, it was the aroma of garlic wafting over the entire square. Of course, I had no choice but to indulge in Marseillaise's house specialty: the garlicky, saffron-infused fish stew known as bouillabaisse. Of all the dishes I had eaten over the course of our three-week trip, this one was filled with all the savory and briny goodness of the sea. For me, this was a rare bonus. The dish included both fish and shellfish, plus olive oil, onions, tomatoes, garlic, parsley, saffron, fennel, thyme, bay leaf, and orange peel. It was a meal that could easily accommodate two! But in this case, Melody preferred to indulge in a *pissaladière*, a pizza with caramelized onions, black niçoise olives, and garlic. But please hold the anchovies, and instead, layer on the grated Parmesan and Gruyère cheeses. *She was getting her verve back!*

If we learned anything about the foods of the Provençal people, it was that they embraced all the many fruits of their blessed earth and sea. And I'm sure that they must also abide by the old adage, "If you feed your babies garlic, you can find them in the night!" Our husbands would definitely know of our arrival the following day long before they set eyes on us!

We drove back to the airport to turn in our rental car and gathered our key for the hotel room. We were worn out but felt we had used our time wisely. Walking down the lobby hallway, Melody spotted a shop that sold suitcases. Her suitcase was coming apart at the seams.

"Does this have anything to do with the full-size iron you've been traveling with?" I asked her with a smirk.

She began to giggle, and then we both began to chortle, and we were doubled over with laughter, when tears began to stream down our faces. Hanging onto the wall of the luggage shop for support, we tried to right ourselves, although we were still blocking the entrance to the shop. Finally, the luggage clerk popped her head out the door and asked if we wanted to come in. We nodded, yes, but had not contained ourselves yet to figure out an answer—in any language. I indicated that we would be right there by raising my index finger, and then wondered if that gesture, too, was translatable to what I meant. She nodded in her best French possible, and we finally made our way into the shop where Melody purchased a fine, much larger suitcase in which she could haul her Provençal treasures plus her iron.

That evening we ordered room service and settled in for our last night in Provence. As always, we had much to talk about.

"So, Melody," I asked her, "what would you say was your favorite part of this trip? I know you enjoyed the camaraderie with the other troopers on our tour. You're always so much better at mixing with new people than I."

Melody sat back on her plumped-up pillows creating a nest on the bed, while sipping a cup of green tea (was that a sprig of lavender on the side?). She said, "I did enjoy getting to know them. I think the connection to those lovely ladies and Russ made the trip all the richer."

"And I get to see many of them when I return home, which will be so nice," I said. I lazed back in the only chair in the hotel room, and we began recalling some of the fun memories we had shared all together: Getting to know each other at Alain Ducasse's bastide in Moustiers, getting caught in the rain at the ceramic factory, tromping through the flower market in Aix-en-Provence; laughing with and at all of the antics of misunderstanding of French in each of the cooking classes, almost getting trampled by the horses in Arles by the Gardiens; digging into the cooking at the amazing class given in the Roman stable. Then there was the class in Les Baux held at La Riboto de Taven and learning of the culture of the witch that lived in those caves. So many memories, but all of them included the constant language of nodding, bobbing, and smiling to make up for our lack of language.

"But, for me," I said, "I think it was meeting many of the locals: whether it was patient Timon, our stalwart van driver, or the chefs in the cooking classes, or simply attempting to carry on a conversation in a restaurant or in the hotels. And there were our lovely tour guides who put up with our antics. And dear Denis and Solange Brihat, who gave us so much of themselves through her sharing of traditional food memories and his talents in photography . . ."

"And, we can't forget Sharon and dear Lise," Melody said. "Those two pulled together a mighty fine culinary tour and we were the richer for the experience." I nodded in agreement.

"And then," Melody said, "there was our mad hatters dash this morning when we realized mad bulls were threatening to run," Melody said with a guffaw. I laughed, as it was one more time our lack of language *could* have jeopardized us.

"Do you want to come back to Provence again?" I asked Melody.

"In a heartbeat, dear sis! In a heartbeat!" She stood up from her pillow nest and came to my chair to give me a long hug. Yes, we would be back!

THIRD TRIP *to* PROVENCE, June 2006

THE GRAND CREW
or
GRAND CRU

CHAPTER THIRTY-EIGHT

A Sailing Journal Revealed:
A Perspective of Two

The following journal was written by my husband, Winston, revealing his plan and after the completion of sailing along the Côte d'Azur. His words are italicized. But it was also my dream so I couldn't help but pop into his journal to tell you the whole story. Be advised. This is a 'He said, she said' type of story, with added comments from our passengers. Enjoy! C.B.

I have always dreamed of sailing in the Mediterranean with good friends. In June 2006, that dream came true. The idea to take this trip began while I was reading a US Sailing newsletter when I should have been working. I saw a small announcement that stated if you had the required US Sailing certifications you could send in an application, along with a passport photo and twenty-five dollars. Then, you would receive a document stating that you were a certified helmsman in Mediterranean waters. So having all the required certifications, I sent a passport photo, the application, and the requisite twenty-five bucks to US Sailing and received my secret decoder ring, the certificate. It looked like a passport and was authorized by US Sailing and recognized by the EU. W. Bumpus

Winston's dream of sailing along the Côte d'Azur began the first time we set foot in Nice, France, ten years before. It was our first foray into Provence, and we experienced a sprinkling of time in the mountains, on beaches, visiting wineries, and tromping around in search of Roman ruins. But I must confess, Winston's heart and mind were always far out at sea. And on the days when I spent hours basking on the beaches improving my tan, he spent time under the beach umbrella dreaming of the day . . . the day when he could take a sailboat out on those azure blue waters. Oh, yes, this was the beginning of a grown man's most ultimate dream. Oh and I must tell you, it was like an itch that needed to be scratched. The wheels in his head began churning. Charts were ordered, and plans were hatched.

Once I received it, my next question was where to sail and when. I had purchased a 38' Hunter sailboat in 2001 while living in the San Francisco Bay area, and had moved it to Lake Travis in Austin, Texas in 2003, so surely, I had earned my stripes. I had also chartered boats from Moorings Yacht Charters before, and I knew what a first-class operation they ran. So, I began looking at their website while dreaming of trips I could take. What jumped out at me was a one-week trip out of Nice, France. We would sail west along the Côte d'Azur on a one-way journey, from Nice to Hyeres.

Once I figured out where to sail, I needed to think about the most important part. Who would be the perfect crew? My wife, Carole, was up for it. And we had gotten to know and include a dear French couple, Laurent and Karyn Foucher, as part of our sailing adventures while living in Austin, Texas. We had sailed together on our Hunter 360, and they were very capable sailors. We had done several overnight trips and regattas together on the boat and had always enjoyed their skills as well as the camaraderie. But they had moved back to France, and we missed them so. W. Bumpus

Yes, this seemed like a dream come true for both of us, as we both had longed to sail along the French coast. You see, I, too, enjoyed sailing, but this was something I had never considered. But now? Would we? Could we?

The Fouchers were a delightful French couple, a tad younger than us, but that was a plus. They would have more energy and strength, I figured. And, like Winston had written, we had thoroughly enjoyed our time together.

Then, I thought, wouldn't it be great to sail with them again? And wouldn't it be handy to have some French native tongues on board to help converse with the harbor masters, and in figuring out the various systems? W.B.

Yes, as much as we liked to pretend we could speak French, we still only had a smattering of one-liners, like *Ou est la toilette?* (Where is the toilet?) or *L 'addition, s'il vous plait* (The check, please). But if anyone had given us instructions in French, we would have fallen into a fetal position and whimpered. Well, maybe I would, anyway!

I then thought about another dear friend and business associate, Jim Turner, who had just announced he was getting a permanent hall

pass and was retiring from his career at Cisco. He and his wife, Sandy, were also sailors, although they were classic wooden boat day sailors. Cruising would be new to them, but I knew they would be a terrific addition to our crew. W.B

I was thrilled about inviting them too! We had also spent some marvelous time with Sandy and Jim at their home on Martha's Vineyard and Winston had enjoyed sailing with Jim on his little Herreshoff 12 1/2, so I knew they had a heart for sailing. Do you know what it is like when you meet someone, and you immediately click with them? For me, that was my relationship with Sandy. And for Winston, he felt the same about Jim.

I picked a date in the middle of June as I thought the weather would be good and I also thought it would be a time when the marinas and anchorages would not be so crowded. As it turned out, everyone's schedule was open, and boats were available, so we had what I called a Grand Crew. It would be the six of us.

Next, we selected the boat, and what a boat it was. The Moorings had a great boat for three couples, a Moorings 443. This was a beautiful 44-foot mono hull with three cabins, each with their own head and shower. It was perfect and brand new. W.B.

Can you imagine all the fun just picking out a boat? We were like kids drooling over our choices of Baskin-Robbins ice cream. But to have room enough for each couple on board, which normally can be a cramped space, was a true step up in our boating world.

In early January 2006 everything was set, and the boat was re-served. I ordered all the charts and books I could find on the region. The Rod Heikell book Mediterranean France and Corsica *was wonderful, with diagrams and aerial photographs of most harbors. The book was filled with great information on everything from food, weather, harbor facilities, along with phone numbers and VHF channels for the various ports. I also ordered the three British Admiralty charts, 2165, 2166, and 2167. This gave me plenty of information for planning purposes as I dreamed of our upcoming trip. And all in English!*

I also chose the Moorings' one-way option that, for a small additional fee, afforded us the ability to travel one-way down the coast, starting in Nice and ending our trip a week later at the port in Hyères, about 100 miles down the coast. W.B.

At this point, I remember Winston and I perused the charts, and we began noticing the names of familiar places like Nice, Frèjus, St. Maxime, St. Tropez, and Porquerolles, as these were cities in which we had spent time during our first trip to Provence.

CHAPTER THIRTY-NINE

Day of Reckoning!
Nice, France

"... For me, upon the sea of history,
Thou wast, Provence, a pure symbol
A mirage of glory and victory
That in the dusky Flight of centuries
Grants us a gleam of the Beautiful."

—FREDERIC MISTRAL

We all six met up in Nice, France. It was mid-June on the Friday night before we were to gain possession of the boat, and Winston was excited, but also a bit nervous. He did overthink these things! Bless him! Fortunately, we had time to gather ourselves after our overseas flight. Or so we thought!

As our taxi pulled up in front of the Park Hotel near Old Nice, we stepped out to be greeted by our friends who had already arrived and were waiting to welcome us! Wild shouts and mad bellows arose from two different balconies, where our Grand Crew stood. Suddenly the two couples, who had never met before, turned on their balcony to see who else was greeting us. This, as it turned out, was their first meeting. The excitement rose.

Karyn and Laurent Foucher, who live in western France, had been the first to arrive by train, but not before they had taken their two young daughters across country to stay with grandparents. No trip is without tangled arrangements.

Jim and Sandy Turner, who had been spending a few days in the Marais District of Paris, had also traveled down on the TGV to join us. This was their first trip to Provence, and the first time they had traveled to the French Riviera. I believe Sandy was almost giddy with excitement. She confided in me later that standing on the balcony overlooking the sea was the first of many experiences she thought had come right out of the movies.

"Like Winston always wanting to sail the Med," she said, "since childhood I've always envisioned myself on the Med in the same way as I had seen in Cary Grant movies. Of course, there's a bit of a disconnect with that vision, as he was with Grace Kelly or a Bond Girl, rather than, well, me." She paused. "Though this fantasy is no longer what it once was, what was left of it was all about to begin," she laughed.

We had arranged for all six of us to stay in the Park Hotel in Nice, as that was where we had begun our first Provençal trip in 1997. We had chosen it for convenience, as it was located only a block from the Côte d'Azur, within walking distance of Old Nice, and was within a short drive to the Nice public marina. But also because the rooms were gorgeous, both the bedroom and bathroom were spacious and the balconies, which were wrapped with beautiful black wrought iron, as the other couples were already finding out.

After quickly settling our bags into our room, we all met up in the lounge for a drink, where introductions flowed like the wine we were being served. Everyone was so excited to finally be together and happy to be a part of this *grande* adventure. Within minutes, it felt like a connection had been made between us all. Winston looked at me, smiled, and lifted his glass. "We did it, kiddo," he said. "We are finally here with our Grand Crew!" We all lifted our glasses in salute. Tchin-tchin!

Weaving personalities together with six people, four of whom had never met, was never an easy feat. It could either make or break a vacation. Especially if you were in confined spaces, like a . . . a sailboat for a week. But we hit the mother lode with these friends. All were like wiggly little puppies with anticipation of going to the dog park, but in this case, it was to hop on a sailboat and sail for a week.

As Winston mentioned before, we had met Karyn and Laurent while living in Austin, Texas. They, too, had been transferred to Texas because of work, and had joined the Austin Yacht Club for the same reason we chose; for the love and fun of sailing and for the camaraderie that was always available. Laurent had grown up sailing on the Bay of Biscay in Brittany, so he was a thoroughly seasoned sailor. The waters off that coast were bitterly cold and the winds were merciless. Karyn was raised in Le Havre on the English Channel, and only knew cold water sailing. So when they arrived in Texas, both were introduced to waters that were so warm, that they couldn't help but fling themselves off the boat, especially to cool off during those sizzling hot summer months.

We had brought our 38-foot Hunter all the way from San Francisco, and we made the same discovery: our boat actually had a swim ladder. This was a concept that I had never considered—for the same reasons the Fouchers had not. So we laughed about those memories as we geared up to testing out the temperatures of the Mediterranean waters soon.

Jim had been born and raised in Texas and mostly knew warm water sailing. But Sandy had grown up in Marin County north of the Golden Gate Bridge, where the cold fog chilled the air and water. Sailing for her did not begin until the two moved to their summer home in Martha's Vineyard.

After an hour or more catching up, we all realized how famished we were, so we began strolling through the park and down the streets together to Old Nice. I noticed how gloriously beautiful the weather was. The air that early evening was humid and warm, but just enough to be pleasurable. And as we locked arms together, we wandered along those age-old streets and allées of Old Nice, the Cours Saleya. It was an exciting way to get acquainted, and all three couples instantly came together. The famous farmers and flower markets were closed for the day, but the streets were filled with children of all ages kicking and bouncing soccer balls with reckless abandon. It was that special time of year for the World Cup and all things soccer, or football, as they say, were filling the heads and streets of the locals. Televisions in nearby bars were blaring game results and the sound of the roars, which swept out to greet us, was joyous!

As we moseyed up and down the thoroughfare eyeing one outdoor restaurant or bistro after another, our own personal favorites were lobbed into the mix of options. If ever there was a sublime way to get to know one another, it was within the sharing of ideas of your favorite foods.

Finally, we all voted to eat the first of many shared meals at a restaurant known as Le Monde du Moules, or the World of Mussels. We feasted on six different varieties of the same thing! Moules et frites, moules in marinara sauce, moules in white wine and garlic sauce, moules in saffron sauce, moules in wine sauce over pasta, oh my! And all were sopped up with large chunks of crusty—yes, French bread. My choice, which I believe was the best, was pasta with moules in a saffron sauce! *Délicieuse!*

After our main course was finished, and in between bottles of shared wine and dessert, we women noticed an art market forming in between the restaurants and cafés. I believe my husband was surprised when I returned—on the first night of our trip—with two gorgeous but large watercolor prints of local seaside villages.

"How could I resist?" I asked him. "This one is of the very village that enticed us to sail the Côte d'Azur in the first place: Villefranche-sur-Mer!"

"But, of course," he responded as he launched into the telling of the lovely coastal village we visited only a few miles to the east of us in Nice.

"After our two weeks' time spent in Provence, on our last day Carole and I decided to drive to the edge of the French Riviera; just before we would cross the border into Italy. We had had a seaside lunch at a charming restaurant . . ."

"Of which," I put in, "he sat facing the steep cliffs and mountains of Italy, while I, contently, faced back toward Nice. It wasn't until after almost a two-hour lunch, that he decided to change seats with me, so," he had said, "I could see the view! As I sat down opposite him once more, I realized the three young bare-breasted women had been lazing out on chaise directly behind my chair. Now, he says . . ."

"Oh, it wasn't two hours," Winston stammered. Somehow, this discussion will never find agreement, but we both laughed at the retelling.

"But what does this have to do with this little coastal village in your painting?" Sandy asked.

"Ah, so," Winston continued, "following lunch we drove through the decadent city of Monte Carlo, and passed the

Royal Palace of Monaco, before heading back on the road toward Nice. It was then that we decided to turn off the highway once again to visit Villefranche-sur-Mer."

"This coastal village," I put in, "is noted for not only its beauty and wealth, but is also famous for having one of the deepest harbors in the area." The men nodded at the importance of a deep harbor. Too many times stuck in low waters could bring about that appreciation.

Winston continued the story, "We threaded our way down the steep, winding streets, found parking, and began a walk along the harbor. Like a magnet I was drawn to the water."

"Yes," I chimed back in, "the pull of the beauty within the charming harbor directed our steps. We followed along the port, once again enjoying the lift and bob of the boats along with the clang of the halyards against the masts. I knew Winston could never get enough! And I knew more sailing lessons were in his future."

"That's for sure," Winston said. "This was in 1997, and I bought our boat, *Dolci Sogni,* in 2001."

"Ah, yes," Jim said, "I believe you invited us to your birthday that year in Sausalito, and it was the first time we saw your boat."

"And," Sandy said, "that was the first time I met you, Carole!"

I beamed. "All for the love of boats!" I said, "and we are all the richer for these connections."

"Hear! Hear!" Laurent piped in, and "Tchin! Tchin!" we all said as we lifted our glasses.

"So, like I said, Winston," as I brought the topic back around, "when I saw this print, I couldn't resist!" He smiled sweetly and said, "I know!"

Sandy, who had also purchased a couple of smaller prints, changed the subject by stating, "This evening sets the stage for our many upcoming dinners, hopefully at outdoor restaurants in large village squares shared with other restaurants. I'm so enjoying the live music, the twinkle lights lighting the dark, plus all this camaraderie." Yes, we were going to have a great time together.

"Mais oui! This makes me so 'appy," Karyn said, speaking English with her lovely French lilt. "I am loving getting to know y'all. Oh, and tomorrow I have so many ideas for food for our boat."

That's what I loved about friends. They ate food together, they talked over food, and then they discussed what their next meals would be! *Ah, mais necessaire!*

After we completed our dinner, we continued to wander through the streets, as they were alive with activity, and we were not ready to return to the hotel. I believe it was midnight when we ended the evening with limoncello as a nightcap. At least for some of us! The camaraderie especially among the men had become fluid.

"Ah, remember London?" Jim asked Winston while lifting his glass of limoncello. The two laughed as they told of some others on a particular business trip, who had truly succumbed to the delectable, yet insidiously potent, drink.

Winston laughed and repeated the mantra that we learned when first sampling limoncello in Florence. "Just make sure you are within crawling distance of your bed. It's that potent!"

It was then that, I believe, Laurent began telling one of his funny little stories—probably about bouts of drinking. "Pastis is like that; maybe not as deadly as the Green Fairy, or absinthe," he began as the evening slipped into morning. When Laurent begins a story, you can't help but stick around, as they were not to be missed. With each of us leaning into the story, Sandy mused, "Isn't it nice to sit and savor this magical experience?" And savor we did!

CHAPTER FORTY

The Dream Begins

"People who love to eat are always the best people."
—JULIA CHILD

The next morning, Saturday, after a continental breakfast at the hotel, we strolled to old Nice again, and through their farmers and flower markets, which were, at that point, up and running. The booths were filled with a vast array of olives, cheeses, fruits, meats, seafood, and stalls of beautiful flowers. This was the joy of being in the South of France with all these fresh foods readily available. In earnest, we shopped for boat supplies (which meant wine) and included a wonderful selection of olives, olive oil, tapenade, an array of local cheeses, fresh baguettes, and other delicacies, as we wanted to be well provisioned for our sailing adventure. It would not be long before we were stepping aboard, Grand Cru. W.B.

Ah, yes, the morning was filled with golden diffused light that wafted off the Baie des Anges nearby and greeted me where I stood on the balcony for one last look. This was the day! Everyone was feeling at their best and energized to start the trip. Despite our jet lag, we were determined to keep up. Our foray through the color-filled flower, spice, fresh fruit, and produce markets was so photogenic, it was difficult to put down our cameras and get down to the business of selecting our choices for the trip. We sampled one of the famous Niçoise specialties, *la socca*, which is like a giant pizza but made with ground chickpea flour, olive oil, and salt. The mildly nutty aroma that floated off the *socca* was a call enough to sample, as it was sautéed in a frying pan right below our noses.

We then quickly zipped back to the hotel to pack and before we knew it, we had loaded ourselves and our bags into two taxis. While driving east down the Promenade des Anglais to the Vieux Port, we passed the enormous Monument aux Morts Memorial, a monument to those who had died during WWI. I tried to catch a real glimpse of it, but we whipped around the corner, and before I knew it, we had piled out of the taxis and onto the dock of the harbor.

At the Moorings facility in the Old Port, Winston ventured into their office and within moments, we were warmly greeted and directed to the boat we had chartered. Like Winston had said, it was a Moorings 443 sailboat called Grand Cru. It was perfect in every respect, including the name. Grand Cru refers to a classification in wine of the most superior grade. The boat was brand new, like advertised, and was more spacious than we expected. It looked to be perfect for us three couples, just as we had hoped.

"What could be better than having dual helms," Winston gushed, "and seating for six in the cockpit under a large Bimini with a connected dodger?"

Dual helms means two steering wheels, and the cockpit is where everyone sits on deck during the time of sailing. The Bimini, which is a canvas that acts as a roof, is handy to avoid rain or too much sun. We had learned this the hard way while sailing in Texas. And a dodger is the all-important windshield. Plus, we had been told the elements on the Côte d'Azur could become extreme—such as rain and the fierce winds of the Mistral.

Now, the cockpit. This was the place we would share every snack, meal, and glass of wine, morning coffee, or croissant, when the weather was good! Ah, yes, life was going to be sweet! Yes, there was a lovely galley and salon below, but why be inside when the weather was beautiful?

We tested out the cockpit by having a picnic with sandwiches. Thank goodness one of us had had the presence of mind to think ahead. Then Winston went back to the office to do the necessary paperwork and to discuss our sailing plan. They were very organized, and everything was done professionally, but it helped that Win brought along Laurent, in case he needed help with translations. Thankfully, Win said later, their English was excellent. Ah, but Laurent provided moral support and possibly a much-needed crutch. This would be the first of many times Laurent would be called upon.

In the meantime, Sandy stood up and announced, "While the boys are outfitting the boat, it's time for us to outfit the galley." She said that with such panache! I loved that, and even though she probably had never outfitted a galley before, she was correct. We ladies grabbed our purses, checked for appropriate credit cards, and abandoned Jim on board to keep watch over the boat. With the assistance of Niccolo of the Moorings, we were shuttled off to a nearby grocery store to purchase the additional provisions. Yes, a full week's worth!

Now, I had done this before when we sailed in the BVI, and it was always a fun but daunting process, but you must be stout of heart. Every country has its own way of setting up their stores. That included how they cut their meats, displayed their produce, arranged the canned foods, and more. You must cast aside your thoughts of what might be found in the US as you are not in Kansas anymore. You need to adapt to the products available. And, of course, none of them were familiar, plus we couldn't read the labels anyway! Ah, but good luck to us! Or, in this case, *bon chance,* because this was where our dear heart, Karyn, truly shone. She was French and, yes, she spoke the language! Score!

We entered the grocery store, known as the *épicerie,* which was dark and quaint, yet crowded. I had expected us each to take a shopping cart and head off in different directions, our provision's list divided into three. But Karyn was at the ready and wanted to lead the charge. So Sandy and I scoped out each aisle, then reported back to Karyn to alert her where certain items, like fresh fruits and vegetables, were located.

We also needed dry goods, like boxes of rice, pasta, and couscous—yes, you must have plenty of couscous and other specialty canned goods. Karyn insisted! We both walked around the store looking for boxes of couscous, but no, we were not even close. Suddenly, Karyn popped up at our sides and shoved a couple of hearty cans of . . . yes, couscous, in our faces.

"You won't be disappointed," she said to us. "Trust me!" And then she pivoted off down the aisle searching for pâtés and eggs.

"Oh, I thought that was a can of pork and beans," Sandy whispered to me. We giggled; yes, we did have a lot to learn. But we were having such fun, as it was much like a scavenger hunt blindfolded. Even though neither Sandy nor I had ever heard of many of these items, we followed Karyn's instructions and tossed them willy-nilly into the baskets. And then, of course, we needed to get plenty of coffee for the French press coffee pot, plus tea, spices, beer, soda, wine, and a whole lot more wine.

Yes, it was jaw-dropping to tally up the bill, but then we were dividing it by three! And mind you, we were also taking into consideration that we women were NOT going to be cooking every day on the boat, as it was our vacation. So, surely, we were saving money now, so we could spend it later at restaurants. And we were on vacation!

After completing the provisioning along with taking a thorough inventory of the boat, we were ready to go. At least we thought we were ready. Just before we were about to pull away from the dock, one of the staff came running back, shouting, "Monsieur Bumpus! Monsieur Bumpus! You cannot leave!" Stymied about the delay and wondering if I had failed to submit all the proper forms, I broke out in a sweat. Did I give them all the appropriate papers? Had they decided to reject my EU special certificate to sail on Mediterranean waters? Shortly, another staff member came running up the dock holding a gift bag. He shoved it into one hand and shook the other, and said, "No self-respecting sailor on Mediterranean waters can sail without this! Bon voyage." It was a bottle of Ricard Pastis. And, as Laurent and Karyn pointed out amidst our laughter, "He's right; no one can sail the South of France without Pastis!" W.B.

Niccolo, from Moorings, answered our phone call, picked us up, and delivered us back to our boat. And then he led the charge to unload all our boxes and packages onto the boat. Nice service!

Whew! That was a scary moment for us, and especially for Winston who was meticulous about completing the tiniest of details. And there he and I were, jet lagged from our flight the day before, standing out in the heat of the afternoon, needing naps, all while taking possession of a brand-new boat. Our knees had turned to jelly in that panicky moment. Ah, but the feeling quickly subsided, we all laughed, and thanked the staff profusely in our best non-French way of doing things. And off we went! Bon voyage!

CHAPTER FORTY-ONE

Off We Went—
From Nice to St. Jean Ferrat

*W*e thanked them, started the engine, and waved au revoir. The forward chain to the dock was removed, we untied the aft dock lines, and were off. I couldn't believe we were doing this. Was this a dream? Good friends, a great boat, and the beautiful Mediterranean waters ahead of us with a full week to sail!!

By the time we left the harbor it was about three o'clock and so a short trip to a little cove for the night was our destination. The folks at the Moorings had suggested an anchorage just about five miles to the east of Nice. The winds were light and easterly, so we motor-sailed for an hour or so along the coast taking in the beauty of the terraced green hills. We found a good place to anchor just off Cap Ferrat, amongst the mega yachts and weekend sailors where we settled in for the evening. W.B.

Winston took to the boat like they were old mates, and *Grand Cru* glided away from the slip, down the fairway, and through the ancient port of Nice. Why, sailors had sailed in and out of these waters for over three thousand years, and wasn't it something that we were one of them! Ah yes, the afternoon was filled with sunshine and great expectations. Our motor-sail was quite relaxing, and we women sat on the bow of the boat. Lovely bow babes we were! We cruised past some of the loveliest of coastal promontories, known as caps, and passed the bay of Villefranche-sur-Mer. We then rounded the rugged St. Jean-Cap Ferrat and headed into the bay of Beaulieu-sur-Mer with Roquebrune-Cap-Martin and Monaco only a few nautical miles away.

Ah, but first things first! Once we anchored, we opened the bottle of pastis as a celebratory drink and for the first time on this trip allowed ourselves a few moments to relax. Some of our crew swam in the waters behind the boat while others read and rested while taking in the views. We ate a leisurely dinner onboard, and everyone settled in. This time of year, the sun sets late, so we watched it fade in the west. Then, like this was not magical enough, the full moon rose over the spit of land jutting out from Cap Ferrat. We were mesmerized. W.B.

Yes, we anchored toward the back of the little bay of Beaulieu amid both small and large mega yachts. It, at first, felt a little intimidating, but then we shed those thoughts, along with our clothes, and put on our swimming suits. After a celebratory sip of pastis and hors d'oeuvres made of rich black olive tapenade smeared onto slices of baguette, some of us entered the water. Dived right in, we did! And came right back up shocked at how cold the water was! "Where are we for Pete's sake?" we shouted at each other. What were we thinking? Shortly, very shortly, we were back out of the drink and Karyn served us an amazing meal of pasta with red sauce, and yes, more black olives! She was truly making our lives easy!

But my husband was correct about being mesmerized by the moon; we all watched as the full moon splashed its golden light across the bay and the rugged tip of Cap Ferrat was silhouetted in the afterglow. The seas were gentle, almost smooth, like dark velvet. The anchor lights from nearby boats, as well as the village lights, which were sprinkled along the surrounding hills, wrapped about us like a mantle of diamonds. Melodramatic? Yes, but then where else could we experience such things?

We all turned in for the night. The anchorage was well protected from the south and the west, where the prevailing winds flowed during this time of year. But it wasn't long before the wind began to build. My wife and I had taken the forward V-berth, and we were right below the loud noises of the halyards clanging and the anchor chain rubbing. I went up on deck a few times to adjust them, but realized I only had the choice of listening to humming or clanging depending on the amount of tension I put on a few of the lines. I already had the halyard tied off on the rail, but the wind was building too much to tame them all. Between midnight and 2 a.m., several nearby boats decided to move to another anchorage. I decided we were all too tired and the snores from the aft cabins on my way up the companionway to make adjustments confirmed I was the only one bothered by the noise, so I decided to stay put. By about 4 a.m., I decided to move to the cockpit and was joined by Carole, my lovely first mate. It was a little less noisy and we could keep a half an eye on the boats around us as they were deciding to pull up anchors one by one. We told ourselves we could enjoy the stars and the

setting of the full moon and settled back down and tried to sleep. We were so dead tired. W.B.

Okay, my non-nautical friends, a V-berth is a cabin (or bed-room) in the bow or the front of the boat. It happened ours was also right under the anchor locker that was where some of the annoying noises were coming from. Winston did an exemplary job of trying to tame the winds, as well as quell the noise. The wind was howling and the halyards, or the ropes connected to the sails, were clanging like church bells in an emergency. So, when he decided to sleep in the cockpit to keep an eye on things, I immediately scrambled up the stairs to join him. Ah, but what we witnessed—or rather heard—was another way of life on the water. You see, it was dark as the now silvery moon had disappeared behind a bank of clouds, and because noise travels well over water, we were given a full education on how to pull up an anchor in the dark—in French. Like most frenzied and tired sailors, not all was kindness, and light! No, no! Husbands and wives were stretching their marriage vows as they attempted to corral their boats and take off for a quieter anchorage. We were left behind with tiny us and all the mega-yachts.

I suppose it was okay with us that the Moorings had a rule that you could not change anchorages in the middle of the night. When on unfamiliar waters, it would be easy to harm the boat as well as others. We were so tired that we just hunkered down and tried to catch up on the much-needed sleep for our jet-lagged bodies. W.B.

Before the others had awakened, we slipped back down to our room to finish off a bit more sleep. I was surprised that all the commotion didn't awaken the four others. But then, that had been our goal: to keep the boat and all on board safe. When I heard voices, I rose and staggered into the galley to find the coffee in the French press already half gone.

"How did you sleep?" Sandy asked me, cheerfully. I looked at her, smiled, and asked her the same question.

"Great! I always seem to sleep well on a boat. Right, Jim?"

Jim, who had gone on deck with Laurent and Karyn with his coffee sloshing in his cup, shouted down to us in the galley, "Great night sleep!" It was unanimous that all four had slept peacefully. I was thinking, *I can hardly focus here, and I can't wait for my nap,* but this was our first full day of sailing. I felt Winston and I had accomplished what we set out to do: keep folks comfortable and feeling safe!

CHAPTER FORTY-TWO

Off to Cannes

*A*fter breakfast, the crew was up from a good night's sleep and the captain and first mate, a little sleep deprived, decided the wind was blowing good and in our planned direction, so anchors away. We motored out of the beautiful little bay and into the Mediterranean toward our first major destination— Cannes.

We raised the sails as the wind had settled to about 10 knots and Grand Cru gave us a very comfortable 15 to 20 NM sail down the coast past Nice and toward Antibes. This was our first day of sailing and the boat handled nicely. We talked, sipped our coffee, and took in the magnificent scenery around us like the port of Nice, the terraced hill sides, and the contrasting modern pyramidal housing development near the Marina Baie des Anges. We sailed toward Cap d 'Antibes and looked forward to stopping in Antibes. But much to our chagrin, we got a grumpy harbor master who wasn't interested in interrupting his lunch. Even Laurent could not sweet-talk him. So off we went, heading toward Cannes. W.B.

Our first morning on the boat went well. A breakfast of coffee and baguette slices, slathered in jelly, smeared with wedges of brie cheese, or with the addition of thin slices of ham or prosciutto, was filling. A bowl with fresh peaches and grapes was set in a swinging basket for anytime consumption. So together we reveled in the gloriously sunny morning while enjoying the camaraderie of our friends, old and new.

Once the sails were up, the boat sailed smoothly, as the waters were calm, and we gals were able to move about the boat. Within a short time, we found our special spots near the bow to sit, chat, and enjoy the panorama. We sailed along the French Riviera admiring the luxurious villas, then quickly passed the entrance to the Port of Nice. We then swept past the 105-foot-tall war memorial, Monument aux Morts, which we had seen from the taxis. We could make out the majesty better from the sea. The grey marble structure consisted of an urn within a niche with two reliefs: one representing war and the other, peace. I read later that it had been built to honor over 3,600 men from Nice who died during World War I.

As Winston mentioned, we sailed past the city of Nice, which appeared from the sea like a swath of sparkling white buildings reaching up like fingers into the green Alpes Maritime. We sailed past Cap d'Antibes, where I was anguished that we gals couldn't hop off. I was looking forward to taking my guests to visit the infamous house and museum of Picasso, as I had visited a few years earlier.

"I'm so sorry we can't visit," I said. I pointed to the house on the Cap. "As I stood right on that very terrace, I remember looking out to sea, and longing to be on the water."

"Funny, isn't it?" Sandy asked. "When we're on land, we want to be on the sea; and when we're on the sea, we look to the land."

"An odd, human trait we have," said Karyn dreamily.

At this point, Laurent took out a bit of fishing gear, non-chalantly tossed out a bit of line with a hook from the stern, and popped open a beer. He appeared to have fished like this many times before, and relaxed into the margarita seat, or a seat off the helm on the stern.

"Say, Laurent," Winston asked him, "could you tell the Turners why we sometimes call you Eric?"

"Oh," he said, with a smile gracing his face, "when I was living in Austin, and I wanted to get a reservation at a restaurant, no one could understand my name, Laurent. So, I simply changed my name to Eric, and I have been Eric since. See, there is no more confusion!" We laughed. We understood how difficult it was to be understood in another language, whether in Texas or in another country.

After an hour or so, he checked the line and proclaimed, "I do believe the fish will have to commit suicide to be able to catch us!" We obviously were making good time and traveling too fast for the fish!

While sailing out of the bay of Antibes, we viewed the island of Ile Ste-Marguerite, which was where Fort Royal was located. This fort was famous for being the prison in The Man with the Iron Mask. *We stayed to the outside of the island, as I was unfamiliar with the area and there were several shallows and obstructions on the inside. We rounded the island and sailed toward the Port de Cannes. I had Laurent call the harbor master for instructions and they directed us to the guest pontoon. This time the harbor master was an acceptable fellow. W.B.*

Circling around the little island of Ile Ste-Marguerite brought to view the old fortress, which was part of Fort Royal, the prison where the Man in the Iron Mask was held for eleven long years from 1687 to 1698. Who was he, you ask? Was he the twin brother of the king? No one knows, even to this day. Half a mile away we spotted our goal, the lovely city of Cannes. We were all excited, as we'd had a grand day of sailing, but then . . . a port was a great place to check out the land.

This was my first chance to Med moor. Med mooring, or docking, would become easier as the week progressed, but we were new at this. The process goes like this. We quietly backed the boat up to the dock, but this was followed by much yelling and shouting as our crew attempted to tie up. There was a line attached to the dock. One of the crew members leaned off the boat, grabbed the line, and followed it forward to a chain that was tied at the bow. Two dock lines were attached to the two aft cleats and tied around the two cleats on shore. We got better at the process, and the shouting decreased as the week went on and my embarrassment subsided.

But the Port of Cannes was home to some of the world's biggest mega yachts. The only question was "How many helicopters did each boat have?" The guest dock, where we moored, was directly across from the Cannes center where the famous film festival is held. Once docked and secured, I went to the harbor master's office to check in; another ritual we would repeat throughout the week. The staff was very friendly, and their English was quite good, but once again I brought my crutch, Laurent, along. W.B.

Yes, it was a tad daunting to arrive at Cannes in the inner harbor and be opposite the grand dame of film festivals, the Palais de Festivals. A bit of the kerfuffle (shouting and stuff) with our crew brought us ladies up from our staterooms—as we had been busy changing into our glad rags. We were going to town! There, directly across from the bow of our boat, was the famous, large white circular building that had been a prominent fixture in film culture for years. And there we were, a 44' boat, bobbing at the dock next to yachts three times the size. Not too intimidating!

"So, what do you think of my first Med mooring," my true love, Winston, asked me, a bit out of breath. To be quite honest, since I didn't see the mooring take place, I felt it was a victory for him and I said so. I knew this maneuver had been filling his dreams (or nightmares) for months now, and he must have been successful. We could step right off the back of the boat easily, and I assumed that was the goal.

Ah, but once our *Grand Cru* was med-moored, we women thought it was time to wander the streets of Cannes and get a late lunch. We'd already fixed three meals in one twenty-four-hour period, so surely it was time to seek something different. So, even though Winston, Jim, and Laurent did the manly thing of going to check in at the harbor master's office first, we were itching to go. The expected thing to do is to check in at the office, give over your driver's license, or some such thing, but we were antsy.

We gals slipped off the boat to peek, and Sandy, always the astute observer, said, "Good gawd! It appears our beautiful 44-foot boat looks like a Mini Cooper pulling into a parking lot of Bugattis and Lotuses with helicopter pads tucked into their trunks!"

We laughed. She was right! We were the smallest boat in the marina, with boats averaging 150 feet and up. But we still felt we had arrived!

When we finally hopped off *Grand Cru* to find lunch, it was nearly 3 p.m. on a Sunday and many restaurants were closing. So we skittered down the dock to make our escape, and in the process bypassed twenty enormous yachts, one more extreme in accoutrements than the others. Most only had a liveried staff on board, busily cleaning and polishing the bright work awaiting their owners' arrival. Wicker baskets sat proudly on the dock filled with neatly placed Topsiders or boat shoes of all sizes, awaiting the arrival of guests. We walked off the docks and past the owners' Jaguars, past the Palais de Festivals, and into a park that was hosting an arts fair. We women slowed, but the men were now the ones rushing us women to get to a restaurant.

Laurent spied an open restaurant and headed straight in to clear the way. The restaurant owners apologized, but informed us that they only had cold, fresh seafood! Yes, most of it had been cooked, but we were so hungry we opted for anything. Before we could bat an eye and order a couple of bottles of rosé, two enormous three-foot-wide seafood platters, or *plats de fruits de mer,* were placed on stands in front of us, with lobster, langoustines, crab, snails, clams, mussels, cockles, welks, and *bulots*, which we were informed were sea snails. Oh my! Small terrines filled with cold sauces, like mayonnaise and aioli, were scattered about the table for dipping.

"Karyn, how do we eat these little, tiny snails, these *bulots?*" I asked our expert.

She reached over and picked up a large cork that looked much like an odd hedgehog. It had been conveniently placed near the middle of the table and was covered with small straight pins. She withdrew one of the pins, lifted it high in the air, then proceeded to stab the innards of the snail, before popping it out with a finesse we had rarely seen. We each took up our own weapon of culinary delight, grabbed one of the many crustaceans at hand, and dug deep inside the shell. Ah, but, not so fast!

"Now, I must give you a *leetle* hint," Laurent said, with that delightful accent of his, continuing our communal lesson. "It takes a twist of the wrist to hook the little bugger. But once you score, you lift it high, then safely drag it through an aioli or mignonette sauce before popping it into your mouth. Voilà," he said as he completed his demonstration.

Since the explanation was over, and we were completely starving, we all dug in with pure enjoyment!

"This is an orgasmic delight—with lemon," Winston said. We feasted until we were almost sick, and then Winston and I headed back to the boat to nap. The others, having had plenty of restful sleep the night before, took their time to shop in the arts market.

Although we had showers available onboard our boat, there were larger showers available for us to use in the harbor at Cannes. To gain entrance one needed only to press a buzzer at the entrance to the shower room and tell the guard the name of your boat. He would then buzz you in, and voilà, a luxurious shower. This became our first challenge at French pronunciation. Our boat's name, which was Grand Cru *was not easy for us to pronounce in French as we were to accommodate the word with rolling "Rs" in the word "cru" correctly. If we weren't careful, we would be telling the guard we had a "big butt." W.B.*

As an aside to you non-sailors, this may seem like a non-issue, but if you are wanting to shower in a large clean shower room, with plenty of hot water, towels, hair dryers and all, but don't speak French well, this can become a challenging thing! So, when Winston and I went up to the harbor master's office and asked at the window for entry into the showers, we proudly announced the name of our boat. Now, mind you, we were surrounded with yachts that had gold-plated faucets and shower heads, and sixteen bathrooms each, whilst ours had three nice but much smaller versions of the same. (No gold-plated faucets, though!)

But the attendant's window was quite high off the ground and had dark glass on the window that prevented us from seeing inside. To reach the microphone, I had to stand on tip toe to announce our boat name, *Grand Cru*. Why me? Between Winston and I, I was the best French speaker. But the funny thing about pronouncing that word—yes, it has to do with the rolling of the r's—but if you don't huck the word out from the back of your throat, you are not saying *Grand Cru* correctly. No, as it turned out, the way I was pronouncing it translated to "fat butt." So, picture me repeating the word over and over, imagining the invisible attendants were most probably rolling on the floor laughing at my blunder. Yes, life had a way of keeping one humble! But repetition eventually got us in!

Refreshed after a nap and a shower, we all dressed up for the evening and headed out for what? Yes, a late-night dinner along the famous Boulevard le Croisette, the grand street that borders the sea. We found a charming outdoor brasserie across from the sea, in front of a myriad of fine restaurants in the middle of the boulevard. Canopies stretched over cloth covered tables with crystal wine glasses and twinkling lights lining the trees above setting the ambiance.

We all six indulged in—yes, anything but seafood! We had had our fill over the past forty-eight hours, so we succumbed to grilled steak, pommes frites, and bottles of wine. We completed the evening with a stroll along the water with the almost-full moon rising above us. When we couldn't imagine the day being any more spectacular, a full display of fireworks shot up into the night calling out to us from Antibes.

CHAPTER FORTY-THREE

From Cannes to Fréjus

J im and Sandy loved getting up early, and on the next morning in Cannes, they slipped off the boat after 7 a.m. to find a patisserie, or bakery, where they purchased wonderful, still-warm-from-the-oven croissants to go with our French press coffee. A great start to the day! This became their morning ritual whenever we were in port, and those of us who were not mutually eager to rise early were grateful. After our breakfast on that beautiful sunshiny morning, we were off to our next stop, the ancient town of Fréjus. The trip was another perfect sail about twenty miles down the coast. The winds were light and, on our beam, made for a gentle sail. We took in the scenery and sailed for about five hours to the next port of Fréjus. W.B.

The morning was golden, and our crew was in great form! Sandy and Jim were bubbling about their adventure into town to find croissants.

"The best part," Sandy said, "is that all we had to do when purchasing the croissants was to point and indicate the number needed. Easy in any language. And when it came to paying?

Why, we just stuck our hands out with numerous euros on it, and they picked off what they needed. *Très facile!* It beat the blank stares we would get if we attempted speaking French."

Before taking off for Fréjus, the only long walk I took was back to the port bathrooms, to get another look at some of the most awesome yachts up close. Literally, enormous boats, and like Sandy pointed out, each had their own welcome mats with the name of the yacht plus straw baskets filled with evenly placed boat shoes. Now, I don't know if this means anything to you, but there was room in this marina for seventy superyachts with a maximum length of 459 feet, with a maximum draft of sixteen feet. *Grand Cru* was a 44' yacht with a six-foot draft that meant that we couldn't sail in waters less than six-feet deep. And, as we pulled out of the port and back into the Côte d'Azur a few minutes later, we passed much larger anchored yachts that were well over-sized for the slips in Cannes. One was flying the Russian flag and could have easily been 600 plus feet.

My husband refers to draft as the depth of water a vessel needs to float, or to not go aground. Now, because the sail was long (five hours), we all took it easy. And after tidying up the galley and our staterooms, we women found our normal perches in which to observe as the world went by. We were sailing along a coastline that had been the object of adventure since long before the Greeks, much less the Romans. And the hillsides, which were interspersed with white craggy cliffs and green meadows, were covered in bushes of yellow broom, or genet. This bright yellow bush was most connected with lavender for the traditional Provençal color scheme.

It was my day to make lunch, so I resorted to simplicity: I made a cold pasta salad with chopped up cold cuts from the marvelous salamis, mortadellas, and cheeses we had picked up in Nice. With olives, a few capers, and a light vinaigrette, with splashes of olive oil, salt, and pepper we were good to go!

Just as we dropped our sails and were about to motor into the port of Fréjus, I sprained my ankle. Even though I was in excruciating pain, we then motored in and Med moored in a designated slip in the marina. It was a terrific marina and had a lot more boats our size. It was fun to be in Cannes, although we felt this was more our speed. I also marveled at the French for using the Mediterranean mooring system. They get almost twice as many boats in a marina than a typical US marina. And, fortunately, even with a bum ankle, our crew was easily able to bring our boat to the dock. W.B.

When we sailed into Fréjus, I was busy admiring the harbor that sported a beautiful mix of new condos, shops, and restaurants all with exterior colors in eye-popping pastels. All the better to find your port in a storm or fog. Winston and I had been looking forward to sailing into this harbor at Fréjus, since we stood on those very docks dreaming of an adventure such as this. This very moment! Winston was in rare form, commanding the helm, leaping up and down off the *lazarettes* (seats) until he suddenly stepped down into the wheel well, twisting his ankle. Just at that moment, we all were running back and forth up and down the boat, fending off other boats, and helping guide the boat in, not aware of his condition. Sandy still has nightmares of that docking as it was the first time she had been asked to help.

"My job," Sandy said, "was to use a boat hook to fend off the bow of the boat from the neighboring boats as we slid in between. I confess I was busy watching Winston back the boat expertly into the slip when Laurent yelled out to me. Yee gads, the bow of the boat was in danger of collision. Fortunately, Laurent saved the day by alerting me and rushing over to push off. Whew! And then we realized our captain had sprained his ankle and was in agony."

I had been so looking forward to showing the other four around Fréjus, I must confess, I wasn't as compassionate to my dear husband as I should have been. Thank goodness for him, Karyn leaped off the back of the boat with an empty bucket, and immediately hefted the cold water up to the others. Gently, I slid Win's shoe off and he quickly plunged his foot into it. The men took charge of checking in with the harbor master and returned with a bag of ice, while Sandy plumped pillows and I raced down to our stateroom for our mighty Advil. Everyone was there for Winston. Even me! He had attained the rare Captain, the mighty Captain status.

It was a wonderful marina with lots of facilities and close walking distance to the old town of Fréjus and the site of some old Roman ruins. The rest of the crew went to town after checking in with the harbor master. The captain, which was me, stayed back on the boat, soaking and icing my swollen foot. The crew had a good long walk into town and saw several medieval and ancient sights. Folks decided to have dinner on board as it would be easier than carrying and dragging the captain around. W.B.

After about an hour, Winston insisted that we go into town without him. I can still picture him lying back on the seat of the boat, looking longingly after us as we headed over the bridge and into town. We tromped through some of the same overgrown fields he and I had visited before, where we found some of the most amazing Roman ruins. As I had done on a previous trip, I dug out my guidebook and read, "As it turns out, the history of Fréjus began long before the Romans, and the creation of the port and harbor were something ready for the taking by the Romans when they showed up 2,000 years later." We turned and looked back toward the port. I continued. "We will be able to see the Roman imprint in amphitheaters, aqueducts, theatres, along with their city walls, city gates, lighthouses, and no less than five public baths."

Like scavenger hunters, we moved from place to place as we inched farther into the old town of Fréjus. We wandered in and out of the eleventh century Episcopal abbey with its beautifully carved doors and cloister with mythological paintings that commingled with the medieval Christian motifs. We then stopped off at a boulangerie (which, fortunately, still had baguettes at that late hour), another cheese shop, and headed back to the boat. Win was attempting to be comfortable with his foot awkwardly in a bucket while lying down—not an easy feat. So dinner on board that night was prepared by Laurent and Karyn that consisted of merguez (a spicy Moroccan sausage) on a bed of couscous—a full-blown North African experience proceeded by yes, Pastis, foie gras, and local rosé! Life was sweet! Even Winston was able to enjoy himself..

CHAPTER FORTY-FOUR

Sailing Away to St. Tropez

*T*uesday morning it was off to St. Tropez a short fifteen miles down the coast. We left later as we had a short day's sail and folks wanted to do a little shopping at the unique shops in the marina. It was another perfect morning and a gentle sail down the coast. As we came close to the entrance to the Golfe of St. Tropez, we could see what appeared to be a regatta of some sort. As we got closer, we could see that there were over one hundred boats involved and they were sailing to windward in our direction. And then as they rounded the mark one-by-one, they popped their spinnakers. What a magnificent sight. As we sailed, we continued to watch this beautiful race as we made the point, at Pointe des Sardineaux, and began sailing toward the port of St. Tropez. As we got closer, I had Laurent call the harbor master at St. Tropez to see if we could find room on the guest dock. "Impossiblé," they said. It would be impossible as the Rolex Cup was currently there, and the marina was filled to capacity. But if we called the harbor master at St. Maxime across the bay, he was sure they would be able to find room for us. Which we did, and they did allow us in, eventually.

An important thing to keep in mind as we traveled along the South of France was to never expect to do business during lunch time, as everything closed and that was that. We slowly motored in circles around the bay, while we had lunch on board. We waited *until after 1400 (2 p.m.) before Laurent could call the harbor master, and we were excited to get a spot. My wife and I had visited this charming town before and to be able to stay here was a treat for us. It may have been a disappointment to the others, as we were set on going to St. Tropez. But once we got settled and moored on the guest dock in St. Maxime, we discovered there was a water shuttle that left every twenty minutes from the very same dock and was a quick ten-minute ride to St. Tropez. Score! W.B.*

The morning we left Fréjus, we skirted past its twin city port, St. Raphaël, which was noted for being the first port for Julius Caesar in Gaul. Winston and the guys put up the sails and headed west toward St. Tropez. Almost immediately the Massif des Maures, a most impressive mountain range that stretches from Fréjus to Hyères, became our constant companion. Roughly translated as the Moorish Mountains, those steep craggy red rocks rode hard on our right side the full distance.

As Winston described, on our left, or port side, we came upon a most amazing sailboat race, which we later learned was called Les Voiles de Saint-Tropez, or the Giraglia Rolex Cup. The regatta consisted of a week-long set of races, beginning with inshore races in the St. Tropez Bay followed by the primary event that began in St. Tropez, passed through the Îles d'Hyères, then headed toward the island of Giraglia near Corsica, and finished off in Genoa, Italy, a total distance of 243 nautical miles.

We were most fortunate to witness the beginnings of this lively race. When boats pop their shoots, it means they put up the forward-most spinnaker, which was most often extremely colorful. To be sailing alongside this race was an exhilarating gift.

Once we were finally able to pull into the harbor of St. Maxime, I spotted the arched bridge in the distance, where we had spent our first beach day a few years back. We had loved the idea of being able to come to a nice relaxing beach, rent a chaise and umbrella, plop down in the chair, and be waited on by bar staff. No paper wine cups here; no, only regular wine glasses for these folks. But everyone else was focused on getting to St. Tropez. Or, as Laurent and Karyn called it, "St. Trop."

We hopped on the water shuttle and zipped across the bay to the port of St. Tropez. The racing yachts were packed in like sardines. They were rafted up three and four boats deep, all flying colorful banners announcing various manufacturers and other races. We toured the town and shops, marveled at the racing yachts, and stopped to have a drink in a little café in the middle of the town. Summer was approaching and the weather was hot. I couldn't imagine how warm it must get in August when the toute de monde (all the world) was in this little village. I know I was glad to be here and couldn't believe we were lucky enough to arrive during the Rolex Cup. I was still hobbling with my sprained ankle but trying to make the best of this magical moment. W.B.

Everyone in our group was ready to party, or at least shop. And the speedboat ferry that raced us from St. Maxime to St. Tropez seemed to know we were in a hurry. I can still see Sandy and Karyn laughing as the wind whipped at our hair. "This feels so *James Bond*," Sandy shouted over the roar of the engine.

The Vieux Port of St. Tropez was decorated in a multitude

of colorful pennants as the docks and the town were filled with the magic of this race. The streets near the quay were crowded with Rolex Cup sailors, as well as those who wanted to rub shoulders with sailors. The camaraderie was boisterous at times. Clearly a good time was being had by most all.

Further around the harbor, houses of every subtle color lined the water, and those of us who had not been here before looked for traces of Bridget Bardot. Or at least what the village had looked like when she had been made famous here. We walked together through the crowded streets, although walking on cobblestones was too much for Winston's ankle. He opted to get off his feet and sat down at an outside bar only a few blocks up from the port. Once he had a drink in hand, we all took off to check out the village of St. Tropez. We women were in the mood for doing more than serious window shopping. As it turned out, Jim and Laurent had similar interests in mind. We headed up toward Rue Général Allard, where pretty pastel-hued shops were occupied by internationally famous brands: Christian Dior, Tommy Hilfiger, Breitling, along with an array of Parisian couture. We found Jim popping out of the Lord Jim shop and snapped his photo.

And then we decided to lower our standards and headed into smaller gift shops and art galleries. One gallery caught my eye, and I purchased two sailing prints for Winston. We crossed another street and passed a dusty boules court where old men carried on like they had every day of the year: ignoring the tourists. Even when the oblivious traipsed through their game.

Of course, we took turns checking in on Winston. He seemed to be very content people watching, as long as his glass of cool rosé was in hand. Later, when we all returned to the quay, we joined him for cool drinks. But then Karyn and I wandered off again through a quay-side art show where I bought two more paintings by St. Tropez artists. We might not be part of the festival in the village, but the village had created a most entertaining afternoon. And now, my collection of art pieces had risen to . . . What? Yes, six pieces, some large, some small. Now, how was I going to get these back home?

We finally hopped back on the shuttle and zipped back across the bay and to the boat to relax and for me to rest my foot. We had dinner that night in a little nearby restaurant in the old section of St. Maxime. And I limped back to the boat for a good night's sleep. W.B.

The afternoon in St. Tropez had taken the steam out of all of us, and the temperatures had increased to the degree that unless we were moving on a boat across the water, it was stifling. We hunkered down under the *bimini* for some appetizers and more wine, and shortly made our way to a local restaurant within walking distance. It was a small family-run place up a slight incline in old St. Maxime. We found the people friendly, and the food was good, not memorable, but that was all we needed.

As the sun began to set, the air cooled and we relaxed even more with our friends. Again, fireworks lit up the bay after we had turned in for the night. If we had had more energy, we would have dashed back up on the deck to capture the action. Instead, we dreamed in technicolor—of fireworks and colorful sails popping in the Rolex Cup race!

CHAPTER FORTY-FIVE

From St. Tropez to Port Cros

*I*n the morning as we awoke, we saw and heard all kinds of officials, the fire department, the police, etc. going up and down the dock pointing in the water and shouting at each other. It was like we were in some strange French film without subtitles. Our French friends hadn't risen yet, so we Americans could only guess. I expected any minute to see Chief Inspector Jacques Clouseau come racing in. We sat in the cockpit of our boat nonchalantly sipping coffee and eating our fresh croissants when Laurent and Karyn rose to let us know the water shuttle had had a diesel spill while fueling. (Yes, the same one we had been on the afternoon before.) Everyone was trying to figure out what to do and how to clean it up. We were informed that the port was about to close. And not wanting to stay there with the Keystone Cops, we cast off and left the harbor just in the nick of time.

It was a blessing, as today would be our longest day to sail. It would be over 30 NM to our next destination, a little cove on the island of Port Cros. It was another beautiful morning as we motored out of the Golfe de St. Tropez. Laurent made another pot of strong French coffee in the larger French press, and we settled in.

We sipped our coffee and marveled at the scenery around us. We motored south until we cleared Cap Camarat at about 10 o'clock and then we motor-sailed pass Cap Lardier. The winds picked up and we shut off the noise maker and sailed. W.B.

It was quite frantic, but almost comedic as we raced to get off the docks in St. Maxime in time. The port officially closed just as we pulled away. Ah, but the morning was beautiful, as usual, and the day was going to be long as Winston mentioned—30 NM (nautical miles)—which usually meant about a five-to-six-hour sail.

But we thoroughly enjoyed the relaxing mood of the crew and the whole experience of gliding through those azure waters chatting, laughing, telling jokes, reading a little, and just enjoying each other's company. Have I mentioned that Laurent had quite the repertoire of jokes? He also liked to tell what he called funny little stories. We always knew we were in for a treat when he began a conversation with that line. His French accent only enhanced the telling, and the matter of misunderstanding each other's culture only added to the enjoyment and hilarity. Plus, as it turned out, he could be quite a gourmet chef. En route for lunch, he prepared a fine salade Niçoise with canned tuna, canned green beans, sliced cornichons, sliced tomatoes, hard boiled eggs, and a dash of vinaigrette! Voilà! Both he and Karyn had brought their culinary game to the boat. And now Sandy and I understood the necessity of canned foods.

We could see our island destination, Port Cros, ahead and the larger island of Levant. The island was a strange combination of purposes

as it was divided into a military camp and a nudist colony, strange bedfellows, indeed. We tacked back and forth heading windward, and what a glorious sail it was. The wind was up to 15-20 knots, so we made good time. As we approached the island of Port Cros, we had the choice of two anchorages and as the wind was blowing from the east, we decided to anchor in the cove to the west called Port Man. It was early afternoon, and the anchorage was already crowded. But after checking out a few likely spots and dropping the anchor a few times just for practice, we found a good spot. We set our anchor so it would hold, allowing for plenty of room to swing if the wind clocked around. The folks were tired from the fresh air and sunshine, and we did not want to fool with the anchor later.

After getting settled some folks took a nap while we dropped the dinghy and attached the motor as others wanted to explore the island and the shore. As I sat there looking back over our stern, I saw in the water what looked like a yellow racing mark. Then I saw a boat near it that looked as though it could be a race committee boat. I had been racing a little at our yacht club in Austin and had volunteered many times; I was familiar with the sight. But we didn't see any boats. W.B.

Yes, we were a bit weary from the long, hot day of sailing! As soon as Winston set anchor, several of us were diving off the boat into the refreshing blue waters. Again, the water was colder than expected, but invigorating to say the least. Some rested, some read, and some went off with our dinghy to explore. Quite honestly, I had even forgotten we had a dinghy on board, but it was a delightful way to check out the protected little pirate cove we found ourselves in. And we weren't far from a favorite place of ours, Porquerrolles. Ah, but not until tomorrow.

Then Laurent said, "Look, there, you can see a large sailboat heeling over beating toward us." The boat was still hard to make out, but it was heading our way. We grabbed the binoculars and could see more boats farther behind. We watched, with awe, as the boats began to fill the horizon, tacking, tacking toward the yellow mark a quarter mile off our stern. Then it dawned on us, this was the windward mark of a regatta. We pulled out the newspaper we had picked up the day before in St. Tropez and realized, this was the windward mark for the 250-mile Rolex Cup, on their way to Corsica and on to the finish line in Genoa, Italy. W.B.

After watching yesterday's race to St. Tropez, we thought we had seen the last of the Rolex Cup. But here they came again! But we felt this was an extraordinary stroke of good luck to be sitting next to the very spot where all the racers would make a fast turnaround, then sail 250 miles away to Genoa, Italy! We had participated in racing our boat, Dolci Sogni, on the San Francisco Bay, and with Karyn and Laurent when we lived in Austin. So, this was, indeed, a thrill!

We sat and watched as boat after boat made it to the mark, tacked, and popped their spinnakers. The sky filled with color, and we sat in amazement. We did not plan this; we could not have planned this. Sitting on our beautiful boat, Grand Cru, anchored in this charming cove, on an island off the coast of France, while watching the Rolex Cup yachts make the weather mark on this beautiful day was truly a high point of the trip. W.B.

I know we're babbling on about this, but it was an extraordinary event to witness. Not even when we were back in San Francisco and participating (Winston was course marshal) in America's Cup did we get so excited! I later read that all the boats in the Rolex Cup were lengths from 32 feet to over 70 feet and the smaller boat won the race, two separate years.

Later, a 70-foot racing yacht, with a capable sailor and his mate, a young woman, pulled in and set their anchor near our port stern. My thought was this would be good for now, but if, or when, the wind shifted in the night, we might be a little too close. I could see he flew the flag of the Yacht Club of Monaco, so I figured he knew better than I. Plus, he could afford to pay any damages if he swung and hit us. I felt that I was being overly cautious, and his boat had anchored last, but, if things changed, I would ask him to move. It was a beautiful yacht, and they were a beautiful couple. Once they settled in, we saw they had a third crew member, a young child. So, we guessed wife? Girlfriend? Mistress? The imagination is always better than reality; we never asked and never knew. W.B.

This racing yacht was not equipped for much of anything but racing, so we were thinking it a bit odd that a family of three would be spending the night on the boat. But, like my husband said, they knew the territory and the rules on the water, which included the last one to anchor accommodates all others around it. On occasion, we would see the lithe young woman step up on deck in her string bikini, and other times the young child would pop up and take a pee off the deck. But other than that, they kept to themselves, and we *were* in France.

The evening sunset was stunning, and as we gently bobbed

in place we feasted on pasta with tapenade and salmon whipped up by our illustrious chef, Karyn. Of course, we had more cheeses (the French eat their cheeses *after* dinner) along with more wine. Plus, the chocolates Sandy and Jim had brought from Cacao et Chocolat in Paris. Did I tell you how much we enjoyed the collaboration of all these culinary talents?

In the night, the winds clocked around from east to west again and as I guessed our neighbor's 70-foot boat stern was swinging close to our bow. We seemed to be clearing just fine, but we would keep an eye on it as we would be leaving after breakfast. The most amazing part of this beautiful yacht was what was written on the transom. At first you saw in big letters Mean Machine. *Well, it was an impressive sailboat and we thought it to be the perfect name for this boat. Then Jim handed me the binoculars and said, "Take a closer look!" What was actually written on the back of the transom was,* Mariposa, Tender to the Mean Machine, Yacht Club of Monaco. *Holy cow! This was just the tender? A seventy-foot sailboat was their dinghy? We couldn't imagine what size the* Mean Machine *might be, but it did remind us that we were in a land where no one could be too rich or too beautiful. After breakfast, we asked the tender captain to start his engine and move his boat just a little as we would be motoring forward to his stern in order to pull the anchor. Without hesitation, he accommodated our request and off we went! W.B.*

When Winston and I first came up top that morning, Laurent and Jim were excited—almost giddy—to point out an oddity. It was before our first cup of coffee, and before our eyes had adjusted to daylight, but they quickly focused our attention on the stern of the 70-foot boat, which clearly said it was a tender (or the dinghy) to a much, much larger ship of two or three hundred feet. All from the Yacht Club of Monaco. I looked over at our little eight-foot dinghy strapped-down on our bow, looking like a large dead fish. *No matter!* I thought. I was pleased we had such conveniences, no matter the size. When you need to go ashore, you need to go ashore.

But my next thought was, *Where is my coffee? Had I missed breakfast? Did I sleep in too late?* Later, Jim cleared up my confusion.

"This morning," he said, "we awoke and went on deck to enjoy the morning and admire the spectacular boat that had anchored next to us during the evening. When it was about time for you shipmates to arise and join us on deck, Sandy went below to make coffee and bring up the remaining croissants. Looking high and low, she could not find them. As you recall, we had raced away so quickly from St. Maxime the day before that we had not refurbished our stash of fresh croissants, so we were counting on these extras. When Sandy remarked about the loss, Karyn nonchalantly said that since the croissants on board were a day old, they were clearly inedible. So she had thoughtfully fed them to the fish. Clearly the French have a much narrower definition of edible than we Americans!" Jim laughed.

Yes, no matter how hard we try, we will never understand each other's national quirks and peculiarities! And don't you just love them despite it?

Chapter Forty-Six

Îles de Porquerolles

*We were off to our next destination, the island of Por-
querolles. My wife and I had visited this island a few
years before, but only by ferry. It has a wonderful little
town and a good-sized marina. We needed to sail only another 10
NM to our next destination, but the winds were still from the west,
so we would have to beat to windward, head directly into the wind.
But it was another beautiful and glorious morning. W.B.*

Do you know the French pronounce the names Port Cros and
Porquerolles (sounds like pork roll) almost the same way?
Pucker your lips and attempt it. But, let me warn you, any self-
respecting French man or woman will quickly collapse with
laughter, as there is no way you, an American, can handle it!
Accept your plight!

*We arrived during lunch time and Med moored in an open slip as
directed by the harbor master. Laurent had talked with them on the*

phone, but the directions were not clear. So, after going down the wrong fairway, we turned around and finally found a spot to dock. Not too much yelling and screaming took place. We were getting better. And our neighboring boats were helpful. We had a wonderful lunch in a harbor side café. There were never enough moules for me. After lunch, some folks toured the town, which had lots of shops and historic sites to see. I found a bench and was content to watch a game of boules and save my ankle. W.B.

Thank goodness we had Laurent and Karyn aboard, as even they had trouble discerning some of the instructions we were given. Eventually we backed into a slip with plenty of onlookers, which can certainly make one nervous. But these folks also gave us a great deal of help by grabbing lines and helping us to tie off. But what was this? "Do we have to walk the gang plank to get off the boat?" I squeaked.

Yes, was the answer. But, with help from our neighbors who laid down a board called a *passerelle,* we popped off the boat. It was lunchtime. Winston and I headed to the same restaurant, Il Pescatore, that we had eaten at a few years before. It was convenient to the docks, it was seafood, and we were there. The moules with a piquant saffron sauce were scrumptious.

Have I mentioned just how hot one feels once you step off a moving boat or walk a short distance from the water's edge? The air that afternoon simply clung to us like a layer of gauze, and no matter how much water we would drink, it was never enough.

After our déjeuner, we slowly sauntered up the incline of the main street, which was lined with palm and pine trees, and into the old town of Porquerolles. We took our time to appreciate how serene and quiet the island was. Once again, a lovely, tropical paradise.

On our trip in the past, Winston and I had bravely hiked up to the old fort at the top of the island, but this time our energy level was lower. No matter! While Jim and Laurent headed in one direction (probably to the old fort), and Winston was resting his ankle at the boules court, we gals headed up through the streets in search of a pharmacy for a pain killer for Winston. Unfortunately, this trek became an adventure in absurdity. As it turned out, only the local doctor could dispense drugs for pain, even for sunburn, and he was not available at the time. (It was during the three-hour lunch break.) If we hadn't had Karyn with us, I doubt we could have figured any of this out.

An elderly man who had also climbed the same steep hill to find a doctor, was told he needed to wait for an hour or so. "Go down and sit on the long bench, in the shade of the fig tree right below the road, which leads to the ancient fort," Karyn translated. He looked chagrined but took the advice and slowly ambled back down the hill to await the doctor's return.

Instead of joining him we decided to go shopping, so we continued down the middle of the main street. The only traffic we encountered were bicycles with brave tourists astride. At one point, and to Sandy's complete amazement, a woman came up to her and asked her in French for directions. Sandy apologized and said she did not speak French.

"How was it that she thought I was French?" she asked us after Karyn responded to the woman and sent her along. "I can't believe someone took me for a French woman!"

"Is that a good thing or a bad thing?" I asked her.

"I don't know. I've always been taken for an American, maybe because they hear me speaking English. But I am certainly not a Grace Kelly type of American, yet I feel . . . thrilled for the mistaken identity! To be mistaken for a local!"

I thought about this conversation as we continued down the hill. We never know how we project who we are to others, but it's rather a fun thing to consider.

The buildings, which lined the streets in the main part of the village, were a combination of storefront or restaurant on the lower level, with apartments above. Each was a shade of either pink, salmon, rust, or terra cotta, with shutters in varying shades of blue, setting each establishment apart. Burgeoning, fuchsia-colored bougainvillea inched up the sides of each structure or hung down from the balcony. We peered into the windows of boutiques and arts and crafts shops, but they, too, were closed until 3 p.m. The only place we could spend our money was at a lone farmers market. So we purchased some eggs for tomorrow's omelets and fresh tomatoes, basil, and buffalo mozzarella for a snack or a salad. We would get the pain relievers later.

Learning the systems in each harbor was always part of the adventure. We attempted to find and figure out the showers. And the systems for showers in these French harbors were as many and different as there were varieties of French cheeses. Laurent, who had figured it out, explained this latest set up to us, and even with that bit of information I screwed it up. In Porquerolles, there was an outer door that led to an inner door that led to individual showers, for both men and women, which was a little disconcerting for my puritan upbringing. But there was also an enclosed individual room for the shower, so it made more sense than having separate shower rooms. So you found an open room and got all your clothes off and then went to put the money in the slot to start the shower, and then you realized . . . you needed the token. Yes, the one that

Laurent had attempted to describe. So back on with the clothes, gather up your stuff, back outside to purchase the token, then back to the showers to start all over again. W.B.

Yes, this was the delight (or dilemma) in trying out new harbors, as they all came with varying degrees of conundrums. And this shower set up involved both Winston and me, as we went to the showers together. I was still thinking that the rooms would be separate with distinct, or should I say discrete, men and women appurtenances. Think again! We both went into the shower room together, and each chose an individual shower stall. After Winston realized he needed a token and was forced to put his clothes back on to go outside to the token dispenser, he did so. But he only had change for one token. I, then, scavenged through my purse to pull out the necessary euros, and headed out to repeat the drama. But mind you, by the time I returned to my designated shower stall, it was already in use. So I stood around lamely staring at the walls waiting my turn. When all was said and done (and we were fresh and clean), we had a good laugh, but then, what would we have done without Laurent there to help?

Laurent and Karyn were to leave the following morning to catch a train to attend an important family wedding. This was our last night together, so we made the most of it with a wonderful dinner under the stars at a great restaurant on the island. W.B.

It was hard to believe that our week with the Grand Crew of the yacht, *Grand Cru,* was coming to an end. Yes, we had become very dependent on Laurent and Karyn for their handy translating skills, but we would most miss the laughter, the talks, the funny little stories that Laurent would tell, and the incredible French dinners Karyn prepared for us. Most of all, they had become like family, and we would miss them—and their sweet spirits.

So to remedy the situation, we opted for a fantastic final dinner seated on the front veranda of Restaurant L'Oustaou de Porquerolles, where our view was not of the sea, but across the street to a boules court (where Winston had spent the afternoon) and the Catholic church beyond. No matter! We knew what the sea looked like.

While feasting on a most scrumptious meal, including foie gras, beef marrow, lamb, and local fish—our last shared culinary delight—we also indulged in sharing some of our favorite memories together during the trip. As this was one of those things my husband and I liked to do, we began with questions like, "What was your favorite beach, favorite restaurant, favorite shower system, favorite moment, and favorite story?" We all shared several bottles of fine wine, and our stories got richer and funnier than even we could recall. We lifted our glasses in toasts until late into the night. These cheers were for a week well spent and well sailed with Captain Winston at the helm and with good friends all around. Oui, tchin-tchin!

As you can imagine, we held onto each other as we ambled back down to the boat, clambered aboard—and in this case, staggered back over the *passerelle,* or gang plank.

CHAPTER FORTY-SEVEN

Hyéres Bound

*T*he following morning, we noticed the weather was be-ginning to deteriorate. We needed to have the boat to the endpoint of our trip at the Moorings facility in Hyères by that afternoon. The original plan was for Laurent and Karyn to take a ferry back in the morning and we would head back to Hyères a little later in the day for the one-to-two-hour sail from Porquerolles to Hyères. We checked in at the harbor master office and discovered there was a storm brewing. So we decided to leave earlier than later and have Laurent and Karyn go with us for the last leg. They would arrive in plenty of time to make their train and we would get to Hyères before the weather worsened. It was a good plan as the weather did get rough and a good old-fashioned thunder and lightning storm picked up later in the day. We ar-rived in Hyères late in the morning. Had time for Laurent to make us one more good pot of French press and we were able to complete the trip with our entire crew. The staff at the Moorings office in Hyères was as helpful and friendly as the staff in Nice. W.B.

Ah, but not so fast! Yes, we all were racing around getting our boat ready to take off from Porquerolles, and much sooner than we had anticipated. Our neighbors in the harbor were also walking around the dock debating whether they would stay put for another day or do as we were doing . . . race the storm across the short strait to Hyères. In that bit of haste, we heard a shout from an outbound boat. A young boy, who had been assisting as it was leaving, was left standing on said boat. His father went racing down the dock as the mother screamed for the boat to stop. Instantly, Winston and Laurent joined the father in grabbing a line thrown from the departing boat and quickly tying off. In no time at all, the boy was back in his mother's arms. We were a bit shaken, but counted our blessings, and our passengers, before we took off with—yes, all six of us on board.

This was the first time during our entire week of sailing that the weather had changed even a little bit. No strong mistral winds roaring in from the north. No hot sirocco winds blasting in from the Sahara Desert. Not even a sprinkle late in the day. We had experienced nothing but beautiful, calm mornings, warmer afternoons, with a bit of haze before cloudless evenings filled with stars.

I believe we were all relieved to get to Hyères once the storm started in earnest. We considered ourselves fortunate! We arrived in time for Laurent and Karyn to pull their bags off the boat and prepare for their train trip north.

It was not as easy to see them go! We had had such a good time together! Why, we were finishing each other's sentences, whether French or English, laughing at each other's jokes, whether they were funny or not. But how were the four of us going to manage without translators by our sides? We still had another week in Provence.

⚬⚬⚬

"Life itself is the proper binge."

—Julia Child

"This was the trip of a lifetime," Winston stated to our little enclave. We all were standing together on the road with Laurent and Karyn, their bags at their feet, awaiting a taxi. "It was a dream come true," he continued. "Our boat was perfect, the sailing spectacular, the sights, the food, and the views along the Côte d'Azur were breathtaking. But the best thing of all was sailing with you, our grand crew."

Tears bloomed in all our eyes as we took turns hugging our dear friends goodbye. I think if Winston had said, "Let's continue sailing for another week," we all would have jumped at it. *Alors*, the taxi arrived, and we kissed them bon voyage before slowly walking back to the marina.

We still had one more night on the boat before we were to leave, and on the following day, Winston, Jim, Sandy, and I were going to continue for another week's tour of Provence. The promises we made to take our dear friends, Jim and Sandy, to some of our favorite haunts on their first foray through Provence were enticing, indeed.

In the meantime, it was time for lunch. Quite honestly, we didn't realize how handicapped we would be without the Fouchers—until that first lunch without them. Do I dare mention this was within the first hour of sending them off to the train? We opted to walk to a restaurant near the docks in Hyères, Café du Port, where we tried our hand at ordering *sans* French. A couple of us ordered pasta with seafood, but Sandy struck out on her own and ordered a *polpi* salad. Thinking she had not indulged in enough green leafy vegetables over the past week, she thought a nice refreshing salad would fit the bill. Quite honestly, I was thinking I should have done the same, but I succumbed once again to a favorite pasta dish.

No, she had no idea what the word polpi meant. When a medium-sized platter was placed before her with cold pink, purple, and white tentacles sprawling overall, we realized she had been served an octopus salad. The fact that it was cold was also a jolt, but thank goodness, the little creature had been cooked beforehand. As I said, we had been on our own for less than an hour when we realized we were doomed.

Well, the rest of the day was set aside as a day of organization. Clothes needed to get washed, and showers needed to be taken at the marina's private showers. But once again we hit another conundrum. The harbor master at this boating facility was kind enough; he just didn't realize how unenlightened we were. It seemed that Winston, who was the registered boat renter, was required to show his Carte d'Identité to obtain a key fob for the showers. So Winston and Jim raced back to our boat, which was, unfortunately, docked in a slip a lengthy distance from the harbor master's office. I watched as my husband limped (yes, he was still limping from his injury on the boat in Fréjus and I had failed to get him medication), down one ramp, along the fingers of perpendicular docks separating rows upon rows of boats, then onto the last dock to pop into our boat, *Grand Cru*. It was quite some time before they reappeared.

They searched high and low throughout the boat looking for what they considered the necessary documentation for the boat but failed to find it. When they both returned empty-handed to the harbor master, Winston shrugged his shoulders and said in English, "I can't find the Carte d'Identité! I'm not sure what you need!"

The harbor master's good humor began to slip, and he shouted the words, "Carte d'Identité" over and over with increasing volume.

This time Winston and I made our way down to the boat to search for what he thought were papers specific to the boat we had chartered. After much scrambling through every nook and cranny, we once again came up empty-handed. With our heads hanging low and wishing we could beam Laurent or Karyn into handling this situation, we again faced the harbor master.

I can't remember what the harbor master finally said that made a click in the little grey cells of our brains. Carte d'Identité meant our Identity Card, or a driver's license. "That's it! They want your driver's license, Winston! Hurrah!"

Ah, but where was it? Only he would know, as he had locked it on the boat. "I'll be right back," he said.

I sat back down with Sandy until this dilemma was resolved, and Sandy leaned over to me and said, "From the outside, this search for the Carte d'Identité looks a bit like the Keystone Kops with a limp." I laughed, knowing full well she was correct. Winston did have a limp!

Once we got this dilemma settled, Sandy and I went back to the boat to pull our dirty clothes together, along with a book to read, and headed to the nearby *lavanderie,* or laundromat. Again, we were feeling a bit skittish about making change— like putting coins into the machines—but somehow, we managed to pull together adequate euros to make the transaction. If we hadn't had each other to laugh and make the best of it, this would have felt insurmountable. And both of us had traveled in France numerous times before.

Later in the afternoon, we finally got around to taking showers. And again, our experiences encountering shower shenanigans in tropical locales—like Cannes and Portquerolles— left us feeling insecure. By now, the Fouchers were completely out of range for helping us out.

"I guess we're on our own, honey," Winston said to me as we collected our towels, flip flops, coins, and headed to the shower facility.

"Those are words that make me quake in my boots," I responded.

But when we arrived, we realized we remembered enough details from past transactions that we were able to get into the shower rooms, find separate changing booths, get the showers to work with special tokens, and negotiate our way through a gender-neutral shared experience. Hurray!

Now, to have dinner! After all the hoo-ha of going up and down the ramps, and with rain beating a light tempo on our boat, the four of us opted to stay on the boat and have left-overs for our final evening.

That's always one of the dilemmas of sailing for a week with good friends who love food. You end up with more food left on board than you realize. You see, at every village we ventured through, we each feared getting stranded without enough food. More likely, we were enticed by yet another delicacy. So, the coffers were . . . should I say, far from empty?

"There's nothing better than cream of refrigerator," Winston announced. With that declaration, we dove into the reserves and had a splendid feast. Even the wine locker had not been depleted! Hurrah! Like they say in New Orleans, *laissez le bon temps rouler!* or let the good times roll!

We awakened the following morning with the sun rising brightly over the marina, with a light breeze humming through the halyards. It was if there was an automatic signal of the boats' anticipation of her next adventure.

Even though disembarking from a boat was not as much

fun as embarking, we were energized to begin the next leg of our on-land adventures in Provence.

Ah, but not so fast! We'd have to save these stories for another time! And believe me, there will be another time! I have so many more stories to tell. Stay tuned.

The End

Citations Acknowledgment

I am grateful to all of the locals who were willing to weave their stories about their traditions, history, and folklore that made the journey so much more memorable.

Acknowledgments

Having just completed the writing of these three separate memoirs, I realized how much time had flown by since I took each of these trips. The full book spans memories from 1997 to 2006, but sadly, several of my travel compatriots have passed away or I have lost track of them. But, nonetheless, I want to acknowledge and honor them.

First is Dan Rockwell, my brother-in-law, who was the stalwart humorist in the first trip to Provence. He was always a quiet one, but his quick wit and sense of humor kept us on our toes or rocking back on our heels in laughter. He was the beloved husband to my sister, Melody Rockwell, who still carries on his spirit with delight. He passed away in the spring of 2017.

Sharon Shipley was the reason I traveled with the culinary group to Provence. She was an accomplished chef; ran a cooking school called Mon Cheri in Sunnyvale, California where I met her; and wrote an award-winning cookbook called *Cooking with Lavender*. Obviously, a Provencal aficionado! Following our culinary tour, I joined her to travel through both France and Italy, as she collected French recipes, *cuisine pauvre,* or the Italian recipes, *cucina povera,* while I captured the stories of the people that pepper the pages of my *Savoring the Olde Ways series*. She passed away in 2007 and has been greatly missed.

I want to thank my sister, Melody, whom I adore, but also because I owe her a debt of gratitude for her help with this book, and traveling with me not once, not twice, but three times to Provence.

And, then there is Lise Croll, who was the French translator and travel agent extraordinaire beginning with the culinary trip to Provence. Having been born and raised in France, she was the most knowledgeable and helpful of my new friends while traveling in France. She continued to be not only my travel agent, but a dear friend for many years.

I also want to mention the many travel mates that sprinkled the pages of each of the three sections and gave the stories the delight of the experience: Bob and Shirley (pseudonyms) in the first trip; Karen, Russ, Joan, Pam, Colleen, Chris, Margie, and Iris in the second trip of whom I, unfortunately, have lost track of where they are after twenty years. Nevertheless, their contributions to this book are invaluable. And, I can't forget the dear couple Solange and Denis Brihat in Bonnieux, who so cordially invited me into their home and shared the many family traditions along with recipes. It was a true joy!

And then there are Jim and Sandy Turner and Laurent and Karyn Foucher who were and are not just good friends, but were the fellow sailors on the third trip along with my beloved, Winston Bumpus. They say it takes a village to write a book, and as it turns out, those villagers are the true characters and an enrichment to the story.

I also want to thank the entire She Writes Press publishing team including Brooke Warner, Lauren Wise, the cover artist, Stacey Aaronson, and all those amazing women in the background who have made my five, now six books, possible! Thank you.

About the Author

photo credit: Chris Loomis

CAROLE BUMPUS began writing about food and travel once she traveled to Provençe on a Culinary Tour in 2000. Her historical novel, *A Cup of Redemption* (2014) was based on an elderly French woman's life stories while teaching her to cook *cuisine pauvre*. *Recipes for Redemption: A Companion Cookbook to A Cup of Redemption* (2015) followed with those recipes. Book One, of her *Savoring the Olde Ways Series*, called *Searching for Family and Traditions at the French Table* was published in 2019; the second of this series was published in 2020, and the third book, *A September to Remember: Searching for Culinary Pleasures at the Italian Table* was published in 2021. All books have been published by She Writes Press and are now distributed by Simon & Schuster. A retired family therapist, Bumpus lives in Redwood Shores in the San Francisco Bay Area.

Visit her website at www.carolebumpus.com.

Looking for your next great read?

We can help!

Visit www.shewritespress.com/next-read
or scan the QR code below for a list
of our recommended titles.

She Writes Press is an award-winning
independent publishing company founded to
serve women writers everywhere.